Migration
& Identity

Memory and Narrative Series
Mary Chamberlain and Selma Leydesdorff, series editors

Trauma: Life Stories of Survivors
Kim Lacy Rogers and Selma Leydesdorff, editors
(with Graham Dawson)

Commemorating War: The Politics of Memory
Timothy G. Ashplant, Graham Dawson, and Michael Roper,
editors

*Environmental Consciousness:
The Roots of a New Political Agenda*
Stephen Hussey and Paul Thompson, editors

*Memory and Memorials:
From the French Revolution to World War One*
Mathew Campbell, Jacqueline M. Labbe,
and Sally Shuttleworth, editors

*The Stasi Files Unveiled:
Guilt and Compliance in a Unified Germany*
Barbara Miller

*The Uses of Narrative:
Explorations in Sociology, Psychology, and Cultural Studies*
Molly Andrews, Shelley Day Sclater, Corinne Squire, and
Amal Treacher, editors

Narrative and Genre: Contests and Types of Communication
Mary Chamberlain and Paul Thompson, editors

*The Clash of Economic Cultures:
Japanese Bankers in the City of London*
Junko Sakai

Narratives of Exile and Return
Mary Chamberlain

Migration & Identity

Rina Benmayor &
Andor Skotnes, editors

With a new Introduction by the editors

Memory and Narrative Series

Transaction Publishers
New Brunswick (U.S.A.) and London (U.K.)

Second printing 2007

New material this edition copyright @ 2005 by Transaction Publishers, New Brunswick, New Jersey. www.transactionpub.com

This edition reprinted by Transaction Publishers by arrangement with Oxford University Press.

First published by Oxford University Press in 1994. @ The Several Contributors, 1994.

All rights reserved under International and Pan-American Copyright Conventions. No part of this book may be reproduced or transmitted in any form or by any means, electronic or mechanical, including photocopy, recording, or any information storage and retrieval system, without prior permission in writing from the publisher. All inquiries should be addressed to Transaction Publishers, Rutgers-The State University, 35 Berrue Circle, Piscataway, New Jersey 08854-8042.

This book is printed on acid-free paper that meets the American National Standard for Permanence of Paper for Printed Library Materials.

Library of Congress Catalog Number: 2005041914
ISBN: 1-4128-0464-7
    978-1-4128-0464-6

Library of Congress Cataloging-in-Publication Data

Migration and identity / Rina Benmayor and Andor Skotnes, editors; with a new introduction by the editors.
        p. cm. —(Memory and narrative series)
    Originally published: Oxford ; New York: Oxford University Press, 1994, in series:
    International yearbook of oral history and life stories; v. 3. With new introd.
    Includes bibliographical references.
    ISBN 1-4128-0464-7 (pbk: alk paper)
        1. Emigration and immigration. 2. Immigrants. 3. Group identity.
    I. Bemnayor, Rina. II. Skotnes, Andor. III. Memory and narrative.

JV6035.M537   2005
304.8—dc22   2005041914

Contents

Introduction to the Transaction Edition   vii
RINA BENMAYOR and ANDOR SKOTNES

List of Contributors   xi

1. Some Reflections on Migration and Identity   1
   RINA BENMAYOR and ANDOR SKOTNES

2. In Search of Safe Haven: Exile, Immigration, and Identity   19
   IVÁN JAKSIĆ

3. The Apple and the Olive Tree: Exile, Sojourners, and Tourists in the University   35
   FRANCESCA BATTISTI and ALESSANDRO PORTELLI

4. The Senegalese Immigrants in Bari: What Happens When the Africans Peer Back   53
   DOROTHY LOUISE ZINN

5. On Becoming a Citizen: The Story of Dona Marlene   69
   EVELINA DAGNINO

6. Identity, Racism, and Multiculturalism: Chinese-Australian Responses   85
   JANIS WILTON

7. Ethiopian Jews Encounter Israel: Narratives of Migration and the Problem of Identity   101
   GADI BEN-EZER

8. Family and Identity: Barbadian Migrants to Britain   119
   MARY CHAMBERLAIN

9. Puerto Rican Women: Migration and Changes in Gender Roles   137
   ELIZABETH CRESPO

10. Identity and Gender in the Mexican-American *Testimonio*: The Life and Narrative of Frances Esquivel Tywoniak   151
    MARIO T. GARCÍA

11. Central American Refugee Testimonies and
    Performed Life Histories in the Sanctuary Movement   167
    WILLIAM WESTERMAN

12. Between Identities   183
    HOMI BHABHA interviewed by PAUL THOMPSON

Introduction to the Transaction Edition

Revisiting *Migration and Identity*

RINA BENMAYOR and ANDOR SKOTNES

More than a decade has transpired since the original publication of this volume. And yet, the introduction we wrote some eleven years ago feels unusually relevant today, as the twenty-first century sets in. If anything, economic and political migration has increased across the globe, intensifying fear and reaction, and, at the same time, creating more zones of cultural contact with creative constructions of identity and belonging. Rather than becoming outdated, the essays in this volume marked the onset of "globalization" in the 1990s, and its social, cultural, and political consequences.

A decade ago, Western Europe was just beginning to see waves of undocumented migrants reach its shores. Today, this economic migration is as commonplace in Italy or Spain as it is on the U.S. Mexican border. In the United States, the 2000 census shows that Asian and Latino migration to the United States continues to grow, with Latinos promising to become the largest "minority" by 2020. As the United States has worked to consolidate its position as the "remaining superpower," it has everywhere pressed its doctrine of (selective) free trade, opening much of the world to the rapid movement of U.S. and Western capital, followed by the rapid migration of impoverished "third world" workers, seeking to survive by working in what is becoming a global network of *maquiladoras*.

The years 1993-2005 are now indelibly marked by September 11. Anti-immigrant demagogy and hysteria were again amplified in the United States by this watershed event, and have likewise been on the increase elsewhere. Popular initiatives designed to deny undocumented immigrants basic social services, and to compel officials and professionals to report suspected "illegals" to the authorities have, in recent years, become commonplace. New laws—such as the infamous Patriot Act in the United States—sanctioned by the so-called "war on terrorism" are greatly expanding the national security apparatus in many developed countries, and are subjecting many immigrants—especially Muslims and Arabs—to governmental harassment, special procedures, expulsion, or, in some cases, long-term detention. Anti-Islamic racism and right-wing xenophobia have both grown apace across North America and Europe.

Additionally, news of devastation and forced migration due to war has pervaded the last decade. From the wars in the former Yugoslavia, to the genocide in Rwanda, to the decades-long civil war in Sudan, tens of millions have fled their homes to cross borders of all types, and all too often to end up living and dying in the squalor of refugee camps. Then there is Afghanistan, Iraq, and Israel/Palestine.

Not all is dismal, though. In a number of countries, progressive movements with deep roots among displaced peasantries, migrating workers, and urban immigrants have won important victories. In our introduction a decade ago, we noted, as did Dagnino in her essay, that the *Partido dos Trabalhadores* in Brazil had a strong base among these constituencies; since then the PT has won important electoral victories including the presidency of the country.

Overall, then, the last decade has seen millions and millions of people grappling, in circumstances sometimes extreme and sometimes routine, with the realities of migration, with people from cultures very different from their own, and with their identities as migrants. Migration continues to be, as we argued some eleven years ago, a fundamental feature of our times.

In the last decade, the framework of transnationalism has come to describe much more accurately the realities experienced by most migrant groups. Transnational scholarship has amply confirmed that migration is a bi-directional phenomenon and that even those who have been outside their native countries for several generations actively maintain transnational circuits of kinship, economy, and culture (Rouse 1991; Basch et al. 1994; Smith 1999; Portes et al.1999; Faist 2000). Our understanding of national and ethnic identities, as a result, has become more complex and multicultural (Hudson and Réno

1999), intersected by gender (Hondagneu-Sotelo 2003), generation (Chamberlain 1998), and racial constructions (Cordero-Guzmán and Smith 2001). Increased attention has also been paid to theoretical framings of how migrants constitute themselves as new social actors and citizens (Hall and Held 1990), reasserting and redefining who they are and what they want to become. Concepts of "cultural citizenship" (Flores and Benmayor 1997) and "flexible citizenship" (Ong 1999) signal ways in which people are thinking and feeling "beyond the nation" (Robbins 1998). For migration scholars from across the humanities and social sciences, life stories, oral histories, and personal testimonies are still primary texts for understanding how migrants construct identities in the context of globalization and transnationalism.

As noted in our original introduction, the essays in this volume exemplify the attention of oral historians to the impact of economic and political migration, war and displacement, cultural contact, and new hybrid identities. The essays suggest a "doubling"—to borrow Homi Bhabha's term—of our own identities and practices as investigators, analysts, and social activists. In some instances, scholars whose own lives are marked by migrant experiences have turned the microphone on themselves, using oral history and *testimonio* as a vehicle for new theorizing about identity, history, and solidarity (Latina Feminist Group 2001). The exploration of memory has moved to the center of oral history work, including studies of migration and globalization (see Chamberlain and Leydesdorff 2004 for an excellent overview). Marking this same trend, the International Oral History Association's bi-annual conferences attest to a proliferation of interest in migration and its cultural implications on all continents. Themes like "Memory and Globalization," of the 2004 conference in Rome organized by Alessandro Portelli, attracted perhaps the largest number of scholars in the Association's history and emphasized the interdependence of memory, narrative, and politics in our field. In the closing plenary, Estela Carloto, president of the Grandmothers of the Plaza de Mayo, gave a deeply moving presentation of a new Archive of Memory to the "*Desaparecidos*" in Argentina. This archive, comprised of audio tapes, testimonies, and photographs, is more than a public commemoration of those who were brutally murdered by the dictatorship. For the many children of the disappeared who were stolen from their parents and illegally adopted, the archive stands as a resource to enable them to discover who their birth parents and families were and to reclaim their histories and identities. Other projects like the massive 9/11 memory project of the Columbia University Oral History Research Office, and the complex work of oral historians with "Truth and Reconciliation" commissions in South Africa, Rwanda, Argentina, Guatemala, and Chile, remind us that the memory and testimonies of migrants, refugees, victims, and survivors are fundamental to our humanity, our identities, our practices as oral historians, and our futures.

References

Basch, L. N., Glick Schiller, and C. Szanton Blanc. (1994). *Nations unbound: transnational projects, postcolonial predicaments and deterritorialized nation-states*. Langhorn: Gordon and Breach.

Cheah, P., and B. Robbins. (1998). *Cosmopolitics: thinking and feeling beyond nation*. Minneapolis: University of Minnesota.

Chamberlain, M. (1998). *Caribbean migration: globalised identities*. London & New York: Routledge.

Chamberlain M., and S. Leydesdorff. (2004). "Transnational families: memories and narratives." *Global Networks* 4, 3: 227-241.

Cordero-Guzmán, H., and R. Smith. (2001). *Migration, transnationalization, and race in a changing New York*. Philadelphia: Temple University.

Faist, T. (2000). "Transnationalization in international migration: implications for the study of citizenship and culture." *Ethnic and Racial Studies* 23: 2, 189-234.

Flores, W.V., and R. Benmayor. (1997). *Latino cultural citizenship: claiming identity, space and rights*. Boston: Beacon.

Hall, S., and D. Held. (1990). "Citizens and citizenship," in S. Hall and M. Jacques (eds.), *New times: the changing face of politics in the 1990s*, 173-188. London: Verso.

Hondagneu-Sotelo, P. (2003). *Gender and U.S. immigration: contemporary trends*. Berkeley: University of California.

Hudson. R., and F. Réno. (1999). *Politics of identity: migrants and minorities in multicultural states*. Houndsmill, England, and New York: Palgrave.

Ong, A. (1999). *Flexible citizenship: the cultural logics of transnationality*. Durham: Duke.

Portes, A., L. Guarnizo, and P. Landolt. (1999). "Introduction." Special Issue: Transnational communities, *Ethnic and Racial Studies*, 22:2, 217-37.

Rouse, R. (1991). "Mexican migration and the social space of postmodernism." *Diaspora*, 1:1, 8-23.

Smith, R. (1999). "Reflections on migration, the state and the construction, durability and newness of transnational life," in Ludger Pries (ed.), *Migration and Transnational Social Spaces*. Ashgate: Aldershot, 187-219.

List of Contributors

FRANCESCA BATTISTI is studying English and American Literature at the University of Rome, La Sapienza.

GADI BEN-EZER is a clinical and organizational psychologist who has been working with Ethiopian Jews for the last twelve years, and he has written extensively on their absorption and adaptation after migration to Israel. He has acted as consultant to various Israeli and international agencies, and teaches at Ben Gurion University in the Negev. During the last three years, he has been on leave, currently researching at Essex University, and earlier in the Refugees Studies Programme at Oxford University.

RINA BENMAYOR is professor of oral history, Latino studies and literature in the Department of New Humanities for Social Justice at California State University Monterey Bay. She is currently president of the International Oral History Association. Her recent publications include: *Telling to Live: Latina Feminist Testimonios* and *Latino Cultural Citizenship*.

HOMI BHABHA is an Indian writer and literary critic who lives in London. He teaches at Sussex University and his books include *The Location of Culture* (1993).

MARY CHAMBERLAIN recently returned to England from living for three years in Barbados. She has taught at the London School of Printing, the University of the West Indies, and now teaches at Oxford Brookes University. Her books include *Fenwomen* (1975), *Old Wives Tales* (1981), and *Growing Up in Lambeth* (1988).

ELIZABETH CRESPO teaches Puerto Rican Studies at John Jay College of Criminal Justice, City University of New York. She is currently working on a book about two generations of Puerto Rican women.

EVELINA DAGNINO is a political scientist teaching in the Politics and Culture Postgraduate programme at UNICAMP, the University of Campinas, Brazil.

MARIO T. GARCÍA teaches history and Chicano studies at the University of California, Santa Barbara. His books include *Desert Immigrants: The Mexicans of El Paso* (1981), *Mexican Americans* (1989), and *Memories of History: The Life and Narrative of Bert Corona* (1994).

IVÁN JAKSIĆ teaches history at the University of Notre Dame, Mishawaka, Indiana. His books include: *Academic Rebels in Chile, The Role of Philosophy in Higher Education and Politics* (1989). His current work is on the relationship between exile, language, and notional identity in nineteenth-century Latin America.

ALESSANDRO PORTELLI teaches American studies at the University of Rome, La Sapienza. He is editor of a journal of popular culture and song, *I giorni cantati*, and his books include an oral history of Terni, *Biografia di una città*, and *The Death of Luigi Trastulli and Other Stories* (1991).

ANDOR SKOTNES is associate professor of history of the Americas at The Sage Colleges in Troy, New York. He teaches courses in working-class, African American, Native American, and Latin American history and culture, and in oral history.

PAUL THOMPSON is research professor in sociology at the University of Essex, and a fellow at the Institute of Community Studies in London. His books include *The Voice of the Past*, *The Edwardians*, and *The Work of William Morris*.

WILLIAM WESTERMAN is completing a research doctorate at the University of Pennsylvania in Philadelphia, on Quaker involvement in refugee issues, from the 'underground railroad' of slavery times to the current sanctuary movement.

JANIS WILTON teaches social history at the University of New England, Armidale, Australia. She has especially focused on researching the experiences of Australians from non-English-speaking backgrounds. Her books include *Internment* (1986), *Immigrants in the Bush* (1990), and *Olde Worlde and New Australia* (1984).

DOROTHY LOUISE ZINN is a doctoral researcher in anthropology at the University of Texas at Austin. She has been working on migration, unemployment, and patronage in southern Italy.

I

Some Reflections on Migration and Identity

RINA BENMAYOR and ANDOR SKOTNES

It's mid-1993, and as we write this introduction, we wonder about the continuing resonance of the theme—Migration and Identity—which we chose some three years ago. But a cursory look at the daily news confirms that, in fact, the issue looms large everywhere and will continue to do so.

The *New York Times* recently reported that Asians are the fastest growing immigrant group in the United States today. Only a short time ago, we were being warned that 'Hispanics' would constitute a full 25 per cent of the US population by the twenty-first century. The persistent metaphor of 'invading hordes', whether 'brown' or 'yellow', permeates the media and the 'white' mind. Its analogue in Western Europe is the hysterical fear of Islamization among whites in France, Great Britain, and Germany. Meanwhile, 300 'illegal' Chinese immigrants run aground in a leaking freighter off Queens, New York, after a journey of more than 100 days, and eight die before the rescue; the captain and crew have been arrested and the survivors—like thousands of Haitian refugees before them—have been carted off to detention jails by Immigration. Some proponents of the unsettled North American Free Trade Agreement (NAFTA) claim that it will stem the tide of undocumented Mexicans and Central Americans who run or wade across into 'el Norte', evading the infra-red eye of the border patrol. Likewise, some hope that the Treaty of Schengen will close Europe forever to the relatives and even children of immigrants who have already arrived.

The news continues. Famine and civil wars have pushed Somali clans off their lands, turning them into economic as well as political refugees, if indeed they have managed to stay alive. The four-year-old civil war in Liberia has claimed the lives of another 300 refugees in a massacre no one claims as theirs. CNN gives us up-to-the-minute, daily images of genocidal ethnic cleansing and forced removal of peoples from their homes in the former Yugoslavia. Neo-Nazi skinheads in Germany burn Turkish immigrant women and children in the latest wave of racist violence. Meanwhile, the French Government announces the creation of a special police division to stem the tide of non-EC undocumented workers. Foreigners will be required to carry residency permits on their persons at all times for police checks.

Other reports indicate that today, one-half to two-thirds of immigrants crossing borders (the 'South/North' 'East/West' narratives continue) are women and children—the feminization of global migration? Migrant women everywhere punch into their global assembly factories, if there is one within commuting distance. When the factories relocate and the region 'restructures', they will be left more likely to face chronic unemployment or perhaps another migration. Meanwhile, black African day labourers gather on street corners in southern Italian towns, waiting to be 'picked' for walnut-picking. Latino men do very much the same on the street corners of Los Angeles, as do migrants from the countryside in front of the National Cathedral in Mexico City, and in downtown Rio de Janeiro, Bangkok, and Manila.

The scenarios of mass disruption abound. At the same time, resistance is manifest, and more creative, hopeful responses appear. Indeed, political resistance, cultural transformations, and constructions of complex identities are at work everywhere. Poor, disenfranchised communities, predominantly communities of 'colour'—to use the US terminology—continue to press for basic issues of justice and equal rights (even if they have to riot to do so: Rodney King). The Turks of Germany, like other migrant communities in Europe, oppose Fascist terror in tenuous alliances with German anti-racists. The importance of building bridges across national and ethnic lines could not be more apparent, even when it seems so hard to achieve. The dwellers of the shanty towns, the *villas miseria*, the *favelas* of Latin America—and, no doubt, of Africa and Asia as well—create new communal forms that are often political and sometimes have dramatic effect, as in the case of Brazil where social movements find expression in the increasingly successful Partido dos Trabalhadores. The emigrants and return-migrants of Barbados continue to lace together a complex network of communities in the Caribbean, Britain, and North America. Some immigrant groups in the Netherlands, France and Germany achieve a degree of economic integration and become upwardly mobile, without homogenizing culturally; the relatively affluent ethnic Chinese of Australia are in the process of rebuilding their connection with their ancestral home after several generations of detachment. Mexicans as far north as Brooklyn, New York, construct transnational identities; they are Latinos in New York and at the same time continue to be active citizens in their towns and villages in Puebla, Mexico.

Problems of migration and the resulting reconfigurations of social identity are fundamental issues for the 1990s. The collection of essays in this, the third volume of *The International Yearbook of Oral History and Life Stories*, explores these issues in a number of recent social settings, from a number of methodological perspectives. These essays are focused 'case-studies', that aim to contribute to the general understanding of migration. They offer glimpses into the interior of migration experiences, into the processes of constructing and reconstructing identity, without forgetting that, both theoretically and empirically, the problem of identity is a complex and multi-faceted one. They all rely heavily on oral history and personal testimony, highlighting the experience of individuals and small groups, without ignoring the tension that exists between the local and the global. In the introductory pages that follow we, as special editors of this volume want to take turns offering some thoughts on these three elements—the general phenomenon of migration, the construction of identity, and the relationship of personal testimony to the global experience—and thereby suggest some framework for thinking about the essays in this collection.

RB and AS

As a historian, born of several migrations, I believe that migration demands the kind of close, detailed study offered in the following essays. As a social scientist working in the broad traditions of Marxism, though, I feel that a dialectic always needs to be established between the detailed and the general, the local and the global. Of course, the authors in this volume frequently point to the general implications of their localized studies and suggest more global conclusions. However, in this introduction, I want to strengthen the global side of the equation a bit by offering a few general comments on the question of migration and, along the way, explaining some of the parameters we set for this volume.

The main point of our opening paragraphs above was to show, with a number of examples, that migration is a basic feature of social life throughout the world today. Moreover, by means of these examples, we want to suggest that the sheer scale and geographic sweep of current migratory movements indicates that the causes of these movements are fundamental, located in the basic structures of an increasingly interlocked world system. These points may not appear to be controversial at first glance, but they run against the grain of much common-sense thinking about migration and are ultimately subversive of certain widely held conceptions. Against all evidence, there is a strong tendency, especially in the 'advanced' countries, for observers and 'opinion-makers' of all sorts—journalists, politicians, scholars—to treat migrations, no matter what their scale, as isolated, random events, outside of the central thrust of social development. Massive population movements are viewed *de facto* as accidents of history, the result of unusual circumstances, catastrophes, deviations from the norm. After all, the dominating discourses of world capitalist culture tell us that modern society is supposed to be stable and prosperous. Despite the fact that the economic power brokers of the advanced countries frequently foster immigration to form pools of cheap labour power, or stimulate it through their interventions in underdeveloped economies, we are encouraged to believe that something as disruptive as migration has to be marginal, transitional, aberrant. Moreover, we are encouraged to think of the migrants as deviants, as the cause of disruption. Migrants themselves are subject to these ideological notions. Towards the end of his essay in this volume, Iván Jaksić, who details his own odyssey from political exile to immigrant, tells of the watershed in his life when he realized that his individual migration experience was a common one, 'part of a much larger human experience'. We all need to embrace this insight for what it suggests about the world today—and for the perspective it throws on the essays in this volume.

It is necessary to add that there is nothing historically unique about the dramatic importance of migration to the current world situation. While there have been quantitative ups and downs, massive migration has been a constant to the last five centuries of world history and has frequently been a key determinant of global developments. Take the Americas as an example. Between the late fifteenth century and the present, the social and ecological realities of these continents were totally and repeatedly remade by the successive movements of hundreds of millions of Europeans, Africans, and Asians to and throughout the 'New World'. Moreover—and this reality is often obscured by the popular notion that the countries of the Americas are 'nations of immigrants'—the indigenous peoples of the Americas were forced to migrate and remigrate to survive waves of genocidal colonialist onslaught; this migration, too, continues to this day. In other words, one cannot think accurately or effectively about society and history in the Americas without thinking about migration.

It is not just the Americas, though. Everywhere modern social relations have penetrated, massive and repeated population dislocations have resulted: from the countryside to the city, between socio-economic regions, across national boundaries, between major ethno-linguistic spheres, from continent to continent. Migrants have moved long distances or short, once or several times; they have often returned to their point of origin, and the process of leaving and returning has sometimes continued over generations. Whether large-scale or small, forced (and it has very often been forced) or voluntary, compelled by war, famine, social disruption, or the hope for a better life, the complex phenomenon of migration has been fundamental to the whole modern epoch. Such an understanding locates the essays in this book, all of which focus on recent decades, as studies of the latest phase of a long, multi-faceted, world-historical process. And again, this historical understanding of migration is potentially subversive for it challenges certain popular myths of progress and of historical development. Moreover, the essays in this volume study many forms of migration resulting from many different causes; two essays—one by Dorothy Zinn, the other by Francesca Battisti and Alessandro Portelli—even suggest similarities and partial convergences between migration and tourism.

One of the most important myths challenged by this epochal view of migration is the notion that the nation-state—a culturally homogeneous society occupying a distinct territory, governed by a unitary state structure—is at once the natural and ideal basic unit of modern political organization. Of course, outside of the partial exception of a few Western European countries, very few contemporary states were constructed encompassing anything close to an ethnically homogeneous population. But, the myth tells us, as society stabilizes and develops within the framework of a state, ethnicities assimilate, nationalities fuse, and the nation consolidates. Now it often doesn't work this way for reasons of class, racist, and ethnic oppression that is internally structured into various nation-states. But it especially doesn't work this way because massive migration is a permanent feature of the world system, constantly undermining tendencies towards ethnic homogenization in a given country, and condemning the nation-state, as an ideal and a reality, to varying degrees of perpetual and endemic crisis. If one lives within the ideology of the nation-state, one can never admit this endemic crisis and, to come full circle, can never view migration in its modern, epochal forms and complexity as anything but marginal, episodic—and destructive. All of the essays in this book, in one way or another, include stories of cultural and ethnic tension related to the contradiction between the reality of migration and the myth of the nation-state. These range from stories of explicit racial rejection, like those of Dorothy Zinn's Senegalese informants in southern Italy or Gadi Ben-Ezer's Ethiopian Jewish (Falasha) interviewees in Israel, to accounts of the subtle and complex ambivalences of self-identity as in Mario García's essay about a young Mexican-American woman weaning herself from her local community in order to escape poverty.

Now here are a couple of comments on some parameters we as special editors, in consultation with the *Yearbook* editorial board in Europe, set for this collection of essays on migration and identity. Although the migrations studied in this volume cover, in their origins and destinations, much of the globe, the majority of these essays (six out of ten) are largely on American—North, Central, South, and Caribbean—experiences. There are several reasons for this emphasis. While there has been much transatlantic editorial interaction, we as primary volume editors live in North America and the main frame of reference for our intellectual work is the Americas. Secondly, the international literature in oral history has tended to be more heavily comprised of European-based experiences. Our relative focus here on the Americas is offered as a step towards globalizing the dialogue.

But there is another reason as well. At a recent panel on the quincentenary of Columbus and the Conquest at my college, an African historian from Nigeria and a North American ethnographer of the Mayan peoples both suggested that the study of the migration-related experiences of the Americas may offer particularly important insights to the whole world because of the range of these experiences, the degree to which migration has structured American societies, and the resulting complexity of multiculturalism within these societies. They are by no means alone in making this suggestion. Similar sentiments are being voiced by European intellectuals in countries that are grappling with unprecedented in-migrations of peoples from Africa and Asia, often from formerly colonialized societies. We feel that there is something to these sentiments, that they should be tested, and that at the very least an emphasis on the diverse migration experiences of the Americas is a good way to stimulate further intercontinental comparison. We offer this collection in this spirit.

Beyond the emphasis on the Americas, this volume focuses on voices and experiences often underrepresented in studies of migration history: those of 'marginalized', 'post-colonial', 'Third World' peoples 'of colour'. The multiplicity of ambiguous terms and quotation marks in the last sentence requires explanation, and that explanation takes us back to certain fundamentals of the epochal history of migration. What we are talking about is 'race', not as a biological category, but a shifting line of demarcation, culturally constructed and reconstructed over the last five centuries. From the European expansion of the fifteenth and sixteenth centuries, hierarchical conceptualizations of race and colour have evolved to sanction and promote European colonialist and neo-colonialist practices—and the migratory movements that resulted. A kind of internally complex, ever-changing grand master narrative of colour was established and continues to function to this day.

Of course racial conceptions are inconsistent between societies and even within societies. A friend was born and grew up in South Africa where he was officially classified as coloured (of mixed descent); when he moved to the United States he 'became' black; when he lived in Brazil for a period, he was surprised to discover that Brazilian friends considered him to be white. At every stop in my friend's journeys his socially-defined racial identity was different, but (and this is the critical point) at each stop his racial identity closed certain possibilities to him and opened others. Elizabeth Crespo, in her essay in this collection, tells a similar story (with similar consequences) of a Puerto Rican woman who became 'coloured' and the object of racial discrimination when she moved from the island to New York. On a world-wide scale, too, racial conceptualization is often vague and contradictory: Latin-Americans, who commonly view their societies as mixtures of all 'races', are often viewed by the dominant ideologies of Europe and North America, as unvaryingly 'brown'. Like ethnicity in general, racialized ethnicity is constructed and reconstructed as a dominant group defines the subordinated as outsiders, the foreigners as strangers, and the content of these definitions changes with various global, national, and regional frames. Also like ethnicity in general, racialized ethnicity can become a basis for community, for resistance, for the assertion of self-determination by the oppressed, and definitions can be transformed in the context of particular struggles. Despite all the complexity, inconsistency, and even absurdity, racial categorization is none the less pervasive and fundamental, and draws basic demarcations between migratory experiences.

This volume, then, has been shaped from the perspective that migration is a critical problem today; that it has been central to the whole modern epoch; and that for us now, it is especially important to comprehend the variety of migration-related experiences of peoples relegated to the subordinate side of the colour line.

AS

Returning for a moment to the relevance of our theme, we should point out that our desire to put together a volume on migration and identity arose from an understanding that these two issues are profoundly interconnected. Bringing these links into view helps to recast both concepts analytically. The dominant tendency, both in popular thinking and in much of the literature, is to define migration as a single movement in space and a single moment in time. The focus falls on the act of crossing, or the more or less finite period in which relocation takes place. Underlying this approach is the assumption that at a certain point, migration ends and a process of assimilation/integration and upward mobility begins.

As I have learnt from working in the Puerto Rican community in New York City for more than a decade, migration—especially for subordinated, racialized groups—is a long-term if not life-long process of negotiating identity, difference, and the right to fully exist and flourish in the new context. This understanding of migration is borne out by many examples in this volume: the examples of Puerto Rican women in New York, West Indian families in Britain or in the Caribbean, Brazilian peasants in the urban metropolis, Chicanos moving within their colonized lands, and even transnationalized 'Third World' students and intellectuals. Being a 'migrant' is often a negative identity imposed by the dominant culture on generations of descendants of those who made the trip. Thus, in our usage, the experience and effects of migration are long-term and critical in shaping and reshaping both collective and individual identities. Seen this way, migration becomes a more dynamic concept.

Something similar can be said for the way contemporary global migration has disrupted static conceptions of identity, challenging notions of cultural homogeneity, essentialism, and stereotype. Not only are nation-states being forced to confront their own myths of cultural unity or racialized purity. New generations born out of mixed ethnic/racial, and cross-cultural marriages resist conformity to an 'assimilated' norm (whether that of the dominant society or of the home culture) and affirm instead a more consciously complex notion of who they are. Indeed, cross-cultural marriage itself is a key arena in which migration-related identities are refined, redefined, and transformed, as Catherine Delcroix *et al.* showed in an earlier article in *Life Stories*;[1] in such cases, the potential for remarkable multicultural syncretism exists, as does the possibility for acute contradiction, and even worse as we are reminded by the excruciating tragedy of Bosnia.

In response to this complexity, critical analysis has now come to pose identity as constructed, multi-faceted, negotiated, situational, or, according to some, fragmented. It is around this latter point that the politics of identity plays out. On the one hand, social movements of disenfranchised people are placing a wide range of identity issues on the public agenda—from those that address class, race, sexual, and gender inequality, ethnic and religious persecution, to those that arise around vital human concerns for health, the environment, ageing, and so on. Through such struggles, people constitute themselves as social subjects and actors, reasserting and redefining who they are and what they want to become. On the other hand, the crisis of political models and systems, from socialism to national liberation, has made it much more difficult for these movements around identities and rights to have substantial political impact and to make major structural improvements to people's life chances. None the less, as several essays in this book point out (especially those of Evelina Dagnino, William Westerman, and Gadi Ben-Ezer), communities continue to organize around claims to human and cultural rights. They challenge entrenched institutions and dominant ideologies. They confront the state, and in the process, redefine notions of citizenship and participation that are based on new concepts of equality through difference.

By way of commenting on the contemporary politics of identity, let me turn for a moment to the media, to one of my particular TV addictions, because popular culture sometimes helps us to crystallize the conundrums of current cultural conflicts. 'Northern Exposure' is a top-of-the-charts series that takes on, chiefly through parody, many of the post-modern identity debates. Cicely—a fictional town in northern Alaska, founded at the turn of the century as a community of free thinkers by two northern California lesbians (!!)—serves as a metaphorical identity frontier where an array of Native inhabitants and socially 'dysfunctional' migrants from the south comically confront personal and collective cultural politics. In the following instance, the play is on the significance of 'tribal' membership in the world of the future. Speaking are Fleischman (F), a 'yuppy' Jewish doctor from New York who agonizes over being the only Jew within a four-hundred-mile radius (!), and Ed, a 'homeboy' and aspiring Native American 'Woody Allen':

F. What does belonging to your own tribe mean to you? . . .
ED. Well, I was raised by the tribe, but since I didn't have parents I was passed around a lot.
F. I never really thought about it, belonging to a tribe. I belong to the Jewish tribe, so to speak, but I'm also an American, you know? But what does that mean? I mean, is there an American tribe? More like a zillion special interest groups. In my own case, I'm a New Yorker, I'm a Republican, a Knicks fan. . . . Maybe we've outgrown tribes, you know, the global village thing. Telephones, faxes, CNN. I mean, basically, we all belong to the same tribe.
ED. That's true. But you can't hang out with 5 billion people!
F. That's a good point.

The episode ironically poses the tensions between the realities of an increasingly interconnected world and the global village as a new master myth of centrifuge; between the defence of tribe (read ethnicity) and the complexity of identity struggles today. Fleischman finds himself caught between affirming his Jewishness, of which he is always ferociously proud, and loving his assimilated American identity defined by multiple 'interest groups'. Unable to position himself effectively, he ends up erasing the tension, and the identities, with a global construct. On the other hand, Ed, who pursues the world of mass communications as his medium of expression, questions how one is to find solidarity, a collective voice, and agency in such a homogenized arrangement. 'Hanging out', he suggests, is still one of the basic processes that constructs the tribe and enables it to act, to negotiate power and difference in humane terms.

Parody aside, Homi Bhabha incisively points out in his interview in this volume, that the social struggles of the future will be built around much wider and more ambiguous ranges of identity. What kinds of collective arrangements will emerge to challenge global strategies of homogenization and control? At the same time, how are the essentializing identity myths of ethnicity, nationality, and even gender or sexuality being questioned or deployed? And, ultimately, how does a more complex understanding of identity and difference shape a postmodern politics of liberation?

These are questions we are all asking and which the essays in this anthology pose. Although from different historical and cultural perspectives, all of the essays recognize that identities are not homogeneous or fixed, so that there are many ways of being black, Mexican-American, Chilean, Chinese, Australian, a Jew, a woman, a lesbian, a *favelada*, a migrant, a labourer, a student, a refugee. But none of these aspects of social identity defines the whole of an individual or communities. Rather, what we see is how, in specific situations and moments, people strategically foreground different dimensions of their individual and collective memories to construct who they are and what they are fighting for.

Each essay really explores a many-layered understanding of identity, memory reconstruction, and the situational aspect of both as political strategy. For example, several of the essays explore gender in relation to other identity struggles. That is, we see how gender identity modifies and mediates ethnicity, class, and race. Elizabeth Crespo illustrates how, in the context of colonialism and migration, race and ethnicity reduce the space that gender and class open up for working-class Puerto Rican women to 'study' and thus counter patriarchal controls over their lives. In Evelina Dagnino's account of a shanty-town woman's politicization in Brazil, we hear Dona Marlene directly connect her struggle for the human rights of migrant *favelados* to new conceptions of the role of women in the 'private' sphere of the home. In his essay, Mario García argues for re-examining what could be called a typical story of ethnic assimilation. For young Fran Esquivel Tywoniak, García's subject, leaving her migrant community meant escaping from the cultural restrictions of gender and class, but not without deep implications for her sense of ethnic and racial identity. And Dorothy Zinn examines how young Senegalese men reconcile their participation in the informal street economy in the south of Italy via their gendered responsibility to be providers in the home context. At the same time, they are not simply fulfilling a gender role, but redefining their exploited class position in the host country through male-sanctioned codes of travel and wanderlust.

Another group of essays examines different ways in which racialization is imposed upon im/migrant people of colour in the Americas, Western Europe, and Australia and how it in turn disrupts the coherence of national, ethnic, and class identities. For Iván Jaksić, political exile from Chile dislocates his national and class roots; but in accepting that he has become an immigrant, he must also position himself with respect to the way he will be either stereotyped in the US context as 'brown' and 'Hispanic', or privileged by virtue of his professional class mobility. Gadi Ben-Ezer's migrant Ethiopian-Jewish interviewees portray how racism and cultural difference topple the myth of a unified Jewish state and of the ethnic or religious homogeneity. From being people without a land in Ethiopia, they find their sense of religious identity and basis for inclusion challenged in Israel. In Ethiopia they were marginalized as Jews; in Israel they are discriminated as blacks. For the ethnic Chinese of Australia, Janis Wilton contends, race became the suppressed identity factor in the effort to achieve upward mobility and stability. The suppression of racism indicates through negation its ubiquitous centrality.

Mary Chamberlain's article on Barbadian family migration and return-migration also illustrates the complexity and contextuality of identity construction through an important elaboration of intergenerational scope. The manner in which families evolve and alter transgenerational migratory traditions and identities is, no doubt, a fruitful direction for future research. Chamberlain's interviews illustrate how several succeeding generations of Barbadian families follow similar migratory routes, thereby building distinct family traditions of migration—although the exact meanings of the migratory journeys differ from generation to generation. The detailing of family migration stories shows how the children of Barbadian migrants along with myriad other second-generation or immigrant minority youth in the British metropole deal differently with class and race, and construct identities that are complex, transnational and cosmopolitan, as well as located in a generational youth culture.

Similarly, the Third World intellectuals and students whom Francesca Battisti and Alessandro Portelli interview in Rome take us on a journey across many borders—national, cultural, and historical. They exemplify how social subjects inhabit many worlds and identities, and that from this condition of 'hybridity', of hyphenated identities that encompass much more than just nationality or ethnicity, oppositional voices emerge. The voices of the foreign students in Rome articulate a healthy critique of the idea of cultural unity. One of Battisti and Portelli's informants, Gifi Fadi from Syria, simultaneously challenges the European pureness of Italian civilization and opens space for himself within Italian culture, as he remarks on Middle Eastern words and symbols inscribed on the Roman Forum and indeed in the founding myth of Romulus and Remus. Homi Bhabha's own life story and his more theoretical comments on how the 'doubling', rather than the multiplicity, of identity capture the complexity of these cosmopolitan, post-colonial experiences and produce new possibilities for conceptual understanding.

Again, the identities we are speaking of are not simply a result of crossing geographic borders. Borderlands (real and symbolic) become the sites where more complex processes are lived out. Elaborating on the metaphors of borders and *mestizaje* (creolization), Chicana and Puerto Rican feminist writers 'of colour' have significantly advanced critical thinking. Carving theory out of their complex personal histories and experiences of migration, colonialism, and patriarchy, they have deeply influenced contemporary cultural studies, infusing it with a sophisticated analysis of identity. They take us beyond the notion of hyphenation as an adequate description of cultural diversity. Profoundly marked by centuries of imperial and colonial domination, Puerto Ricans and Chicanos resist the '-American' qualifier. Rather than hyphenation, they speak of plural identity. Gloria Anzaldúa, a renowned Chicana writer, comes from the 'borderlands' of Aztlán, the former Mexican territories of the south-west United States. This territory, historically and metaphorically, produces what she calls 'a new consciousness of the mestiza'. Inhabiting the hybrid terrain of borderlands means that the new mestiza 'has a plural personality, she operates in a pluralistic mode'. This important writer and theorist claims an identity that is, at once, indigenous, Mexican, US, continental American, lesbian, female, and brown. Through this multiplicity, she sees herself as involved in creating 'yet another culture, a new story to explain the world and our participation in it'.[2] Speaking from the in-between spaces of 'borderlands' not only constructs new centres. It expresses an infinitely sharper view of history and of an unequal world.

In similar fashion, the Puerto Rican poet Aurora Levins Morales presents herself as a 'California Puerto Rican Jew', claiming diversity as a cultural resource. Her view has resonance particularly for people like myself, whose roots, migratory histories, and cultural experiences do not easily fit into any sort of homogeneous community, whether dominant or oppositional. Like Anzaldúa, Levins Morales uses metaphors of terrain to construct a political sense of coherence and wholeness—in multiplicity, and from her many historical roots. She says:

I am not african. Africa is in me, but I cannot return.
I am not taína. Taíno is in me, but there is no way back.
I am not european. Europe lives in me, but I have no home there.
I am new. History made me. My first language was spanglish.
I was born at the crossroads and I am whole.[3]

Propositions such as these are quite different from existing paradigms of assimilation, pluralism, and liberal interpretations of multiculturalism. Like Dona Marlene who, in Evelina Dagnino's essay, speaks from the *favela* experience in Brazil, these poetic voices emerge from long histories of oppression. They do not advocate integration into existing arrangements of power that define peoples' social places and identities. Rather, they destabilize national ideologies of coherence and threaten the norms of the dominant 'core' culture. Here, US historian Arthur Schlesinger's defence of the motto of the United States, 'e pluribus unum', as the essential and necessary terms for cultural nationhood comes to mind. In contrast, subordinated cultures and voices call for new terms of inclusion, new citizenship, new social arrangements, and new stories from which to construct equality.

RB

This brings us to our final point, the role of oral history and life stories in the studies in this volume. We particularly want to note that these studies, by drawing heavily on personal testimony often highlight individual experience. In part, the value of such an approach is that it allows glimpses into the lived interior of migration processes. It allows understanding of how moving matrices of social forces impact and shape individuals, and how individuals, in turn, respond, act, and produce change in the larger social arena. These personal stories allow some sense of how individual migrants, in situations of extreme and sometimes unpredictable flux, make sense of their experiences and thereby continually construct and reconstruct understandings of themselves and their larger social circumstances. In all of this, of course, the individual experience is broadly representative of group experiences. But it is more than this, for the individual experience is always richer, more contradictory, more paradoxical than that which we represent as the experience of a group. This is particularly true of the experience of migrants, who often live dramatic, rapidly changing, sometimes contingent, but also intensely creative lives, and who can never (if indeed anyone can) adopt an 'off-the-shelf' identity. Personal testimony speaks precisely to how im/migrant subjects constantly build, reinvent, synthesize, or even collage identities from multiple sources and resources, often lacing them with deep ambivalence. Knowing something of the utter uniqueness of particular individual migrant experiences certainly enhances our generalizations about the group experience, but it also elicits humility about the adequacy of these generalizations and a realization that few actual individual lives fully conform to the master narratives.

On another level, the essays in this volume indicate an additional, more activist role for the process of personal testimony: that it not only reports on, but actively participates in the process of identity construction. One essay in particular—William Westerman's account of Salvadoran refugees and the Sanctuary movement in the United States—speaks quite directly to the political force of testimony and its transformative character. Fleeing from a civil war fomented by the United States and denied legal status as political refugees, these Salvadorans have nothing but their personal accounts as documents of passage. Their testimonies of persecution, fear for their lives, and the horrors of the journey become their self-made papers, their passports and identity cards in the United States. Such testimony also becomes a political weapon, both to defend the refugee community from deportation back into the hands of their oppressors, and to continue the struggle against their oppressors from afar. Finally, in telling their stories in the safe havens provided by the Sanctuary movement, to audiences largely made up of non-Latino North Americans, these Salvadoran refugees engage in a process of negotiating new identities for themselves in the United States. Thus personal testimony is far more than a neutral object of research.

What is interesting and important here, as well, is that the act of testifying is a traditional means of building and reaffirming identity in many cultures throughout the world. This is particularly true in Latin America, where the *testimonio* is both a folk tradition and a literary form. And throughout Latin America, as among Salvadorans, personal testimony has become intimately linked with resistance, especially in recent decades. Giving testimony is practised in grass-roots communities of the poor—the famous 'base communities', guided by liberation theology—throughout the Americas. It became a principal weapon in denouncing the many dictatorships that were established throughout the hemisphere in the 1960s, 1970s, and 1980s. Testimony was a means of exposing the responsibility of these regimes for widespread torture, murder, and for the 'disappearances' of thousands of people. The Mothers of the Plaza de Mayo in Argentina, the Mothers of the Disappeared in El Salvador and Chile, the life story of Nobel Peace Prize winner, Rigoberta Menchú of Guatemala, exemplify the political force of the word. Notably, most of the Latin-American pieces in this volume emphasize the impact of political movements on identity and stress the role of testimony as a strategy of resistance.

None of this is to argue that oral history, or the oral-history movement around the world, is necessarily political, although in many instances it certainly has been. We are only suggesting that the character of the personal testimony holds a remarkable political—indeed, liberatory—potential, that has been realized to varying degrees, at different times around the globe. By arguing that personal testimony and oral history are not just research methodologies, we are not attempting to denigrate their importance for the investigation of social reality or for presenting the rich complexity of that reality to the reader, so well exemplified by the essays in this book. These essays also illustrate a variety of ways in which testimony can be used, and how overlapping levels of testimony can emerge. Dorothy Zinn's essay shows the most typical use of testimony. She gives voice to her Senegalese interviewees, both by quoting them and by summarizing what they tell her of their migration experiences; she also elaborates a layer of her own commentary and conclusions. It is important to add, though, that like all of our authors, Zinn does not position herself as the detached, neutral observer. That is, she does not pose as the objective positivist, but self-reflectively locates herself as a factor in the research process. Similarly, Francesca Battisti's interviews with fellow-students and intellectuals at the Villa Mirafiori are explorations of their shared position as students of foreign literatures and cultures.

Evelina Dagnino also provides her own level of interpretation and explanation while giving voice to her informant. She goes one step further, for she draws much of the theoretical and conceptual framework for her own explanations from her informant's story. In other words, her informant becomes a *de facto* collaborator in the theoretical and explanatory structure of the essay. The backdrop to this collaboration is the fact that both Dagnino and Dona Marlene have similar political commitments and involvements, although Dagnino tends not to insert herself directly into the text. In contrast,

Iván Jaksić takes a brave turn to the first-person voice, to his very own story, as a way of analysing and coming to terms with the effects of political repression and exile. In his case, the testifier and the analyst are one in the same person, and one of the fascinating aspects of Jaksić's text is the internal dialogue with himself in each of these roles.

William Westerman, however, takes us beyond these issues of representation by suggesting the political responsibility of those of us who gather and analyse oral histories. His essay is openly and explicitly the testimony of a researcher-participant in the Sanctuary movement. His essay is an example of double testimony. Just as the testimony of the refugees is a call to the North American audience to become actively involved in protesting US intervention in El Salvador, so, in fact, is Westerman's. He mounts a frontal challenge to the myths of objectivity, detachment, and observation that still characterize much oral-history scholarship.

Westerman's challenge brings us to our final observation. It has to do not with the politics *of* identity but with politics *as* identity. In the locally focused studies in this volume, the complexities and details of a wide range of identity constructions will be examined. That, as we have said before, is how it should be. However, we want to note that the issue of identity has re-emerged on the global scene and as an object of study at a time of major crisis for a wide spectrum of oppositional and counter-hegemonic movements. Indeed, why this is occurring should be an object of our investigations. Those associated with many progressive social struggles world-wide have recognized the complexity of individual and collective identities. It is no longer adequate to assume identities as essences which command like behaviour. To be a feminist of colour from the working class is quite different from identifying as a feminist (read white and middle class). In a sense, this volume is part of the process of naming these complexities. We (this large, world-wide we) fight many oppressions and are 'doubling' our identities from those engagements. However, in all of this, something seems to have happened to weaken the centrality of a politically defined identity, as well as the recognition that identity is forged through political struggle. Something has happened to weaken a world-view that guides us and allows us to transcend the accidents of birth, the belief in essences, and to resist effectively the force of the myriad oppressive identities imposed from without. Something seems to have happened to weaken a world-view that rises above particularisms to a globalism, indeed, to an internationalism. As our societies become increasingly multicultural, we are challenged to expand our understanding of diversity and difference, which, again, is how it should be and part of our purpose here. But in the long run, identities built around a common politics of human liberation may be our best hope of coalescing and bringing about social change. To the extent that oral history, life history, and testimony—our field and method of study—allow for a 'doubling' of our engagement as investigators, analysts, and activists, we reinforce an already established tradition within our field. But we are also challenged to propose new roles and practices for our own identities in the future.

RB and AS

Notes

We wish to thank the Centro de Estudios Puertorriqueños, Hunter College of the City University of New York, and Russell Sage College, Troy, New York, for their strong material support of our efforts in editing this annual. We would also like to thank our colleagues at these institutions for their suggestions and insights.

1. Catherine Delcroix, Anne Guyaux, and Evangelina Rodriguez, 'Le Mariage mixte comme rencontre de deux cultures', *Life Stories/Récits de vie*, 5 (1989), 49–63.
2. Gloria Anzaldúa, *Borderlands/La Frontera: The New Mestiza* (San Francisco, 1987).
3. Aurora Levins Morales, 'Child of the Americas', in Aurora Levins Morales and Rosario Morales, *Getting Home Alive* (Ithaca, 1986).

2

In Search of Safe Haven

Exile, Immigration, and Identity

IVÁN JAKSIĆ

It was 11 September 1976, when friends drove me to Santiago's international airport. I had a one-way ticket to the United States, and a valid passport with a visa. But 11 September was one week before the scheduled start of my mandatory two-year military service. I had been expelled from the University of Chile by officials appointed by the military regime of Augusto Pinochet, and my part-time job as a secondary school teacher was in jeopardy. My mentor at the Department of Philosophy was in prison and I was expecting the same fate for myself. My choices were either to leave the country or stay and be drafted, something I did not want to do under the current conditions of Chile. I did not know whether the airport police would have the information about my military status and so I reviewed my possible answers. I could say that I was leaving only for a short while, that I would get back in time. But with a one-way ticket? In Chile, where only the extravagantly rich could leave the country 'for just a few days'? What was I going to do in the United States, anyway? I had already been through that airport in 1974, and in similar circumstances, not knowing about the future and not knowing if I would even be allowed to exit. I had been able to leave for Argentina at that time, but passing police inspection now would mean a departure in defiance of military law. Would I ever be able to come back?

The passport inspector coldly glanced at my papers and at my face. He checked his list and looked at me again. My passport had been issued in 1972, and renewed in Argentina in 1974. 1974? When the neighbouring country was teeming with people in trouble with the regime of Augusto Pinochet, who had seized power the year before? The stamps on my passport, and the dates, made him uncomfortable. But my papers were in order and he eventually sent me off to the transit area. I was numbed, suddenly aware that I was in fact leaving for an unfamiliar place that I had never expected to visit. I knew that my life had changed in those few hours. When I boarded the plane I began to realize that the prospect of starting a new life was not an opportunity, but a burden. I struggled to convince myself that my situation would only be temporary, that I would get back as soon as the regime changed or my military situation somehow became normalized. There were also immediate problems. I did not speak English. I did not know the people who had worked so hard to get me admitted into both the United States and the State University of New York at Buffalo. I did not have any money. But most disconcertingly, a sensation of fatigue had overtaken me. I felt as though my youth was spent, that from now on I would live a life I had not chosen.

When I first arrived in the United States, I refused to incorporate any new experiences as my own. I lived as though I were escaping from the reality around me. All I could think about was Chile. My life there had not been particularly happy, especially after the military coup, but I had developed a strong, if unconscious, sense of community and citizenship. Hence, I pictured my situation as similar to that of a plant that could not grow outside Chile and was destined to wither away on foreign soil. Inevitably, that would have happened had it not been for the immediate need to survive. And an essential part of survival was language. Learning English gave me a focus. But most importantly, it allowed me to translate—at first haltingly, but more fluently as time went on—my struggle to stay in contact with Chile, the country where I had lived the only life that held meaning for me. I was only dimly aware that my experience was not unique, and that in fact part of my own family had lived through a similar experience when they emigrated to Chile.

My father's parents had left Dalmatia for Chile at the turn of the century, and had settled in the remote city of Punta Arenas, where many other Croatians lived. Life was hard for them, not just because of the barren, frozen landscape, but because they knew they could never go back to their unstable land. They never did, and that sense of loss and sadness became a permanent part of my father's own personality. He always seemed to be remote, even frightening, in his loneliness. He had lost many of his brothers and sisters to tuberculosis. He and his mother saw my grandfather, who had deserted the Austro-Hungarian imperial army, leave one day for Argentina, and never return. Father struggled to keep the family together. He criss-crossed Patagonia to eke out a living. When he eventually felt secure enough to start his own family, he had only the memory of his lost parents and siblings. As I grew up, he took silent stock of a harsh, unrewarded life. He would sit for hours in the dark, never showing joy or happiness unless he was around friends who had the same origins and experiences.

His marriage was a disaster. Mother was much younger and was also unencumbered by the weight of memories and the meaning of an immigrant experience that father himself could not fully articulate, or even grasp. She wanted a happier life. They made a last ditch attempt to save their marriage by moving to Santiago, only to have father severely injured in a hit-and-run accident just weeks after his arrival. Although he survived, he became even more remote and withdrawn. He knew he could not stop the dissolution of his family. He could not stop his own children from leaving him when mother, who had left him earlier, asked us to join her.

I grew up very alienated from him. My brother and I would visit with him briefly on weekends. He lived a spartan life, moving from one single room to another for years on end. But he wanted to be a giving father and would share with us an unwelcome philosophy of sacrifice and readiness for the hardships of life. We dreaded these encounters but were comforted by his predictable nature.

Shortly after the military coup of 1973 came the day that would forever change our relationship. My college, my professors, my friends had been devastated by a furious onslaught of military repression. I barely escaped arrest and knew I had to leave Chile, and soon. Father had to give me the legal permission required for anyone under 21 years of age who was leaving the country. We met one night to discuss this, and as he prepared dinner he refused to give me permission on the grounds that I should first clear my name with the authorities. I should have nothing to fear if indeed I had done nothing wrong. I told my father that he was naïve, even reckless. We argued as dinner overcooked. That night he had prepared something special for me. He had set the table and arranged the small room to receive his son. But now a dreadful, unbridgeable abyss had opened between us. I left in anger as my dismayed father held the tray of food in his hands. We would not see each other again for years.

My school at the University of Chile had been raided by the regime's secret police, the Dirección de Inteligencia Nacional, or DINA. It was a school, the Instituto Pedagógico, that had become notorious for its radicalism in the 1960s and early 1970s. It was also a teachers' college where students from a working-class background could hope to get a higher education. Prior to college, I had attended a trade school, trained as a machinist, and worked at a factory near the city of Puente Alto. I was thus part of a generation that was painfully aware of its limited prospects. I had been involved in student politics during my trade-school years, and when I entered college in 1970, I quickly identified with peers who were highly critical of Chilean politics and society. There was a tradition of student activism at the Instituto Pedagógico, and the very nature of our disciplines (philosophy, sociology, history, and so on) brought us into direct contact with the problems of Chilean society. The coup triggered a fury of retaliation against us and all we represented, even though we were not aligned with the Socialist government of Salvador Allende: we had in fact been quite critical of it. Our school was closed down in 1973 as part of the general repression of universities, and when it reopened in 1974, the DINA descended on us. That is when I narrowly escaped arrest. I abandoned my rented room for restless nights in different houses until my situation became unlivable. These were the days when I learnt about the detention of friends just as I tried to avoid my own. I did not have the luxury to ask why; I instinctively knew that I had to move on, and help others if I could. Together with my philosophy professor, Juan Rivano, we maintained a very precarious network of contacts until my friend Eugenio, who had been arrested during one of the DINA raids, sent a message from prison that during an interrogation he had been asked about me. I knew I had to find a way out of the country, and soon.

Thanks to the French Embassy in Santiago, and through the mediation of friends, I received documents that allowed me to obtain safe conduct and leave for Buenos Aires, presumably on my way to Europe. Buenos Aires was the most sensible choice. I did not know anyone there, but it was my hope that I would soon find someone who could help me find my way around. It is hard to describe how different Buenos Aires was at that time, especially when compared to the repressive environment of Chile. The streets were filled with people, day and night. I experienced an almost forgotten sense of freedom and safety, but I had nowhere to go and work was difficult to find. I did not have a work permit, and at any rate there were tens, perhaps hundreds of thousands of Chileans, Uruguayans, Paraguayans, and Peruvians, in the same situation that I was, desperate for work. As a trained machinist, I had one advantage over my generally more intellectual peers. But work took me to La Plata, a provincial city where I was far removed from friends who started to arrive in Buenos Aires a few at a time. I also found that the man who was compassionate enough to give me work could not or would not pay me more than a fraction of the minimum wage. Wasn't that the way it had always been in an immigrant country like Argentina? There was something reassuring about being in a situation I knew had been shared for decades by many people in my situation. But it was not easy to work a six-day, ten-hour shift, sleep on the floor at night, and wait for the mail to arrive. I would walk every night into a home that was not mine to see if there would at least be a familiar sign, a letter, a postcard, something that would tell me that I did belong somewhere. But the letters took longer than expected, in part because friends at home didn't feel there was anything worth reporting, and in part because the mail would take weeks to come, and would sometimes arrive damaged. Sometimes it didn't arrive at all. Whenever I received a letter I wrote back feverishly. I wrote about Argentina, about La Plata, about work, about freedom, about how terrific it was to be in a place where I did not have to worry about my safety. This enthusiasm was genuine to some extent. In many other respects it was not: the language I spoke could be the same in Chile and in Argentina, but I was shocked to learn that my Chilean accent and comportment singled me out in ways that would later prove dangerous.

One day, wandering around the streets of Buenos Aires on a weekend visit, I ran into my friend John. It was only natural that many refugees would hang around downtown Buenos Aires, where there was so much light, so much life, and where hotels were cheap. John had jumped the walls of the Ecuadorean embassy in Santiago. He was granted asylum, but the military government harassed him in Quito. He decided to cross the border into Peru and Bolivia, and then into Argentina where he settled uneasily, until one day we ran into each other on Avenida Corrientes in downtown Buenos Aires. We looked at one another in disbelief, and at that moment we realized that we were not alone, that we could probably start all over again, that we might soon find others.

And we did. One by one, our friends and classmates arrived in Buenos Aires. We established a place for meetings, the Café La Paz, on Corrientes near Pueyrredón, where we drank coffee for hours and pretended that things were OK. We exchanged news; we talked as we always did. Wasn't it an ironic twist in the history of Latin-American dictatorships that we could find such sanctuary in Buenos Aires, the very city that had sent so many into exile in our own Santiago since the last century? But in our case, a sense of impending disaster hung in the air. We received the first warnings when the cheap downtown hotels began to be raided. At first it appeared to be routine, nothing more than a regular police search. But then people began to disappear, or were found riddled with bullets. Carlos Prats, the Chilean general who had remained loyal to the Allende Government in its last days, was killed in Buenos Aires and we knew it was the DINA that was responsible. We started to suspect the Chileans who arrived in our café. We asked ourselves: Where to go? What to do? Juan Domingo Perón, the populist leader who let so many of us come into Argentina had died in mid-1974 and the situation of the country, as well as our own, began to unravel.

The shocking news came when John showed up in La Plata one morning and told me that he had been arrested. He was terrified, he could not stop shaking. But at the police station he mustered enough presence of mind to declare that they should immediately dial the number of a prominent politician to tell him that his nephew was mistakenly being held there. The police decided not to call John's bluff. But they told him to get the hell out of there before they changed their minds. John walked the streets the rest of the night until he could catch the first bus to La Plata. He did not need to say much for me to realize that there was trouble. My own roommates were restless because a few days earlier a group of unknown but presumed leftist radicals burned the state capitol building in La Plata, causing increased surveillance and harassment of foreigners. The city was occupied. Military patrols combed the streets while unmarked civilian cars drove slowly by. Gunfire pierced the air. Distant shouts could be heard. John confirmed what I most feared: we were not safe; we should try to leave as soon as we could. Argentina was collapsing. He had seen a frenzy of blood and death in the eyes and behaviour of his captors. He hugged me, knowing we would never see each other again. He found refuge in the United Nations building in Buenos Aires, and I returned to Chile for what would soon prove to be just another temporary safe haven.

It was 1975 then, and for a while it seemed that repression against my college in Chile had subsided, but only temporarily as the regime's attention had simply turned to other challenges. I was even able to resume my studies in philosophy and join a group of former classmates and professors. My most important contact was with Juan Rivano, whom I had met in 1971 and with whom I stayed in touch while in Argentina. I had always admired his scholarship and teaching, and the years before and after the coup gave me the opportunity to get to know him as a person. As one of the most respected philosophers in Chile, he had numerous students representing the entire political and philosophical spectrum. The military government saw him as a threat. The secret police harassed him and his students. Beginning in 1973, his former and current students and associates were arrested. One night in 1975, shortly after my return from Argentina, he was abducted from his home by DINA agents driving unmarked cars. He remained missing for a month. He was then held without charges for a year in various makeshift prison camps.

I visited him every time they would let me in. During the visits, he would counsel me and others about our situation, which had grown ever more precarious as the military government proceeded to purge us methodically from the university. He would help the others in prison, keeping up morale and passing on messages to the outside. I once carried one of those messages: a phone call to a family simply to tell them that their relative was alive. I still cry when I recall the anguish, followed by relief and gratitude, in the voice at the other end. The fear of those endless months and years, though it still wakes me or darkens my mood, is nothing compared to those few moments of human contact. The oppression of those years, the anger and impotence I felt when looking at my mentor across a prison's fence, gave me a glimpse of the depth of humanity in the face of adversity.

It was during the time when Rivano was in prison, in March of 1976, that I was expelled from my college. As I tried to register for the academic year, I was told by a military-appointed official that I was no longer a student and that I was barred from entering the campus. Shortly thereafter, I was drafted. My whole world once again collapsed, and the implications for my safety were obvious. There was no choice for me but to leave again.

In the United States, the memories of repression continued to burden me while new anxieties were added. Orlando Letelier, the former Chilean ambassador to the United States, was assassinated in Washington barely a week after my arrival. The DINA acquired an almost mythical proportion in my eyes. Clearly, Chileans were not safe, even in the United States. Rivano obtained asylum in Sweden. John was given refuge in Austria. My classmates were scattered, all facing uncertain futures. I tended to think of it all as a bad dream. Could we stop time and return to life before the coup? Separately, we all knew that this was impossible. Those of us who were out of Chile could not go back without facing certain arrest.

There were other immediate tasks, however, like re-establishing a network of contacts. In the United States, I tried to establish contact with those few Chileans who had been admitted into the country, and to concentrate on helping families who came in without any contacts or means of support. Some came straight out of prison and needed to rebuild basic trust in people before they could even consider participating in politics. A few of us formed a group that fixed houses and free-lanced as painters and carpenters. Ironically, we ran up against the hostility of those who argued that the struggle against the regime should take precedence. We also encountered the despair, the violence, and the generalized misery of decaying downtown Buffalo. Our new-immigrant ethos was not welcomed in an environment where there were no resources. This was the kind of place one should leave, but most could not.

I was also trying to do graduate work at SUNY-Buffalo. I learnt enough of the language to do academic work, but felt frustrated when I could not put into words my feelings about Chile or about friends and family. I also began to suspect that even if I could articulate many of the things that held meaning for me, I would not find interlocutors. Friendship, just like anywhere else, was based on common experiences. But who shared mine? Who *wanted* to share mine? Every time I spoke of Chile to my Anglo classmates, who were in many ways as uprooted as I was, I felt that my experience was minimized. Where was Chile anyway? they asked. When I ran into them in cafeterias and hallways, the polite hellos hurt me more than the frankest of rejections. And at any rate, why this search for communication and understanding? Wasn't I a 22-year-old adult, and shouldn't I accept my lot and go on?

I could not. I struggled to communicate with others in order to convince myself that I had a life that had only temporarily been suspended. I wanted someone to understand what it was like to see your life suddenly cut down, your points of reference blurred, your ability to express emotions and feelings impaired by the pervasive presence of a different culture and language. In the absence of that contact, the dry yet structured life of the student was one of the few concrete things I had. But there were no central issues that brought us together. We shared in a community of learning, but how come it felt so empty? The cold and the wind of Buffalo reminded me of my native Punta Arenas on the Strait of Magellan, and I felt even more isolated. Not a single familiar face, or promise of return awaited me in my empty room.

One day in 1978, two years after my arrival, a letter came in the mail informing me of an amnesty for people accused of violating military law. It simply read, 'the following citizens are eligible for amnesty', yet those few words, and my name under them, instantly restored me to my Chilean life. I could feel it in my head and in my chest: I could finally go back. I could see my friends, my family, all the familiar places of my young adulthood. I phoned the consulate in New York City to ask how to claim the amnesty. They told me that I had to go to Chile, in person. And I did. I wasted no time.

The day after my arrival I went to army headquarters in downtown Santiago. It was winter and thus the building had the familiar odor of kerosene. There was someone typing on a manual typewriter who stopped when I explained the purpose of my visit. The officer in charge coldly and condescendingly told me that the deadline for claiming the amnesty had long passed. I was disarmed. I tried to say something about being away, not having the information, but soon realized that he was not listening, that he was simply looking at me as a draft evader who had finally come back where he belonged. He issued an order for me to appear in military court, effective immediately. No pleasantries exchanged, no mistake about my condition despite two years of absence. Indeed, I was rapidly restored to the life of fear I had lived before my departure. The city I loved had once again become menacing. I once again felt threatened.

The trial did not last long. I sat in a hallway outside the makeshift military tribunal while my case was being tried. I did not have a lawyer, I did not see the judge, I did not see the prosecutor. All I saw was the sentence, which was handed to me through a window: guilty on charges of violation of military law. Two soldiers then took me at gunpoint to the Ministry of Defence, the dreadful place where so many had been held in the days following the coup. I feared the worst when I was taken to a basement, where I sat for hours, waiting. Then two military officers came to interrogate me. They asked me about my patriotism, they asked me about my activities, they asked me about the United States. I then realized that the Carter administration, which was pressuring Chile on matters of human rights, was deeply resented by the military. They asked me if I was glad to be in my own country, which I admitted with trepidation. They asked me why I had left the country in the first place, to which I could reply with some conviction: to study. But they wanted something more than straight answers. They asked me what was more important, to serve my country or to study. There was only one possible response, and that was to serve my country. In what was supposed to sound like a reward, they told me that they had assigned me to the Buin regiment near Santiago, to serve for four years and to do all that I could for my country. I should be on my way immediately after the medical examination. Then they left me alone.

As I waited for the medical examination I felt as if I had fully returned to Chile. I was even questioning whether I had ever been out of the country. My short life in the United States suddenly appeared as a vague and distant dream. As I stared at the green walls and heard the sound of military orders and boots, I found myself reviewing my past all over again, trying to determine what I should forget, what I should remember if I were asked. I cannot describe the tremendous sense of relief I felt when the medical examiner, upon learning that one of my lungs had spontaneously collapsed a few years earlier, dismissed me as unfit. I was therefore free to go and live as best I could with my unsuitable military record in a military regime. As I faced the dark and cold night, I clearly understood that I had only one way to go. This time there was going to be no return to the Chile I thought I knew.

I returned to Buffalo in the fall of 1978, this time convinced that I should consider a longer stay. In fact, I didn't even think of returning to Chile until six years later when my brother notified me of my father's terminal cancer. It was at that point that I realized, as I thought about my father's life, that I was no longer an exile waiting for the fall of the regime, but rather an immigrant who relived the experience of many other immigrants in history. A silent process of healing was bringing me closer and closer to my father as I recapitulated his life of loneliness, sadness, and longing. But it was not until 1985, more than a decade after our dinner confrontation, that I could communicate with him as he lay dying in his small apartment in downtown Santiago. Outside, shots and clashes between protesters and police announced the rebirth of a nation determined to end the dictatorship. He himself had grown disaffected with the regime. He now knew that I had done what I needed to do back in 1974. On my part, I now knew what his own life had been like after the family breakdown. We chatted quietly for hours, days, weeks, until he died one night just before curfew. I stood by his body all night before I could begin the procedures for registering his death. My own sorrow was constrained by the magnitude of the events surrounding the deterioration of the military regime. I carried my father's ashes, alone, through a city torn by political confrontation. Our estrangement and reunion would forever be associated with the rise and impending fall of dictatorship.

After my father's death I began to look at my life in the United States differently. Until then, I had seen myself as forced by circumstances to live in a place that was not my own. Now I understood that even if I could never be entirely a part of the United States because of language and culture, I could try to make my situation more permanent. I had completed my education in the United States, and although I had to confront not just the usual insensitivities foreigners encounter, but also the stark realities of discrimination, I had never felt that my life was in jeopardy. Most importantly, I now had a family of my own. My wife, who has close family ties to Mexico and our daughter, who is growing up speaking Spanish, made me feel much more rooted to the country. Perhaps I could not relate fully to the festivities, the culture, the comforts of shared values and history. But I could share in a community and build a new life as well as a new identity.

Building a new identity, or at least an identity in addition to my sense of national origin, was one of the unexpected challenges of my experience of immigration. During my first years in the United States, I found strength in my nationality. In fact, I think I became conscious of it only when removed from my own cultural context. At first, I found it shocking that I could look at my own experience from the perspective of someone outside it. I was particularly troubled by the perception that Chile was just another country. I had to recognize, not without tremendous discomfort, that my struggle to stay in touch with Chile occurred at a level independent from the myriad contacts I made as part of my daily routine. I was an island of ongoing, separate experiences. I was even aware of being an island. But what was important to me was to hold on to my background and to my network of friends and family as firmly as I could. Although aware that I could not return to Chile, I fervently hoped that one day I would resume my life in my own country.

There was a turning-point, however, or perhaps two, when I realized that I might be here to stay and that I therefore needed to develop a new public persona that could help me manage in a new environment. First, the amnesty disaster forced me to face the fact that I could not return to Chile as long as there was military rule in that country. Secondly, the final encounter with my father made me realize that my experience was rooted in his own, and through him, that it was also part of a much larger human experience. That was the moment when I changed from an exile to an immigrant. As an exile, I had viewed my experience as temporary, even as a preparation for an eventual return. As an immigrant, I understood that while return was not impossible, I had to come to terms with life in another culture, and participate in it as fully as I could.

It was during this process of adjustment that I realized that the experience of exile can deepen one's knowledge of one's country, and even add a critical element to that knowledge. I thought about Chile so much that even my intellectual orientation changed. Having trained in philosophy in college during the early 1970s, I studied the classics and learned the fundamentals of the discipline in a context of national disintegration. All I had read and discussed about Socrates and about the philosopher's role as social critic prepared me in some ways for what happened to my own mentor, to me, and to my country. But the experience of exile added a twist. In the effort to remain in touch with Chile, and once I could resume my studies, I did not return to the study of philosophy merely for its own sake or for its methodology. Instead, I decided to study the development of Chilean philosophy. I wanted to trace, step by step, the origins and fate of the discipline in the national context. This became my way of coming to terms with what had happened to us as a nation, and, more specifically, to my teachers and classmates.

I became, in US academic parlance, a 'Latin Americanist'. Becoming a member of the profession afforded me new ways of staying in touch with Chile and Latin America. It allowed me to learn more about the history of my country, and most importantly to place it in the broader context of regional and world developments. This experience is as humbling as it is enlightening for anyone who has been raised in the uplifting yet distorted accounts of national history. Belonging to this profession also allowed me to stay in touch as I ran into other Chileans in the hallways and rooms of professional meetings. Every year I met a stream of Chileans who brought news about emerging social movements, about the ups and downs of political alliances against the dictatorship, and about other specific events and their meaning. I also met and befriended North Americans whose knowledge of, and commitment to, the country and region was inspiring. I had never been more in touch with my homeland than during the long years of struggle against military rule.

As the regime itself liberalized in preparation for a protracted transition to democracy, made all but certain after the plebiscite of 1988, I was able to return again to Chile and see my experience of the mid-1970s from a different perspective. This was the time when I could finally meet with my mentor and other friends in our own country for the first time in more than twelve years.

These were much happier days for our nation and for ourselves, but the past could not be erased. The very process of redemocratization in the late 1980s demonstrated the magnitude of the changes in our lives. I had learnt much more, and gotten much closer to friends, than I would have if there had never been a coup. Keeping contact with Rivano and many other friends and former classmates had been a triumph. However, I could not help but long for the life that could have been. Moreover, the very process of redemocratization sometimes brutally forced me to confront memories I had wanted suppressed. The crimes of the military regime were exposed. The names of the dead reappeared along with the gruesome accounts of their abductions and deaths. I relived the fear of arrest, torture, and anonymous death. And as I read the news about findings of remains, or the confessions of former secret police agents, I was haunted by the images of young friends less fortunate than myself. I had wanted to forget the time when I learnt that life could be worth so little. I needed to forget in order to carry on. Now I must find a new balance between life as I knew it growing up into adulthood, and life as I want to respect it and pass it on to my child.

It was this ability to return freely to my country, meet friends, and witness the process of democratization that made me confront and reconstruct the past. Current events have also served as constant reminders of how central political violence, exile, and immigration, can be for thousands, perhaps millions of people. How many exiles are there who must negotiate a transition to immigrant life? How many must forget the horrors of the past in order to reaffirm life and rebuild trust? My father's Croatian background has brought into painful relief the current situation of the former Yugoslavia. How many lives have been forever imprinted with the fear of death and the unsettling sight of uncontrolled violence? How many more from Bosnia or Central America, if lucky to find safe haven, will have to relive the life of countless exiles and immigrants? How will they communicate? How will we listen? How will past and present be reconciled in their lives and the lives of their children? What new subjective and social identities will emerge?

As for myself, I felt the urgent need to remember events I had wanted to forget. I even went back to the places in Chile where I once had been happy and which later turned into places of persecution and violence. This was the time when I could at last confront my past, my fears, and the facts of my survival. I finally felt the compelling need to put my experience into words, even though they at first resisted me.

Writing had been an important part of my life ever since I could remember, but especially since it became apparent to me that my parents were growing apart. I needed to build my own identity in the face of conflicting loyalties. I needed to make sense of the dissolution of what I had thought, or hoped, to be a permanent bond. I poured words on to paper in writings that had little structure but that gave me a sense of self, and relief. By the time I was in college, I felt confident enough to write poetry and prose that built on my own experiences, and that provided me with a sense of direction and to some extent control over my own life. Then came the coup. Writing allowed me, especially in Argentina, to maintain a sense of self and to find a voice that would reaffirm my Chilean identity in an alien environment. A ten-hour work shift did not allow me to write except secretly during breaks or late at night. But I needed it. And by this time I had also developed the sense that writing was not entirely a private matter. During the short period after my return to Chile from Argentina, I wrote a number of short stories about repression. They were all of a testimonial character, some coming from my own experience, some coming from the information I gathered in my visits to the prison camps. They circulated anonymously for a while among classmates and friends.

I came to the United States with a sense of self and of national identity that had developed in close contact with writing in Spanish. Inevitably, the need to learn and communicate in English put my Spanish voice on hold. One of the most difficult tasks in learning a new language is finding a voice that conveys one's innermost feelings and thoughts in a structured way. You speak neutral words that constantly betray you. You make mistakes, you lose confidence, you wonder who you are.

As I grew more confident in the new language, I also realized that my use of Spanish and English fell into distinct spheres. I would dream in Spanish, wake up in Spanish, talk about memories and feelings in Spanish. English became the language of my interaction with others, the language of my job applications, the language of teaching and negotiation. My English was unencumbered by the weight of the past, but I was uncomfortable with the sharp division it introduced into my life. True, English was the first language I could use publicly without fear of retaliation. It allowed me to establish meaningful bonds with society, the kind that I had never been able to establish in two disintegrating nations.

But how could I address, communicate, and resolve personal conflicts and memories? I had to reconsider my approach to English, and at least attempt to incorporate the private into my English self if I ever wanted to both confront the past and present myself as more than public persona. Writing this piece in particular has made me go back and listen to the sort of experiences and conflicts, originally spoken in a Spanish voice, that were such a defining part of my life.

I cannot claim to have achieved the meeting of language and experience any more than I can claim to have dissolved the clouds and burdens of the past. Perhaps there will be a day when the most painful memories will turn into knowledge and wisdom. A day when I will understand what has happened to me as a bridge to communicate and understand the experiences of others. But I have come to accept that the experience of immigration has been a central part of my life just as it was the centre of my father's life. And I suspect that in this nation of immigrants, where so many of us have come from unlikely places to meet in unlikely places for generations on end, there must be a way for us to communicate our experiences, our sense of loss as well as our hopes. Perhaps there is a language that can bring us closer together, if we only dare to speak it.

Notes

I dedicate this piece to Michael Frisch, Ana María Hidalgo, and Alfredo Matilla, whose care and perseverance changed my life.

3

The Apple and the Olive Tree

Exiles, Sojourners, and Tourists in the University

FRANCESCA BATTISTI and ALESSANDRO PORTELLI

> I am fond of writing, or saying, that I am an olive tree, an olive tree torn from its native ground and planted by force in another.
> (Thamer Birawi, Palestinian immigrant, poet)[1]

> The apple breaks away from the tree, and so does the young man, or the animal that can fly. At a certain age, one breaks away from one's parents, he catches a plane and goes, all the way to the North Pole. There is a time for breaking away from the family: a violent impulse, I must go, I don't know where but I must. I don't want my mother to control me, I don't want my father to control me...
> (Gifi Fadi, Syrian immigrant, graduate in medicine)[2]

> My ideal? To travel, what else? To roam about the world freely, contentedly....
> (Valeria Landolfi, Italian student of foreign languages, University of Rome)[3]

> One thing I noticed is how travel-oriented Islamic culture is, how much it is inclined toward travelling, going around, going out....
> (Omar Nasser Miludi, Italo-Libyan student of foreign languages, University of Rome)[4]

Since the student movement of 1990, we have participated in an oral history of the students attending foreign-language departments at the Villa Mirafiori campus of the University of Rome 'La Sapienza'.[5] Departments of foreign languages and literature are, by definition, places where people gather to learn about other languages and cultures; they are, therefore, almost natural places to look for signs of a multicultural imagination. Indeed, a central theme was the students' desire for 'otherness', the myth of travel and cultural and linguistic multiplicity.[6] On the other hand, the University, and foreign-language departments in particular, also have a multi-ethnic and multicultural constituency: they attract both a number of foreign students, and many Italian-born students with nationally or ethnically mixed backgrounds, who wish to take advantage of their native knowledge of languages or to keep in touch with their 'ethnic' roots. We decided to investigate more deeply into these groups and to include also other stories of young Third World intellectuals and educated migrants, to explore aspects of what we perceived less as a dimension of the international labour market, than of the multiplicity and fragmentation of subjectivity in international youth culture.[7] This essay, therefore, will be concerned with aspects of subjectivity: point of view and visibility; displacement and estrangement; language and aphasia; memory and syncretism; family, origins, and ambivalence.

In our time, people, especially young people, travel for many reasons. Tourism and exile, violence and choice, the trauma of emigration and the fascination of seeing the world and seeking an identity are often less the terms of a binary opposition than polarities along a continuum. The same individual may identify both with the uprooted olive tree and with the free-floating apple. Thamer Birawi, who describes dramatically the conditions under which he left Palestine, also speaks proudly of his explorations across three continents: 'Italy is where I am now, but before coming here I had to take a long detour, I went to Jordan, from Jordan I went to Iraq, then I went back to Syria, to Lebanon, to Egypt. I wanted to know, to feel, to master another world.' Another exile, Ribka Sibhatu, left Eritrea 'for one thing, to save my life: but what really motivated me was the search for myself'. She sums up both motivations under one heading: 'freedom'.[8]

In this regard, though our migrant interviewees tend to be older than the average student, shared generational tensions may be as relevant as national or ethnic differences. Both the exiled Gifi Fadi and the student Caterina Duranti use the same verb—'staccarsi' ('breaking away')—to account for their travels. The desire to 'go away, out', which motivates a student to learn foreign languages and to travel abroad may be typical of contemporary, Western, middle-class culture; but it also resembles the 'inclination toward going out, going around' which Omar Nasser Miludi identifies in his father's Islamic background.[9]

Of course, we cannot ignore the differences. Both Thamer Birawi and the student Chiara Midolo wanted to get away; but while Chiara sought some undefined cultural alternative ('everything I was not, everything Italy was not, everything which my adolescence was not'),[10] Thamer had to get away from the Israeli occupation. The perspective of return also differs: the traveller goes home at the end of the trip, while exiles and migrants may never be able to return, at least not to their home as they left it. Indeed, the sheer duration of absence creates a dramatic qualitative difference in experience. Yet the differences stand out more clearly when seen against a background of emotions and desires which are shared or, at least, comparable.

Comparability is heightened by social background. All of our foreign interviewees support themselves by what Ribka Sibhatu describes as 'the little jobs that suit my colour' (she 'does for' a lady in exchange for rent, Birawi works in a pub, Gifi makes a living by teaching Arabic in spite of his medical degree, etc.). Yet they come from middle-class families, and received a higher education before leaving home. Like the Italian students (and unlike the vast majority of immigrants) their motivations for going abroad were not primarily economic: 'When I came here in '69', says Gifi, 'Syria and Italy had the same standard of living, my father made good money, so until he died I didn't have to work to support myself here.' Omar Miludi, son of a Libyan journalist and a middle-class Italian mother, is very much aware of the cultural and economic difference between himself and the black immigrants:

A friend told me once, 'People can tell you're not an immigrant:[11] you wear dreadlocks, you look good. . . .' For the immigrants it's different. All right, I'm coloured, but I go to the university, I speak good Italian, if someone says something to me on the bus I can talk back. She told me, 'They don't look at you the way they look at the immigrant who wipes windshields at the traffic light.' People don't see colour so much as the image of that person that they think is here up to no good, maybe he's pushing dope, while you're the guy who goes to the university, studies, makes no trouble.

On the other hand, these privileged migrants, exiles, and 'ethnics' interact with the larger immigrant working-class communities and feel involved in their destiny: 'It's important to me to see how other people of colour are seen,' says Miludi. While not representative in statistical terms, they represent a shared subjective horizon of possibilities and desire. They stand for the fact that not all non-European presences in Italy can be summed up in the stereotypes of the victim or the peddler-begger-pusher. In admittedly varying degrees, all migrants are bearers of knowledge, and all struggle to retain a degree of choice and control over their lives. This is also why we do not attempt to generalize from a broader sample, but focus on the meanings and implications of a few significant narratives.[12]

In the continuum between exile and tourism, therefore, roles and outlooks may overlap and reverse. Student travellers may experience, by choice or necessity, the condition of the emigrant, while the emigrant may take on the *persona* of the tourist. 'The other day', says Gifi Fadi, 'I was strolling in the Roman Forum, beneath the arch of Septimius Severus, with a young lady from Asmara [Eritrea].' In a book of stories and poems, the 'young lady from Asmara', Ribka Sibhatu, writes: 'Between myself and the Rome of the Republic, of Nero, of Saint Peter's, we have established a marriage in chaos. The ruins whisper a mysterious and moving language to me. . . . Rome has so many eternal tales for the exiles.'[13]. On the other hand, middle-class Italian students may support themselves abroad by working at immigrant jobs: 'I was a dishwasher, I was a waitress, I was a charwoman, I worked as a cook's helper in a fast-food, I was unemployed, I was drawing social security, I was a squatter—I mean, all the things that Italians in London do.'[14]

Yet, the mixing of roles highlights the different backgrounds and histories. For Gifi and Sibhatu, acting as tourists is a way of holding on to their original membership in the educated middle class; for student travellers whose middle-class status is not in question, the 'immigrant' experience is part of their strategy of seeking new selves by getting away, albeit temporarily, from their family and country, and from their class as well.

Manuela Bagnetti, a part-Chinese student, told us of the girl who approached her in the women's rest-rooms of the University and told her: 'I've been noticing you. Are you coloured, or are you normal?'[15] We will begin this section with a theme which is shared by all our interviewees: the question of visibility and vision, seeing and being seen. Italy has not grown used yet to the presence of ethnic difference in its midst: 'I grew up in Italy, my mother is Italian, I went to school here', says Omar Miludi, yet, because he is black, 'I'm the one people look at. After all, you're not the conventional person people expect to meet. Sometimes I wonder—if I were to go into a building and ring the wrong bell, what would I feel if I were the person that opens the door and sees me?' Highly visible strangers in their own country, Manuela and Omar are made to feel at times as if they were standing 'on the parapet, dangling between two worlds' (Lucia Rossi), estranged and displaced. As Franco Esposito Soekardi, who is part-Indonesian, says: 'It used to bother me, when they asked me where are you from, I'd say I was Italian, and they didn't believe me.'[16]

Student travellers also experience displacement and liminality. In their case, however, it results from a voluntary departure from the native context; therefore, rather than feeling exposed to other people's gaze, these intellectual questers (as opposed to conventional mass tourists) turn their own gaze inwards, generating a sort of inner estrangement. 'There are three thousand different ways of living and being, and when you're travelling you become aware of this. You can really be other than you normally are, understand?'; 'For a moment there you stand naked, really naked; you have no shelter, you don't have a family, you're away from home, from your mama, from your daddy, from the money, from all the safety nets you have there. It's a way of measuring yourself, because you understand what your limits are.'[17]

Since identity and personal growth are the main objects of this type of travel, however, the perception of the new contexts remains often rather conventional. Essentially, young travellers seek in the places they visit an alternative to their ordinary experience: 'everything I was not, everything Italy was not'. Thus, in Germany or Britain they find Western efficiency, modernity, user-friendly universities ('a huge library ... comfortable armchairs and gardens, clean bathrooms, available teachers, a laundry service'); in the Third World, they discover alternatives to Western competition and consumerism.[18] Paolo Giacomelli sees in Thailand a 'kindness' to which 'we are completely unaccustomed' and 'a strength, a courage which we have all but forgotten, with our running hot water, mom and dad, our clothes washed and ironed in the closet'; Ludovica Mutarelli remembers New Caledonia, where she grew up, as a 'paradise' of communal solidarity and sharing, inhabited by 'truly mild people'.[19]

Exiles and migrants experience both outer and inner estrangement. They are the object of other people's gaze because of their ethnic difference, but they also see themselves under a new light; most importantly, the fact that their estrangement is more involuntary and less temporary allows them to view their new environment differently from the local people. 'I know Rome very well', says Birawi, 'I hate it and love it. I am an immigrant, I work at night, and I suffer from the cold—I ride my motorbike home each night, to a cold water flat on a seventh floor; there is also an inner cold, not physical, but one of the things I dislike about Rome is the cold, the cold weather.' He writes poems about the cold nights of the migrants in this supposedly warm city:

> In Rome at night the graves open up
> In Rome at night the dead rise
> they walk around
> hands on their heads
> in the rain
> shoeless
> toothless
>
> without a ticket
> undocumented.[20]

Seeing Rome differently may be a way of finding oneself in it. In his strolls around the Forum, Gifi Fadi identifies a Middle Eastern presence at the very roots of Roman civilization: the word 'Arabicus' in the arch of Septimius Severus, the traces of the 'Syrian cult of the sun' and of 'the priests, the singers, the architects of the Syrian school' under Caracalla and Eliogabalus. 'Fifty per cent of the Italian people have Syrian blood in their veins: we find Syrians around Tarquinia, toward Abruzzi, all around Etruria.... The Roman legend of Romulus and Remus... Romol means sand in Aramaic.' Credible or not, this version of Italian origins combines effectively the estranged self-recognition of the traveller and the estranging vision of the migrant and exile, establishing continuity and legitimacy for this Syrian-born Italian citizen.

Indeed, a plurality of modes of perception is the most frequent case, especially for persons of multiple roots. Omar Nasser Miludi is made to feel like a stranger in Rome, but when he visits his father living in Malta he perceives the difference which his Italian upbringing makes:

My father keeps Ramadan, has been to Mecca, he prays, and I don't. And at times it happened that it was Ramadan when I was down there with my father. And you see yourself seated at the table, you eat and he does not. It's ironic. It used to be a shock [to visit my father] and find Arabic visitors, Libyans or Islamic, or whatever, all squatting on the ground eating kouskous, and I didn't speak Arabic, so I couldn't speak, I could only say three or four words. Ironic—I was dressed different, I had different rituals—I didn't know how to eat kouskous, I didn't even know whether I liked it or not. And my father introduced me, said: 'This is my son, who has been living in Italy'.

'I feel completely Chinese,' says Manuela Bagnetti—and five minutes later she speaks of 'us Italians'. According to where she is, in

Italy or China, she shifts to the outsider's position. Thus, the tea-taking scenes in Henry James's *Portrait of a Lady* remind her of 'the darkest period of China . . . because tea is a reminder of the colonial period' of which she heard in her mother's stories. On the other hand, while she fears that the tourist may replace the colonizer, and is proud of riding the trains with the Chinese rather than in the compartments reserved for foreigners, she inevitably shares the traveller's way of looking at people and landscapes, through the glass of a train window, a camera eye, a nostalgic imagination: 'I took so many pictures. . . . And then this land, cultivated inch by inch . . . it's a very rich land, with the river flowing by. . . . The adults, there, live together with the children, the houses are made of one big room'. Again, her image of China is to a large extent a projection of a desired alternative to her ordinary, Italian environment: the commune she visited 'seemed truly an ideal community because the people work and share what they raise, equally—it's not like here, where everything is calculated, a race to see who is, or has, more. . . . There, you see all that we don't have in Italy.'

Franco Esposito Soekardi goes back to Indonesia ('the place of my mythic childhood') in a disappointing search for the 'exotic' part of himself: 'You come from Europe, and Indonesia, which happens to be part of me, appears to you through exotic eyes—this terrible thing of every European who goes to these places and thinks he's God because he has money, and is looking for these [exotic] things and is disappointed because they are no longer to be found. He finds colour TV, he finds parmesan cheese, all the comforts.' It's a good thing, he says, because 'people are no longer starving'; yet, when he reclaims his status as a native he finds that he has become a tourist:

It's not even the colour of your skin, it's the way you act that identifies you. People can tell right away who is a tourist. Last summer, my girlfriend and I—she is Italian—and other friends went back down to Indonesia and we were walking along the beach, and these children who sell things spoke to me in Italian! I got mad, and I asked them, 'Don't you see that I am like you, that I am Indonesian?' He looked at me and said: 'No, I don't'.

When we were small, we lived for ten years in Switzerland, with my mother. We returned to Italy around 1979, '80, and my brother had a language problem, because in Switzerland we spoke French or English, also at home, with my mother, and my father now wanted my brother to speak Italian right away, immediately, and for a year and a half he did not speak at all. My father thought French was a secret language between us (Manuela Bagnetti).

The reconstruction and creation of identity finds in language, and in culture in general, a crucial battleground, especially in the case of young people who make the study of languages their specific vocation. Manuela Bagnetti refers to studies and stories of aphasia, such as Roman Jakobson, Maxine Hong Kingston's *The Woman Warrior*, N. S. Momaday's *The House Made of Dawn*:

My brother's inability to express himself reminded me of Abel in the Los Angeles ghetto.... Momaday explained that Abel's problem is that he is a man without a voice. For us Italians, language is just a way of communicating, while for blacks or Indians in America there is more attention to language at the stage of birth—dialect is the stage of birth, and then the study of aphasia is language in dissolution, and this applies to every language.

What she is dealing with is the linguistic consequences of displacement: aphasia on the one hand, and internal Babel on the other; too many languages or no language at all. The multiplicity of languages is primarily a symptom of possibility: 'languages fascinated me as a different way of communicating, as formal instrument, a sort of mask, you know. I mean: let's see, if I played the part of an English person, what would the result be?'[21] These students' sense of possibility, however, is rooted in the fact that their membership in their native linguistic community is never threatened or questioned. For migrants and exiles, foreign languages are more a matter of necessity than choice; holding on to their native language becomes a matter of protecting and preserving their innermost identity. 'My diaries and my poems', says Sibhatu, 'I often write them half in Italian and [half] in Tigrinya. It depends: when I think of my mother, my words flow in Tigrinya.' The tie of language and roots takes a different twist in the case of Italians of mixed descent: Omar Miludi had to study Arabic in order to speak with his father, and Manuela Bagnetti is studying Mandarin. Learning a foreign language becomes a search for a part of one's roots.

Migrants and exiles exhibit their mastery of languages as evidence that they are educated and world-wise: 'I think I have a very great advantage, in that when I want to write in Arabic I write in Arabic, when I want to write in English I write in English, or in Italian, and I can find the right ways and words. Languages are almost like clothes, when you feel you have mastered something you use it instinctively', says Birawi. Like Sibhatu, he takes pride in his virtually accentless Italian; in fact, most contemporary immigrant writing stresses mastery of the host language rather than linguistic syncretism (when we detected some slight errors in Sibhatu's prose, we suggested she let them be as a reminder of her identity, but she insisted on correcting them). Linguistic signs of otherness must be sought, rather, in certain metaphors drawn from a pre-urban, village paradigm, especially in Gifi and Birawi's speech: language as 'a garden' or 'clothes'; identity as apple, olive tree, 'fruit', bread (the Israeli occupation as 'the oven which matured my generation').

Franco Esposito Soekardi gives a vivid description of multilingualism as possibility. 'In my house we speak a very strange language, a sort of patois. I speak to my sister in Indonesian, English, and Italian. I say the things that come to my mind in the language which has the more appropriate words': for instance, he refers to hard cheeses in Italian and to soft ones in Indonesian because 'cheese is always soft in the Orient'. On the other hand, he remembers his father speaking Neapolitan dialect at the dinner table, and says—*in English*: 'he reared me up as an Italian'. The use of English to describe an Italian upbringing reveals a fracture at the root of his linguistic identity. In fact, the price of polyglottism can be a nostalgia for a truly satisfying language of one's own, or the utopia of a higher synthesis:

Q. What language do you think in?
GIFI. Right now, in Italian; when I must think of something I studied in English, I think in English . . .
Q. What about feelings?
GIFI. More often in Italian. In Arabic, only the children's tales I studied in Arabic: Aladdin and the flying carpet. . . . Years ago, I wrote books both in Italian and in Arabic; and it was a waste of energy, because I am not satisfied with languages as they are spoken today. There will have to be a superlanguage, one which conveys most information with least energy.

A similar process concerns another deep layer of identity, religion; being exposed to more than one religion, in a context of displacement, can result in having none: 'My father was a non-believing Muslim, who lived in a Christian neighbourhood. Really, after studying everything, I can no longer believe in any religion, because they are all the same' (Gifi). As is to be expected from intellectuals in an intellectual environment, the place of religion is often filled by culture. Knowledge is often presented as an antidote to racism: 'I had a hard time, in the beginning, until I understood that racism is ignorance. Yes, studying helped me through many of the difficulties which a foreigner faces' (Sibhatu).

Thus, all describe the university as a friendlier environment, where 'there is less ignorance, or at least, there should be; there is more information, much more politics' (Miludi). Ribka Sibhatu writes:

> The University adopted me. My teachers are my parents and the students my sisters and brothers. When I first started going to classes, I couldn't understand what was said, and Daniela happened to sit next to me. One day, when the professor began to talk about Joyce's *Ulysses*, I asked her: 'Who are Penelope, Telemachus . . .?' She was agape, but she explained it. . . . Later, she corrected my history paper six times, and she even gave me money for books, trying not to hurt my feelings, when I had to stop doing 'the little jobs that suit my colour'.

Sibhatu describes 'self-knowledge' as the most important aspect of both her travels and her studies, and compares her exile with literary precedents: 'It's easy to talk about exile and silence, as Joyce does. But talking about it, and living it, are two different things.' Likewise, Omar Miludi reconstructs his identity through the study of history and literature, drawing especially on Malcolm X's presentation of African history:

> Culture has been a great help to me. First of all, it has helped me claim what it means historically to be black. A few years back, if someone had asked me how come I am in Italy, I would have answered it was because my father married my mother. It is still the main reason, but now I know there's more than that.

If racism is identified as ignorance, culture becomes a weapon. 'I study anthropology for self-defence', says Gifi, and he means it literally. His anthropology is of the nineteenth-century positivistic type, not exempt from traces of anti-Jewish prejudice ('international Zionism will win in the end, because it holds the world economy in its hands'). But what counts here is that knowledge and language are part of a strategy of physical survival:

> Once I was stopped by Nazi skinheads, the Fascist youth movement, near the Colosseum: 'Foreigner', they said, '*quo vadis?*' ['where are you going?'] And they were doing the Fascist Roman salute. So I told them, 'I may be more Roman than you are: look at the Colosseum, it was celebrated by an emperor named Philip the Arab; I have an Italian last name, and if you want to know, it was the Syrians that built up Rome.' They wanted to invite me to dinner that day, I didn't go, but I gave them a lot of information they didn't have. There are three emperors of Syrian descent, I learned that for reasons of self-defence, of survival.

'I come from a family which has two different views of the world. My father was more linked to his culture, more attached to the land; my mother, she said: the world is changing, it is a world of education, not land.' Cultural syncretism has always been part of Ribka Sibhatu's environment, as a consequence of Italian colonialism; but is also a part of the experience of all of our interviewees. We will see in this section how it is perceived as a source of both empowerment and fragmentation.

Sibhatu makes a determined effort to recover and preserve her grandfather's mythical stories ('He said that the West would be the origin of the loss of man. Mankind will get lost on its way to the West'), yet she received from her grandmother a more practical example of how to deal with colonialism, in terms of selective appropriation, economic gain, cultural mediation, and a sense of historical rather than mythical time:

During Italian colonization, in '35, she was the first to learn the language. She was an orphan, so she had to make her own way, and she had the most contacts with Italians. I mean, normally Italians were seen as devilish sorts of creatures; the very fact of being easily angered was typical: among us, when one is angry, one does not show it, one checks oneself. Our grandmother, however, had no choice, if she were to survive. So she worked, as a babysitter, later she became an interpreter; she was twice here in Mussolini's residence, to interpret. So they had discussions between them, and she supported colonization—she had a great deal of money, my grandparents were well off. 'After all [she said], sooner or later they will have to go away, they shall not live here forever. One day we shall have our independence. Meanwhile, until we are free, let us take what they know'.

Mussolini's residence where her grandmother worked as interpreter is two blocks away from the Villa Mirafiori campus where Sibhatu is now studying foreign languages. So when she came to Italy she was not a total stranger: Italians had invaded her country, now she is travelling to theirs, bringing back some of their impact on her homeland. This syncretism has deep historical roots in Africa and the Mediterranean: as Gifi Fadi says, 'I'm not the first Syrian who comes to Italy. Migrations didn't begin yesterday.' And they went in more than one direction: after all, Italy is historically a country of emigrants. Marinella Bucetti recalls:

I was born in Cairo, Egypt, from Italian parents, children themselves of Italian parents who had moved there to work. My grandparents were from Messina [in Sicily], and after the [1908] earthquake they settled in Egypt to stay. They had been there temporarily before: since the beginning of the century, there is this flux of emigration toward everywhere: I have relatives scattered all over the world. I have relatives in Egypt, I have relatives in Lebanon, relatives in South Africa, Yemen, people who speak Italian, French, English, and Arabic. If Nasser had not chased all us foreigners out of the country in '66 we would have stayed in Egypt.[22]

This history of multidirectional migrations, ethnic mixing, and cultural syncretism allows Gifi Fadi to claim Italian roots for his family just as he claims a Syrian presence at the roots of Italian civilization: 'I bear an Italian surname, Giffi—half the people in Abruzzi bear this name. In Arabic, the double consonant falls. These unusual surnames in Syria always intrigued me: like Morelli, which I find both in my hometown and here.' On this basis, he imagines a story of Abruzzi fishermen landing on the Syrian coast a century and a half ago, and concludes: 'My family was Italian, Gifi, back in 1830, my greatgrandfather was Christian, then my grandfather was Moslem.'

In most interviews, ethnic and cultural syncretism is described as a source of strength. Gifi, again, takes it very literally: 'My father used to say, the more you mix the stronger you become, all the ancient peoples who were unable to mix grew weaker and died.' Omar Miludi insists on the potential for self-creation which derives from combining in an individual way the different pieces of his multiple identity, adopting the black images of the Jamaican Rastafarian and the American blues singer—though, perhaps, more through Italian youth culture than through his African origins. He thus turns the enforced visibility and marginality of his otherness into an empowering vision of his unique self:

From this point of view, I am glad, sincerely glad that I am black, I am pleased with my experiences, with what it has brought to me. I mean, if I had lived my life in Africa among so many other blacks, I could not have appreciated it, I would not have been as glad as I am now. Because on certain things you always have to choose, you must always choose something which is much more personal, which others do not share. So you can create a strong identity. If this identity also contains insecurity, it's not important. What counts is that it also contains something strong within you, you are strong inside.

The post-modern sense of fragmentation as possibility, however, combines in these stories with a sense of fragmentation as the result of violence. 'When you have a cultural identity which has been shattered,' says Marinella Bucetti, 'it's harder to know what you are.' Thus, Miludi concludes the discussion of his multiple and open self with a recognition of the historical paradox on which it is based:

The Apple and the Olive Tree

It makes me kind of sad—everybody says, how nice, a black boy who speaks with a Rome accent. I used to like it, now I don't like it so much. Because after all, a black who speaks Roman, I see it simply as something which has been violated. Not negatively, or positively, either. A course which has been changed.

Yes, I'm talking about '66, the six days war, the six years, the six centuries, I don't know. That event was the oven which matured a generation which is mine, which throughout Palestine had almost the same influences, the same handicaps, the same broken dreams, that is, of going home one day to sleep on that pillow, in that corner—forget what happens in the world, whether I have accomplished anything in life or not. . . . In a way, we are still anchored, we are still bound, something in us has been broken (Thamer Birawi).

This final section is concerned with the memory of the cultural and physical violence and loss, personal and historical, which is implicit in the histories of exile and migration, but also, as Miludi reminds us, in the roots of 'mixed' ethnicity. We will also look at the ways in which the narrators deal with this memory and turn it into a source of strength and identity through the use of imagination and symbolism. Let us start with the most dramatic story, that of Ribka Sibhatu:

I was sixteen when I was arrested. Just because an officer was courting me, and I didn't want him. He accused me, he said that I was in touch with the guerrillas. I didn't know anything about these guerrillas. So, the first thing—torture. They cover your eyes, tie your arms around your back, I don't know what they did to me, but torture is the first thing, my back still aches. Actually I was lucky, because I was only tortured twice. I think that the foremost torture for someone who is in prison is psychological: facing death. There is no trial, so every night, each time we heard those feet coming, we thought they were coming to take. . . . Every day life is in danger, in tension, because they take you one by one. So when we hear the handcuffs and the feet—'it's my turn'. And at night, it's not our cellmate we're afraid for: it's ourselves. It's the next day, that we weep for the girl who was taken.

In a poem, Sibhatu evokes her friend, Abeba, who was killed in jail. She explained that the dots between two verses represented both the silence of absence, and the shape of the bullets that killed her. But we might also read them as a metaphor of what was broken within herself:

> For the world to understand,
> while they were digging her grave,
> wrapped in the mystery of death,
> I weave an *aghelghl*
> and send it without *hmbascia*.

> In an intense night
> they took her from me in handcuffs!
>
> . . .
>
> Each day she is absence,
> but in the dark she is omnipresent![23]

Cultural memory, concentrated in powerful symbols, is the only way to overcome the trauma. This is the function of the *aghelghl* and the *hmbascia* (a palm-leaf basket and the ritual bread it usually contains) in Sibhatu's poem. Birawi's story of the Israeli occupation of his native village also focuses on three symbols: the mother, the loss of vision and meaning, the physical destruction of the land.

> Of that day, I remember only my mother. And I remember that she was nervous, she kept coming and going around the house, looking in all directions. And then she goes out into the garden and begins to look down a road, the only paved one, that came in from the village's north gate. She wasn't saying anything, but I knew something big was happening. We couldn't open the door, but there was a hole in it, and I used to kneel at the hole and look outside; that day I went, out of curiosity, and saw military machines, armed men. The village was dead, no one around, a heavy air, I saw these cars come and turn and go. Then we went out to see the signs of this visit, this change, this event. The first thing which struck me—as children, we used to play beside the street, or in the street itself. And when I went out on the street, it was all ground up. I saw the street ground up, where we used to play, because the tanks had torn it with their wheels.

The earth torn by the tanks is a powerful metaphor for the loss of homeland. Exiles and migrants, as opposed to tourists, know that the home they left will not be waiting for their return: 'I used to miss my village', says Gifi, 'I went back twice, and the village I used to miss is gone. My world is dead. It was painful, and later on I was afraid to go back.' 'We went back to Egypt ten years ago, and Egypt was completely changed', says Marinella Bucetti. This makes for a different shape of memory: travellers remember being abroad, migrants and exiles remember being home. Ultimately, it is always a memory of absence, of where one is not: 'in a way, I have never left, though I am away from the place where I was born', says Birawi; 'Nablus is a town I love very much also because I am faraway from that town.'

The loss of home is also cultural loss: the violence of history silences the transmission of culture. Awaiting the invasion, Birawi's mother looks in all directions, but does not speak; afterwards, 'Even the adults could not explain what was happening.' It is up to the younger generations both to make sense of these events, and to attempt to preserve—through memory, writing, story-telling—what is left of the culture of their ancestors.

We had to learn by ourselves that there was an occupation, that there was an army, that this army was our enemy; we had to see the dreadful fear in the eyes of our neighbours, of our brothers and our parents. Our first battle was a battle against the fear of what had happened, to get rid of this fear, and recognize this reality, understand it, and finally control it.

Ribka Sibhatu says that she is studying African literature in Rome 'in order to keep my grasp on this ephemeral culture which is being lost with all its wise men'. While Sibhatu holds on to her oral tradition, Gifi privileges book-learning and written culture ('I was born 16 kilometres from Ugarit, which is where the alphabet was born'). Writing is rooted in absence and loss: Sibhatu sees her work as a writer as an alternative to participation in the liberation struggle ('I mean, I cannot go back, because now I want to write books. And those books will be censored. So, how can I go back? Maybe I ought to fight, but I don't know, I don't believe that my struggling would be of much [use]. It is more useful to write it').[24] Birawi writes hundreds of letters and sent his first writings home for a friend to keep until he returns. His poems turn obsessively on a word—'without'—and on a symbol, the moon, which is both an image of the cold nights of Rome, and the memory of a lost, powerful emblem of Arabic and Moslem culture: 'The moon in Rome | is no moon' for those who are 'on the sidewalk' and 'outside the walls | without clothes | without fear'.[25] These writings of absence, in Italian by foreigners, are the contribution of these intellectual migrants and exiles to the creation of a multi-ethnic literature in Italy.

The theme of loss is implicit in the effort to recover historical and family origins. Manuela Bagnetti begins:

My mother's mother was half French [and half Italian]. At eighteen, she, left everything, because she had fallen in love with this Chinese soldier who had come to the Mediterranean to learn the art of war. He went to military school in Turin, then he met my grandmother and they left, without marrying, he took her to China where he had his concubines, then he left her alone and went to war.

These stories, however, also include the awareness of the irretrievable distance that now separates them from these origins. While young tourists and students travel temporarily away from their families, exiles, migrants, 'ethnics' travel back and forth between the memory and nostalgia of the olive tree, and the desire of selfhood and difference of the apple detached from the branch.

Often, this dual attitude is expressed by references to the mother as a signifier of 'descent', as opposed to the father as a token of difference, change, choice, and 'consent'.[26] Omar Miludi muses: 'My father is dark, he is darker than me. Between my father and me there has always been this thing, that after all I am whiter than him; or perhaps he is blacker than me.' Franco Esposito Soekardi describes an emblematic scene: 'all the family at the table, with my father at the head, almost as the white patriarch'. It is not a matter of colour, since both the Indonesian and the southern Italian extended families are patriarchal: 'but with the eyes of memory I see this family scene, this terrible connotation' of the racial, colonial difference between his coloured self and his beloved, white, father.'[27]

On the other hand, Ribka Sibhatu evokes her mother as the focus of her wish to return, the subject and addressee of her writing. And Thamer Birawi sums up the ambivalence, which is the basic undercurrent in all the stories we have listened to, in a deeply touching final scene:

The very morning I left home, I say goodbye to everyone, and then I say—mother? No one can tell me where she is. The taxi was waiting, so I go into the house, I look in the room—we had a single room—she isn't there, where did she go? Then I think of the orchard, the same orchard where she stood beside me when the Irsaelis came, and I say, 'what's the matter?' 'Why, are you really leaving?' She seemed like a historic hero trying to destroy a whole story. In a word, she says, 'are you really leaving?' And so I left, with these words of hers that still ring in my mind and in my life, 'but are you really leaving?'

Notes

1. Interviewed in Rome, Department of English, Villa Mirafiori, by Alessandro Portelli, 15 Feb. 1992. Unless otherwise noted, all interviews were conducted at Villa Mirafiori, seat of the English Department of the University of Rome 'La Sapienza'.
2. Interviewed in Rome by Francesca Battisti and Alessandro Portelli, 16 Mar. 1992. In quoting Middle Eastern names, we have followed the usage of the informants themselves; thus, while Gifi Fadi still follows the Middle Eastern form of putting the family name before the given name, the others have Italianized the form and reversed the order. In the course of the essay, we will refer to them mostly by family name.
3. Interviewed in Spain, on the train from Salamanca to Madrid, by Francesca Battisti, Aug. 1991.

The Apple and the Olive Tree

4. Interviewed by Francesca Battisti and Alessandro Portelli, 31 Mar. 1992.
5. See Alessandro Portelli, 'Interviewing the Panther: The Italian Student Movement of 1990', in *International Annual of Oral History 1990* (Westport, Conn., 1992), 145–66; Micaela Arcidiacono and Sonia Di Loreto, 'Precious Memories: On the Historical Background of the Italian Student Movement of 1990', and Carlo Martinez and Elena Spandri, 'Authority, Dialogue and Self-Awareness', in *Memory and Multiculturalism*, papers presented at the VIII International Oral History Congress, Siena-Lucca, 25–28 Feb. 1993, 1061–7, 1127–32.
6. Francesca Battisti, 'Another Country: Multiculturalism and Imagination in Foreign Language Students', in *Memory and Multiculturalism*, 1068–75.
7. The narrators discussed in this essay also include two persons who are not students at Villa Mirafiori (Thamer Birawi and Gifi Fadi). However, they were contacted through Villa Mirafiori students and interviewed there. They may be considered as part of the social network which irradiates from the foreign-language departments.
8. Interviewed by Alessandro Portelli and Antonietta Saracino, 24 Jan. 1991.
9. Caterina Duranti, interviewed in Genzano (Rome) by Carlo Martinez, 18 Feb. 1990; Sonia Di Loreto, interviewed by Alessandro Portelli, May 1992.
10. Interviewed by Francesca Battisti, Mar. 1990.
11. The expression used is 'extracomunitario', meaning a non-European Community national. Although technically the term would also apply to Swedes or to US citizens, it is intended to refer euphemistically to Third World or Eastern European immigrants.
12. On the concept of 'horizon of possibility' as a form of representativity in oral sources, see Alessandro Portelli, in Paul Thompson *et al.*, 'Responses to Louise A. Tilly', *International Journal of Oral History*, 6: 1 (Feb. 1985), 32–9.
13. Excerpted in *I giorni cantati*, 23–4 (Dec. 1992), 3. Sibhatu's book, *Aulló: Canto dall'Entrea*, a bilingual collection of stories, tales, poems, both traditional and written by herself, was published by Sinnos Editrice, Rome, in 1993.
14. Tiziana Petrangeli, interviewed by Sonia Di Loreto, 11 Sept. 1990.
15. Manuela Bagnetti was interviewed by Alessandro Portelli, 27 Mar. 1992. This remark was made later in conversation.
16. Lucia Rossi (daughter of returned Italian immigrants to the United States), interviewed by Alessandro Portelli, 17 May 1990; Franco Esposito Soekardi, interviewed by Alessandro Portelli, Rome, Villa Mirafiori, 30 Apr. 1992.
17. Elena Doria, interviewed by Elena Spandri, Mar. 1990; Tiziana Petrangeli, see n. 14.
18. Fabio Ciucci, interviewed by Micaela Arcidiacono, Villa Mirafiori, 26 Mar. 1990.
19. Interviewed by Alessandro Portelli, 26 Sept. 1990 and 12 Mar. 1990.
20. 'Portoghesi', unpublished poem; manuscript supplied by the author.
21. Caterina Duranti, see n. 9.
22. Marinella Bucetti, interviewed by Alessandro Portelli, 31 May 1990.
23. Ribka Sibhatu, *Aulló: Canto dall'Eritrea* (Rome, 1993), 38.
24. Since she was interviewed, the political situation changed, and she was able to go back.
25. 'Lettere', in Thamer Birawi, *Un po' di poesie* (Rome, Ed. Raggio Verde, 1992), 18.
26. Werner Sollors, *Beyond Ethnicity: Consent and Descent in American Culture* (New York, 1986).
27. This tension of identity and difference is accidentally but emblematically embodied in the speaker's Italian surname. A very common name in Naples ('it shows we don't come from the aristocracy'), Esposito is an indication of regional roots; on the other hand, it is one of the surnames that the Church imposed on children abandoned ('exposed') at convents. Thus, it stands both for paternal roots and for ultimate fatherlessness.

4

The Senegalese Immigrants in Bari

What Happens When the Africans Peer Back

DOROTHY LOUISE ZINN

As anthropologist Renato Rosaldo has written, 'No analysis of human action is complete unless it attends to people's own notions of what they are doing.'[1] Unfortunately, research in the area of immigration has often neglected this dimension of study. This essay seeks to demonstrate how the use of the oral life-history of the immigrants themselves is one means by which this gap may begin to be filled. Through a study of the movement of Senegalese men to Bari, Italy, the analysis focuses attention on cultural aspects of international migration which have been overlooked.

In the case of the Senegalese, an economistic 'push–pull' framework does not offer an adequate explanation for their presence in Bari; with high unemployment and few reception structures for immigrants, men from Senegal have none the less continued to arrive in this southern Italian city and support themselves chiefly through self-employment as itinerant pedlars. The Senegalese give meaning to their migratory experience in Italy in positive terms, as they define themselves in part as 'tourists'. At the same time, they discuss their activity in terms of labour migration. As many of their original expectations meet with disappointment, the manner in which Senegalese position themselves as 'immigrants' is another aspect of their own assessment of their presence in Italy. In this analysis, I will explore issues of meaning, subjectivity, and social identity in the context of relations of power and social definitions of space.

This essay is based on anthropological field-work I conducted in Bari, in a three-month period. My project addressed the following question: How do immigrants coming to Italy from developing countries define their motives and expectations, and how do these immigrants perceive these motives in the light of their actual resettlement experience? Using an ethnographic approach, which stressed qualitative data-gathering through interviews and the participant–observation method, I investigated the research question by focusing on one immigrant group, the Senegalese of Bari. I emphasized the life history of the immigrants: reminiscences of life in Senegal, their expectations prior to arrival, and what they experienced in the migration process.

I first met these Senegalese under the palm trees and sunshine of Piazza Umberto I, in the centre of Bari. I wanted to get under way with the field-work, and I knew from preliminary research that the Piazza was their principal place for work and hanging out. As I approached some of the spreads of goods the pedlars had put out, a young man called out to me, 'Ciao, bella!'—a classic Italian opening line. Like most Italians, the young man was unaware at first glance that I was a foreigner in Italy. I look Italian enough to pass for a native, but him— this black man from Senegal—well, it was clear that he did not quite fit the *O sole mio* image, though I have heard some northern Italians say that Africa begins south of Rome (in Rome they say, 'south of Naples').

Thus began my acquaintance with the *copains* ('friends'), the Senegalese immigrants who live in and around Bari. The presence of immigrants in Italy in significant numbers is a phenomenon which has developed along with the expansion of the Italian economy in recent years; the pattern of immigration from developing countries to Italy has followed that of other industrialized Western European nations.[2]

Italian society is experiencing profound effects from the 'new immigration'; the ways in which Italian discourses position the immigrants reflect the reorganization of space and boundaries occurring with greater capitalistic development and the processes of European Community unification. Consider that the Italian euphemism for the immigrants from developing countries is *immigrati extracomunitari*—that is, non-EEC immigrants. As a US citizen, I am technically an *extracommunitare*, too, though in fact no one would really consider me as one. So Italian officialese has developed this expression to refer to those whom many Italians generically designate as *negri* ('blacks'), *marocchini* ('Moroccans'), and *vu'cumprà* (recently suppressed in and by the media as offensive, this word derives from a stereotype of the immigrant pedlars' pronunciation of *vuoi comprare*, 'do you want to buy?'). I say that these terms are used generically because they are often deployed without much regard for actual gradations in skin tone, nationality, or occupation. There is a certain incongruence between these categories, the groups they bind, and the facts of the matter.

On the bumpy road to a new, united Europe, the drawing of boundaries takes on a new dimension; that is, 'us' becomes members of the EEC, and 'them' turns into non-EEC citizens. *Extracomunitario* (read: 'Third World') immigration to Europe is also becoming a major policy concern for the unification process, as the frontiers between member states are opened. European integration is one of the latest sites of the redefinition of space in the epoch of late capitalism. Following Roger Rouse, I refer to literary critic Fredric Jameson's concept of *post-modern hyperspace*, a new kind of social space forming in the wake of transnational capitalism.[3]

In this new space, the chronically depressed Mezzogiorno (southern Italy) shifts from being an area of substantial outward migration to a destination of immigrants from developing countries, despite the incompleteness of its capitalistic development. In analytical schemes which divide the world into 'core' and 'periphery', this area is an uncomfortable anomaly, lying somewhat at the periphery of the core. My analysis is an exploration not only of the Senegalese immigration *per se*, but also of the implications of this migration for the recodification of space in the processes of European unification.

During the three-month research period, I worked with over forty Senegalese, all of whom were single men or married men who had left their families in Africa. I had multiple, extensive conversations with most of the interviewees, and I witnessed the dynamics of their lives over time, even if a relatively brief span of three months. By becoming a 'regular' in their community, I was in a position to observe their interactions with one another and with native Italians. I spoke with the *ambulanti* ('itinerant street pedlars') at work, and even participated in their daily life to the extent of occasionally helping consult their clients on a purchase, translating, and accompanying them to the Police Headquarters. From time to time, informants would invite me to their homes for lunch, to a café, or to an African music concert.

The overwhelming majority of the Senegalese in the area of Bari, as throughout the Mezzogiorno, work as *ambulanti*;[4] they operate either in the city itself, or in the small-town markets and festivals, travelling throughout the region. Typical items among their wares include imitation Lacoste shirts, cheap sunglasses, costume jewellery, hair accessories, belts, handbags, and sometimes African carvings and crafts. Every so often these pedlars make a trip to purchase their goods from suppliers, who are located mainly in the Naples area. A very few Senegalese hold other sorts of jobs; occasionally I met one who worked in a pizzeria or in an automobile body shop; one relatively privileged young man is a scuba-diving instructor. However, these positions are often of short duration or at least substantially supplemented by *ambulante* work, for reasons I will discuss below.

Few of the Senegalese actually live in Bari; many mentioned difficulty in finding housing in the city proper. They cluster in groups in surrounding towns and commute by bus or car into the city. Housing conditions are generally crowded by US or Italian standards, often with five to eight people sharing a small apartment. Despite Italian legislative efforts to help immigrants, real structures are lacking, though a bit of assistance is offered through various religiously affiliated organizations. Most of the Senegalese are card-carrying members of their own organization, 'Mama Africa', which is a mutual-aid group.

I wondered why, with the extremely restricted economic possibilities in southern Italy, the immigrants continued to arrive. That is, why didn't the 'senior' immigrants discourage new arrivals if conditions were so disappointing? I found that many Senegalese *ambulanti*, scratching out a living from day to day, originally had very little understanding of precisely what they would find at the end of their journey. Because of the elements of social stigma involved, the immigrants do not report home what their conditions are really like. Still others then leave Senegal, seeking the 'bella Italia' which they had heard about, only to arrive and face disillusionment. The immigrants hang on in Bari, often in the hope of reaching another, more fruitful destination, or until they can make a face-saving return to Senegal. Thus, the perpetuation of Senegalese migration is due in part to misinformation circulating through the migration network, supplemented by attractive conceptions of life in the industrialized West.

On the whole, the Senegalese immigrants in the area of Bari view their stays as temporary. Some see Italy as a stop before gaining entry into another country. Once they have obtained a permit to stay in Italy, a number of these Senegalese head for northern Italy, where their social networks have indicated the availability of factory jobs. Many choose to remain in Bari, however, in part because they perceive that living conditions for immigrants are superior in the South in terms of climate, housing, and the cost of living.

This is a game which is losing its interest. Presently there will be no back-yard in the heart of Central Africa that has not been peeped into (Joseph Conrad, on the death of travel).[5]

I left my job, I came to Italy to be a tourist here. Later, I'll do France. I want to do all the countries of Europe ('Moustapha', Senegalese street pedlar in Bari).[6]

Italy has long been a touristic destination for the wealthier segments of the world community; in the present day, the tourism industry is a significant sector of the Italian economy. The tourist is a welcome type of foreigner in Italy, in contrast to the mixed reception in recent years of immigrants from developing countries. Ugo Ascoli notes that the boundaries between the two types of foreign groups has been the subject of conflict for Italian policymakers:

Part of the problem lies in the inherent conflict between Italy's desire to be as open as possible to incoming tourists, on the one hand, and the fact that entry as a tourist is one of the easiest paths for potential illegal workers to locating employment, on the other.[7]

When I began to talk with the Senegalese immigrants in Bari, I was surprised at how often, as Moustapha's quote demonstrates, they cast their own experience in Italy in terms of travel, voyage, and visitation. In other instances, even side by side with these discourses of travel, the Senegalese talked about their migratory projects in terms of work and earning money. But it is not, as Ascoli might imply, that they are misrepresenting their motives to obtain an illegal status as a tourist. There have been two amnesties for illegal immigrants since Ascoli wrote his article, and among the Senegalese with whom I worked, all either had their papers in order or were in the process of obtaining them, and their declared motive for stay was *lavoro* ('work').

This incongruence between how the immigrants cast their migratory project as 'tourism' and how elsewhere their motivations are 'work' suggests that we direct attention to what Roger Rouse has described as 'the rhetorical dimension of the interpretations that people give to their own and others' involvement in migration'.[8] All of which leads to the observation that, as I state in the title of this essay, the Africans are peering back. As the ex-colonials (and neo-colonials) increasingly come to Italy, what are they doing, and how do they talk about it?

The migratory project is typically thought of as the migrant's game plan or strategy for his/her movement through time and space; it is shaped by the migrant's capabilities, motivations, desires, and expectations. Yet the migratory project should not be viewed as a single, coherent whole, as it is often presented in the migration literature; multiple projects may be held contemporaneously, and not necessarily consciously.[9] We see a similar fragmentation in some of the conceptions of individual subjectivity which have come out of poststructuralist and feminist theory. As Weedon sums it up, in contrast to humanistic conceptions of subjectivity, in which the individual is an immutable, coherent essence, 'poststructuralism proposes a subjectivity which is precarious, contradictory and in process, constantly being reconstituted in discourse each time we think or speak'.[10] I suggest in this analysis that the Senegalese hold migratory projects which are not always seamless and consistent, and which are a reflection of similar multiplicities in subjectivity. Moreover, I argue that the discursive construction of subjectivity must be viewed in the context of complex relations of power.

As I noted above, the Senegalese position themselves, in part, in the role of tourist. This 'tourist' identity itself allows for play with and the creation of subjectivity, as Adler notes in her contribution towards a sociology of travel.[11] The premiss of Adler's article is that travel in certain contexts may be viewed as 'performed art', in which movement through time and space becomes the arena in which social meaning and subjectivity are constructed. She writes that, 'travel becomes one means of "worldmaking"... and of self-fashioning'.[12] 'Travel lends itself to dramatic play with the boundaries of selfhood.'[13]

Through the tourism/travel motif, the immigrants invest distinctive meanings in their movement through space and time. When I talked with the Senegalese, they often spoke enthusiastically of 'doing' a number of countries in their travels, which seems to imply a conquest of space. As 'Hamidou' responded when I asked why he came to Italy, 'I want to find all the countries of the world. I must get my liberty to go anywhere I want to go.'

Manhood and the construction of adult masculine identity were recurrent themes in my conversations with the Senegalese. They propose their own notion of what they were to become through the migration experience—adult men.[14] The trope of manhood has been a standard in much discourse and literature of travel. Among my Senegalese *copains*, some manhood issues are cast generally in terms of autonomy from the parents, as in the case of 'Ibrahim', who said that it was his own idea to come to Italy: 'I had the idea. I spoke with my mother and father and said, "I really want to go to Italy. I want to understand. I don't want to stay with you forever, because I am a man." ' Other Senegalese, such as my *biliardino* partner, 'Henri', related their desire for greater economic autonomy from their parents.[15] In the Senegalese discourses, manhood—construction of adult masculine gender identity—figures as part of a triad, with travel and knowledge as the other two legs. In our discussions, there was a constant linkage between the idea of travel and gaining knowledge. 'Angelo', 25 years old, has been in Bari for three years: 'I like to travel around the world like this, get to know everything. Then when I return to Senegal I'll understand everything'. Like the 'Grand Tour' of old, travel in Europe seems to be becoming *de rigueur* for the young Senegalese man's position back home.

One element of 'manhood' construction which Adler identifies is the common 'descent into hell' travel trope.[16] While I do not in any way mean to belittle the actual psychic or physical discomforts of the immigrants in their experiences, I would suggest that the way in which they endow this condition with meaning contributes to their development of masculine identity. Difficulties include housing and language problems, financial straits, bureaucratic mazes, encounters with authorities, racism, homesickness, and physical maladies. The expression of problems or suffering reminded me of the manner in which Italian youths often describe their period of compulsory military service—as a period of hardship, a first experience away from the home which forges manhood. Indeed, one of the Senegalese I spoke with made the very same analogy. Another *copain*, 'Cheikh', put it stoically:

If I'd known the work was like this, I wouldn't have come. But after all, it's good to be in Europe, get out of your country, get to know things. You suffer a little bit, but when you return to your country, you know how to live.

The 'descent into hell' trope allows for a positive meaning—construction of an adult masculine gender identity—to be invested in a migratory experience in Bari which offers numerous disappointments.

Overall, I am suggesting that the Senegalese depiction of immigration to Italy as travel or voyage has to do with meanings attached to social identity. However, social identity is related not only to gender, but also to class and race; as many of the Senegalese move through time and space to Italy, they find themselves dislocated in terms of class and treated as a minority racial/ethnic group.[17] Part of what is going on, I propose in the following discussion, is that the immigrants are endowing their travel/migration experience with self-empowering meanings. Such meanings are in contrast to their perception that the Italian audience views them as 'primitive Africans' working as low-status street pedlars, regardless of what socio-economic position or ethnic group belonging they may have held in their own society.

First, the Senegalese are extremely critical of what they perceive as 'exploitation' in their southern Italian environment. The statement by 'Philippe' is exemplary: 'There's a lot of exploitation. You should work maximum 8 hours but they make you work 14 hours, and the maximum, very maximum you get paid is 45,000 lire [then, approx. US$36].' Some of the Senegalese have taken on such jobs, but they rarely stay at them. They say that because of the difficulty of finding work which is 'good'—that is, not exploitative—most choose to make their living as *ambulanti*. Similar assessments of exploitation are offered by unemployed southern Italian youth, who often face the same job prospects as the immigrants, with a bit wider range. Unlike the Senegalese, however, most of these youth have the option of living at home with their parents until they find something better. Of course, 'good' work is in the eyes of the beholder, for working in the peddling trade is not free from the exploitation of the suppliers.[18] The crucial difference for the Senegalese is that as pedlars they are able to be their own bosses; if they are to make miserable earnings with long hours and no insurance at another job, they might as well be self-employed, unsupervised pedlars. Even though they roundly pronounce peddling as low-status activity, something they would certainly not do back home, they perceive in it the advantages of autonomy and deciding how, when, and where to work: their working hours, where to sell, the prices of the goods, etc.[19]

Here I suggest that versions of dual-labour market theory are not adequate to understand the complexities of this situation. Some analysts suggest that immigrants take jobs which native workers are no longer willing to do simply because, due to the temporary character of migration, they do not care about their short-term social status.[20] Piore even states that social status comes only from the home community.[21]

In my view, such analysis is too narrow; as Adler points out, we should pay attention to the role of the audience(s) in the travel performance.[22] Indeed, the Senegalese immigrants have several audiences: themselves, each other, the native Italians, the folks back home, and enquiring social scientists from the United States. The creation of meaning in their migratory projects, including the jobs they perform, is in part a function of these multiple, fractured audiences. The immigrant pedlars may perceive that they maintain their autonomy through a trade-off for this type of low-status work, which in Italy is the almost exclusive domain of foreigners. Contrary to the expectations of dual-labour market thinking, the *ambulanti* do not take jobs from the natives; their activity is in the economic no man's land of the submerged economy, a third labour market. I suggest, moreover, that the immigrants' choice of peddling—however exploitative it may be in reality—is aligned with their quest for autonomy, manhood, and freedom from the obligations they face in the home country. That is, there is a myth of freedom around their entire migratory project which is indeed related to their social status, and which helps us to understand why they do not simply accept the jobs that the natives refuse.

While the myth of freedom gives a positive sense of identity to peddling in the context of the migratory experience, I found that precisely because of a concern with social identity, the Senegalese immigrants who peddled in Bari did not pass on accurate reports about their activities to the 'audience' back home. Many immigrants, like 'Cheikh', said that if they had known that they would end up peddling, they would not have come. Friends and relatives none the less would continue to arrive with high expectations. In short, the immigrants' concern with social status actually has an important role in reproducing the situation.

I have related some of the issues surrounding the social identity of the Senegalese with particular regard to the 'audience' of themselves and those at home.[23] An important dimension of sliding class boundaries, however, is their relation to the Italians around them, both an audience for and co-participants in the travel performance. In this case, when the Senegalese 'peer' into Italy, they offer a critique of those whom they encounter and of what they see. The Senegalese whom I met, most with a relatively high level of education, and/or petit bourgeois family background, often spoke indignantly about what they perceive as Italian 'ignorance'. Discourses about Italian ignorance are also tied into conceptions of travel and knowledge, as I discussed above. 'Philippe' said:

I like to travel. A lot. For me it's normal. It is necessary to know [*savoir*]. Until you leave you're in ignorance—it's dangerous. You'll meet someone in Bari who's 100 years old and has never been to Rome. For example, they don't know where Senegal is. They might ask, 'Are there cars in Senegal?'

Other Senegalese mentioned that people actually asked them if they wear clothes in Africa.

These discourses of Italian ignorance also intersect with the immigrants' evaluations of their encounters with racist ideologies and behaviour. While the Senegalese describe actions in which Italians apparently displayed malicious intent as 'racism', they seem to use 'ignorance' to dismiss more subtle, but none the less offensive (and in fact racist) manifestations when they perceive that good faith is involved. The immigrants are quick to say that, 'There are good people and bad people everywhere', and the racism/ignorance distinction they use in coding encounters with many Italians coincides with the recognition that not all Italians are racist in a conscious way.

As an aside, I would like to touch on the Italian discourses regarding the Senegalese. If I may make a broad generalization, Italians tend to construct Senegalese immigrants as 'good' immigrants, in contrast to some other immigrant populations, particularly North Africans, who are viewed with more suspicion and thought to be more likely to be involved in criminal activity. On the other hand, stereotypical, naïve 'Sambo' images of black Africans are still abundant in Italy, images which have long been recognized as racist and unacceptable in the US context. On one occasion with Italian friends, when one otherwise sensitive person suggested throwing a party in which the guests would come in blackface, I shuddered and tried to explain why I could not endorse the idea.

By positioning themselves as more knowledgeable, more worldly than the Italians, the Senegalese provide an interesting reversal of the racist image that they are 'primitives' among the more 'developed'. Yet alongside and not always distinct from these discourses, in which the Senegalese position themselves with the upper-hand, are self-reflexive references about being an immigrant in which they assess their condition of subordination. This aspect of subjectivity is connected to the recognition of some of the unmet expectations of their migratory projects; it offers a more pointed assessment of relations of power between the Senegalese and the Italians.

The self-consciousness of the Senegalese about their position as 'immigrants' permits them to critique the situation in which they find themselves. In contradistinction to the subjectivity as traveller, expressed in 'I' and 'me', 'immigrant' identity is always framed in terms of 'they, the immigrants' or 'we immigrants', implying a sense of solidarity as they position themselves in political discourses of immigration. 'Pierre' said:

It's tough to find a steady job, for us foreigners who want to work here.... Here in the south, in Bari, about 20 per cent are unemployed. So they, before they give us foreigners a job, they give it to their own.

As 'Philippe' demonstrates, there is an awareness of Italy's emigrant past and a demand for empathy:

I prefer the Italians because they're a little African; they're warmer compared to other countries . . . but I condemn them because they do nothing to aid the foreigners. I've been to France and Germany, and there are a bunch of Italians there. They should think about the past, because they were once immigrants. They should do something because they were in this situation.

These sorts of statements, which I heard from many others as well, say something about the immigrants' own perceptions of the tensions surrounding their presence in tight economic circumstances.

The critiques of the Italian economy and of the 'ignorance' of the Italian people are also embedded in a larger discourse about Italy's lack of development, as the Senegalese put it. There are two principal threads of this evaluation, which often dovetail: first, the disappointment of expectations of what Italy was like; secondly, comparison between Italy and France, in which France is always depicted as 'more developed'.[24] 'Max' said, 'I found that Italy is poor. It's the same as Africa. . . . You see, the Barese themselves don't even work.' Another friend, 'Mamadou', studies economics and aspires to study in Italy. He had been in Italy one year, seven months when I met him, learning Italian and peddling to get by. He says, 'There are some problems for studying here, unlike France. France is much more developed than Italy.' 'Giorgio' complains that he earns a bit, 'but it's not worth a lot because the lira isn't worth a lot. Not like in France. You earn 2 to 2.5 million [lire] in a month.'

The use of France as a reference point by which the Senegalese, even many who have never been there, express judgements about Italy, seems rather obvious in the light of Senegal's close ties to France, its former colonizer. While in this essay I cannot examine in detail the ideological ties between Senegal and France, I would like to point to the colonial legacy as one aspect of 'Europe' as a socially constructed space for the immigrants.[25]

In terms of expectations, Europe (and often the United States along with it) seems to have taken on a generic quality, and Italy is supposed to conform to this European paradise. Certainly this amplifies the immigrants' disappointment of not earning in Bari what friends and relatives earn in France or Germany. As 'Pierre' put it, 'We in Africa always look to Europe. People say that you live well.' 'Cheikh' states that, 'In Europe, money moves [*bouge*]. The buying power that one has in Europe, one doesn't have in Africa.' These assessments of Europe as a spatial entity are based on many ways in which social relations intersect with relations of power. Factors include, as mentioned above, links in the post-colonial era to France and other industrialized Western nations, particularly ties in which Senegal remains economically subordinate. These ties are mediated by Europeans present in Senegal itself, and the representation of Europe that they embody for the Senegalese, as well as by economic investment which creates the sorts of cultural-ideological connections Saskia Sassen has pointed to between so-called 'core' and 'peripheral' nations.[26] Certainly the mass media, which are also party to a general imbalance in North–South access in global communications, have a role in the formation of perceptions of Europe as a pot of gold at the end of the migratory rainbow. When I asked them what they knew of Italy before coming, the Senegalese often made reference to the media, particularly television. The quintessential statement of the role of the media was one friend's choice to call himself 'Blake Carrington', the tycoon protagonist of television's *Dynasty*.

Finally, in examining the Senegalese immigrants' conceptions of Europe, and more specifically Italy, as social constructions of space, we must also address the major importance of information circulating among the immigrants themselves. Information, especially in the form of hearsay, moves through what Roger Rouse refers to as the 'transnational migration circuit'.[27] While much of this sort of information facilitates the immigrant's practical concerns in leaving the country and getting about, hearsay is of immense significance to the expectations and images of Italy prior to arrival. 'Cheikh' said:

At first, I didn't think about coming here. I wanted to go to New York. But it was difficult to get a visa—I had many problems. But then I had a friend who's been living in Italy. . . . He said to come—I could get a visa easier from Italy.

I asked 'Henri' if he knew (*connaître*) Europe before coming. 'Yes. I spoke with other friends who came here before.' I asked what they had said. 'They said it was good. Also, when you come here you find money.'

But, as I noted above, the character of hearsay in circulation is also contingent upon issues of social identity and status back home—hearsay information does not reveal the whole picture of the life of the Senegalese immigrants in Bari. 'Ibrahim' commented on how peddling did not meet his expectations: 'It's a drag. [My friends] didn't explain this work clearly—just that you sell.' 'Alessandro' expressed concisely how the immigrants did not pass back home accurate reports of their activities:

Look. We didn't come to Italy expecting to do what we're doing [as *ambulanti*]. We don't like it at all. We don't want the folks back home to know about what we're doing. We're proud people.

Circulating hearsay, then, like the media, becomes caught up in a complex of social meanings which comprise 'Europe', and which are in part structured around the inequalities of post-colonial Senegal and the industrialized Western nations.

In this social construction of European space, the expectations held by migrating Senegalese offer a more coherent vision of Europe than the Europeans themselves may have ever had, a view which does not recognize the different conditions from region to region, nation to nation. The migrants leave for the Promised Land of Europe, yet once in southern Italy, they find themselves in tough economic conditions somewhat reminiscent of their homeland, as many told me. Peering back as both tourists and labour immigrants, the Senegalese throw into question the neat divisions of the world as 'periphery' and 'core'.

The corner of Europe in which these Senegalese immigrants find themselves, Bari, is not at the end of a line segment drawn from Dakar. It is a dot on the circumference of the four-dimensional transnational migration circuit, a Grand Tour realm composed of home, stop-overs, lay-overs, seasonal moves, places heard of and territories dreamt of, all in constant motion. The life histories of my immigrant *copains* provide a glimpse of this experience; they bring attention to aspects of migration which have been downplayed or ignored in much of the literature, and amplify elements which have been viewed rather unidimensionally. Despite the positive meanings invested by the immigrants, their migration experience is certainly not very easy. I asked 'Ibrahim' if he had thought about going to northern Italy:

I don't know. Maybe tomorrow I'll go North. Or I'll go to Africa. I'd like to have work here and stay, because now I have a lot of friends here. But I'd like to be in Africa, with my mother. I have to deal with what's directly in front of me. I can't think too much about what's ahead.

Though some of the immigrants remain in Italy for a long time, most told me they eventually wanted to return to Senegal. Those who do stay, perhaps to settle permanently in Italy along with hundreds of thousands of other immigrants, will find that access to rights in a Western European democracy is not so easy to attain. The Italians long observed the racial/ethnic problems of other nations and touted themselves as 'non-racist'. But in recent years they have experienced manifestations of intolerance, even acts of violence against immigrants of colour and Italian Jews, as well as the rise of neo-Nazi youth gangs ('*naziskins*'), who are the conspicuous tip of an iceberg of hatred. Italy is a country which has not resolved its tensions between North and South, not to mention those between different classes, genders, and sexual orientations. This is the backdrop to the current challenge of facing people of diverse religions, colours, and languages without relegating them to a new category of marginalization. For the Italians, dealing with difference in the present era will require that they peer back upon themselves.

Notes

Support for the research was provided by an award from the Fondazione Giovanni Agnelli, a Pre-Doctoral Fellowship in Italian Studies. I would like to express my gratitude to Gilberto Cardenas, Roger Rouse, Annamaria Rivera, José Limón, to the editors of the *International Yearbook*, and to my husband, Antonio, for their supportive commentary in the preparation of this essay. *Djere djef* (thanks) and best wishes above all to my Senegalese friends.

1. Renato Rosaldo, *Culture and Truth: The Remaking of Social Analysis* (Boston, 1989), 103.
2. Ugo Ascoli, 'Migration of Workers and the Labor Market: Is Italy Becoming a Country of Immigration?', in R. Rogers (ed.), *Guests Come to Stay* (Boulder, Colo., 1985), 201–5.
3. Roger Rouse, 'Mexican Migration and the Social Space of Postmodernism', *Diaspora*, 1 (1991), 2; Fredric Jameson, 'Postmodernism, or the Cultural Logic of Late Capitalism', *New Left Review*, 146 (1984), 53–92.
4. M. Macioti, E. Pugliese, and E. Melotti, 'Roma, Napoli, Milano: Tre realtà a confronto', in *Stranieri a Roma* (Rome, 1989), 73.
5. Quoted in Judith Adler, 'Travel as Performed Art', *American Journal of Sociology*, 94 (1989), 1366–91.
6. To respect the confidentiality of my informants, I have given them pseudonyms. Some of the names have been selected from among those most common in Senegal.

In other cases, I have adopted some of the Senegalese's own practice of assuming Italian names, either a version of their African name (which may be French) or something else.
7. Ascoli, 'Migration of Workers and the Labor Market', 203.
8. Roger Rouse, 'Migration and the Politics of Family Life: Divergent Projects and Rhetorical Strategies in a Mexican Transnational Migrant Community', unpublished paper (1989), 7.
9. Ibid. 35.
10. Chris Weedon, *Feminist Practice and Poststructuralist Theory* (Oxford, 1989), 33.
11. Adler, 'Travel as Performed Art'.
12. Ibid. 1368.
13. Ibid. 1385.
14. Certainly, as Arthur Brittan notes, 'Masculinity has no meaning by itself—it is always defined in opposition to femininity' (*Masculinity and Power* (Oxford, 1989), 181). The analysis in this essay is by no means self-contained in this regard, and I hope that other study of gender issues in migration might expand on some of the points I make. Additionally, investigation is needed into the use of material and nonmaterial gains from migration to forward projects at home which have gender-role implications, e.g. the purchase of a house for marriage or support of a spouse and children left at home.
15. As Vittorio Morabito and Annamaria Rivera have pointed out to me in personal communications, a strong 'push' factor in the African setting is the immigrant's desire for self-reliance and for release from the obligations of mutual support of the extended family. Ironically, however, instead of an escape, the immigrant finds himself bound to the same duties of mutual support with his fellow-immigrants in the host country.
16. Adler, 'Travel as Performed Art', 1386.
17. I would like to stress that I do not speak of the Senegalese in Bari as a completely homogeneous group. Among them, there are differences in class, level of education, and ethnicity which are all significant in their home country and carry their own implications; the Senegalese also differ according to how they fare individually in Italy. These considerations notwithstanding, I have focused my analysis on some of the discursive commonalities of the Senegalese I met, particularly the *ambulanti*.
18. I would like to acknowledge Rina Benmayor and Andor Skotnes for their insightful remarks on this issue.
19. Roger Rouse notes a similar preference for unsupervised work among the male Mexican migrants with whom he studied, and he looks to this as a site of resistance ('Men in Space: Power and the Appropriation of Urban Form among Mexican Migrants in the United States', unpublished paper (1990), 25, 29). I would also like to mention here that the Senegalese often refer to peddling as an alternative to stealing, which is forbidden by their Islamic principles.
20. Franco Chiarello, 'Teorie dell'emigrazione e flussi migratori: applicazioni e implicazioni', draft paper (Bari, 1990), 8; Michael Piore, *Birds of Passage: Migrant Labor and Industrial Societies* (Cambridge, 1979); Mirella Giannini, 'I lavoratori immigrati: Compatabilità e contraddizioni nel mercato del lavoro in Puglia', in G. Cocchi (ed.), *Stranieri in Italia* (Bologna, 1989).
21. Michael Piore, 'The Shifting Grounds for Immigration', *The Annals of the American Academy of Political and Social Science*, 485 (1986), 25.
22. Adler, 'Travel as Performed Art', 1378.
23. It was not within the scope of this study to investigate the implications of return migration and how the migrants' social status back home might change; this aspect should certainly be taken into account.
24. In case the reader is wondering why the Senegalese do not choose France as a

destination to begin with, I would like to note that France's immigration policies and their enforcement have been quite tough in recent years, while those of Italy have remained fairly lax (though the Martelli law of early 1990 has slowed immigration somewhat). In some cases, Italy may have been a second choice to an intended destination for which a visa is difficult to obtain. Furthermore, as I discuss below, there is the influence of contacts already present in Italy and the information circulating through the migrant social network.
25. Interestingly, the Senegalese critique of Italy, specifically the south, as underdeveloped does not dispel the myth of the European/US paradise, but merely dislocates it to other countries.
26. Saskia Sassen, *The Mobility of Labor and Capital* (New York, 1989), 19.
27. Rouse, 'Mexican Migration and the Social Space of Postmodernism', 10, 26.

5

On Becoming a Citizen

The Story of Dona Marlene

EVELINA DAGNINO

The re-establishment of formal democratic regimes in Brazil and other countries in Latin America in the past decade has brought a new impetus to the discussion about the very nature of democracy. Social movements have been central to this process of democratization, and their role has suggested a new notion of citizenship, one that is being constructed by the disenfranchised and that transcends both liberal bourgeois conceptions and authoritarian practices of the state. Dona[1] Marlene, the protagonist in this essay, has been an active participant in these social movements in Brazil. Her life story, as she tells it, conveys much about the contents, scope, modes, difficulties, and limits of the recent democratization processes—and the emerging conception of new citizenship.

Dona Marlene is a migrant from the countryside to the city. She was forced to move from place to place, in search of a piece of land where she could work and live, finally coming to settle in a *favela*, or shanty town, on the outskirts of the city of Campinas, in the state of São Paulo. For her, as for many, the struggle to survive in the city soon meant a struggle for rights. In this process, the struggle for her own rights as a *favelada* (resident of a *favela*) and as a woman became intertwined, shaping the redefinition of her identity and making her part of a collective struggle for equality. D. Marlene helped to organize one of the more significant popular movements in the region—the Assembléia do Povo (People's Assembly), which emerged in 1979.[2] She has run as a candidate to *vereadora* (a member of the City Council) when the movement decided it needed to reach the institutional political level. But she also participated in women's groups in her neighbourhood and fought for her autonomy as a woman within her own home. For D. Marlene, public and private spheres have constituted a single arena of struggle.

Dona Marlene's story also illustrates how rural migrants arriving in the big cities are submitted to an authoritarian social ordering in a very particular way. Expelled from the countryside by an unjust structure of land ownership, they are again shoved to the periphery of the city and become *favelados*. There they face the constant threat of eviction, sometimes for their own safety, given the risks of landslides and other adverse conditions. In addition to being poor, *favelados* are also seen as idle people, criminals, and prostitutes. With the poor, blacks, women, and homosexuals, they belong to this hidden, dark, excluded part of society, to where non-citizens and disenfranchised are confined. But the precarious physical location of *favelados* illustrates metaphorically their social status: in fact, they do not have a place; they do not belong anywhere. In this sense, this condition of physical placelessness contributes to unmask the reality of their social space as a non-existing place, the place of those who do not have rights. That is why the struggle for a physical place also becomes a struggle for citizenship.

Like many others, Dona Marlene drew on her experience in the countryside, on the trauma of her migration to the *favela*, and on the collective struggle with her community, to challenge the condition of placelessness and non-citizenship. She built a new identity in the process.

When I met Dona Marlene for the first time, in 1979, she was a member of the Assembléia do Povo. The movement had been attracting public attention given its novelty and the impressive numbers it had reached in a few months, bringing together 60 per cent of the city's *favelados*. In their public meetings, gathering up to 6,000 people in front of the City Hall, D. Marlene was a powerful voice. Her speeches combined simplicity and sweetness with a deep intensity. Expressing her own particular mingling of public and private arenas, such a style is not unusual in women who participate in social movements. I followed her struggle thereafter, both in the women's movement and in the Partido dos Trabalhadores, or PT (the 'Workers' Party', founded in 1980), which she joined in 1981. Many years later, studying social movements and their meaning within the process of democratic transition, I realized that recovering the life history of D. Marlene and her personal voice would shed new light on neglected dimensions of democratization as a social and cultural, as well as a political process. The emphasis on the institutional dimension of such a process has obscured precisely what makes it possible: the daily struggle of the people, both in individual and collective terms. What she agreed to share with me was the history of her struggle.

Dona Marlene was born in 1941, in Lagoa Bonita, in the interior of the state of Minas Gerais, Brazil, where she and her family worked the land. This is how she described her life before coming to the city:

My family were squatters (*posseiros de terra*). We lived from the land, we planted everything, we built everything a worker needed.... We used not to buy anything because we produced everything but salt and coffee. There was the pig for fat, sugar cane to make sugar and raw brown sugar (*rapadura*), we grew rice, beans, raised chickens. Most of those people were not used to buying even blankets because we wove.... We were even able to make the fine things on the loom, to sell and to use in the house.... We made pots, plates, cups, coffee pots, everything in clay. On the day of pot-making, the women from the neighbourhood sat down and produced pots all day long, to be fired. Then everybody had their share to take home.

The quasi-idyllic dimension of this description of the rural past certainly results in part from the disruption of the migratory experience and its contrast with later life in the *favela*.[3] The memories of hard toil were overshadowed by those of autonomy, self-sufficiency, abundance, and collective work. One's own efforts and their fruits, be they physical labour or, later, political work, are recurrent sources of pride and dignity.

At age 21, and already married, Dona Marlene made her first migratory move to a region undergoing a boom in agricultural development. As she described it:

In 1962 we moved to the state of Paraná so we could have more land to plant.... As the family was increasing, we had to go after new land [*caçar outros espaços*]. There we had an okay life, we managed to buy two *alqueires* [twelve acres] of land. It was enough to plant what we needed and we could still sell the rest. There were years when we were able to produce 85 bags of beans, 300 bags of rice, amazing, a thing that I had never seen before. We worked very hard.

The boom, however, did not last very long. Modern capitalism continued to penetrate and disrupt the agricultural sector, replacing workers with technology. In addition, landowners refused to comply with the new labour legislation of 1963 and 1964 and thousands more lost their jobs. Dona Marlene and her family again had to leave the land. When speaking about this second migration, her tone changes radically. Suffering, exclusion, and deprivation replace pride; and the sense of autonomy is smashed by the presence of what she consistently—and significantly—refers to as 'the power':

> Whereas man was man, the machine was the machine of power. At that time, I perceived that invasion of the power into the community as if it was, let's say, a moth eating the strength of man and destroying all that; it was impossible even to survive in that place. It was like you were leaving a life, you were losing your life, because that work you had, that power to survive, the machine took them. Then men were leaving for the big city. They did not have a place to live, they did not have anything to eat, they did not have a trade to come to a big city. They came with their faith and their courage.

To Dona Marlene, as to millions of rural workers all over the country, migration to the big city appeared as a new hope but also as the only remaining way out. Arrival in the city clearly had a very significant meaning in her life. She remembered the exact date of her arrival and talked about it in strongly emotional terms:

> I got here on the 24th of May 1967. At the moment when I arrived . . . I felt a very strange thing, like I had a passion inside me, a pain in my heart. As if I was losing everything in my life. I arrived here with nine children; I did not have a place to live; I had only my suitcases in my hand. . . . We got here, we went to that pasture down there and cut grass to make a mattress so we could sleep. This was when I woke up. . . . It seemed as if I had been sleeping all my life. Everything that happened to me I accepted. It was the blow that made me wake up. That blow hurt me.

Described as a traumatic event, this second migration experience seems to have represented a climax to the deprivation Dona Marlene felt in being repeatedly forced off the land. She experienced that process, as well, as a loss of her identity, not only as a person but as a human being. She mentioned insistently the fact of sleeping on grass, as if behaving like an animal expressed the loss of her dignity and her very humanity. The contrast between the sense of community shared in the countryside and the newly experienced feeling of isolation was part of this loss. Nevertheless, this last migration marked a turning-point, and was perceived as a new beginning.

The rupture with the experience of subordination lived in the rural past is certainly a crucial step in the migrants' redefinition of their own identity in the city. To Dona Marlene, her 'awakening' meant a new perception of her own reality but also a willingness to struggle in order to change it. 'When I began to struggle' and 'When I began to wake up' are interchangeable expressions she uses to indicate the same process. Moreover, a critical tone replaces the nostalgic image of the rural past, now seen as one of passivity and submission. The magnitude of this rupture with the past can be grasped through D. Marlene's own assessment of her views about politics while in the countryside:

At that time [when living in her birthplace], I didn't have any idea about politics. I knew from what I heard people saying. We received an order as if it came from the greatest big shot in the world, it was a kind of domination. Then everyone bent their heads down, they would say: 'You must vote for so and so, otherwise you will be arrested.' And everybody voted, like a slave, the slave had to obey the orders from the boss. I was like that, too. Women and men, both had to obey those orders.

In 1967 Campinas had around 350,000 inhabitants and was already going through a significant process of industrial development. This process accelerated in the 1970s, when the municipal government subsidized the establishment of an Industrial District that was intended to create 80,000 jobs. The city became a centre of attraction for migrants, most of them from rural areas and without the necessary qualifications to work in the large industries of the region. As a result, the population of *favelas* boomed to 583 per cent, from 1973 to 1980, with the consequent aggravation of the already miserable conditions of life.[4] Dona Marlene's introduction to the life of the big city began by getting to know the *favela*, something she had never seen before.

I was puzzled as to why people would live like that. I asked them and they said: 'Because here we don't have to pay rent, this is an area belonging to the city government.' They told me that in order to get into the *favela* we had to buy a shack and move in immediately because otherwise it would be invaded by other people. I wanted to move in but my husband did not. He didn't know the *favela*.

'You are crazy, woman! Only criminals and prostitutes live in the *favela*,' he said.

'But why?' I asked. 'Will I become a prostitute if I move into the *favela*? Will you become a thief? You who have worked all your life? It's very aggressive of you to say this, very aggressive. Let's prove ourselves, then, and move in.'

We finally bought the shack, but he quarrelled all the time.

The notion of land, as a place to live and to produce one's livelihood, can be seen as a central element in the cultural universe of rural migrants. It has organized Dona Marlene's life since the very beginning. Combining both symbolic and instrumental meanings, such a notion expresses a continuity between the two settings. While in the countryside, the relationship to the land was intimately connected to the very idea of life and survival. It constituted a fundamental basis of D. Marlene's own identity. Living in the *favela*, and the urban experience as a whole, undoubtedly contributed to redefining the notion of land and added new meanings to it. It certainly became even more important, expressing an obvious material need, but also a need to reconstruct a sense of belonging, autonomy, and dignity:

Then we began to struggle for housing, so nobody could come and give orders in our house. Be it of grass, be it of wood, it is your haven, a shelter where you belong [*um teto que você pertença nele*]. Then we began to talk about a guarantee of land to live on [*a garantia da terra para morar*].[5]

Previous struggles had already taught the *favelados* the relationship between their collective needs and basic social inequality. They had also learnt how the distribution of state resources expresses and reproduces such inequality. Dona Marlene learnt this lesson herself, at her first attempt to fight it:

Everyone drank water from the faucet, but in the *favela* we had to drink water from the well. The water was full of little worms.

'Why is it that everybody can have running water installed and we can't?' I asked.

'Because this is city land and they don't install water here,' people told me.

But that isn't possible, I felt. . . . So we went to the City Hall, this woman friend and I. . . . to ask for information about getting running water.

'We don't install running water in *favelas*,' they said.

Not able to convince other women to join her, Dona Marlene kept insisting alone:

Once I went there and they told me: 'If your water is no good, leave! Leave! And shut your mouth!'

'What right have you to say this?' I asked.

'I am a government employee and that land is the Mayor's land.'

'What Mayor's land are you talking about? If that was the Mayor's land, he would be living there with us, he would be a *favelado* himself! That is the land of poor people like us, who do not have a decent salary. . . .'

'Don't you think you are talking too much?'

'No, I don't think I'm talking too much. I'm speaking of the reality I feel there; if you have the right to drink a glass of water from a faucet, we have it too. We are citizens like you, we are human beings like you. Why can you?'

'Ah, but we live in our houses!'

'This doesn't have anything to do with houses, man!'

The need for land, for a 'shelter that is yours and where you belong' meant a recovery of the dignity lost in the big city. But it also had a number of instrumental meanings to the *favelados*. For instance, in order to get credit in stores you had to present proof of address, usually a utility bill. *Favelados* could not meet this requirement. Seen as a central issue, whose solution would have multiplying effects, and perceived as the correction of an injustice and an affirmation of social equality, the need for land then became a right to land. Affirming this as a right meant asserting its universal character. Such an assertion also implied transcending the mere struggle over particularistic corporatist interests and the competition among such interests for government resources, alleged characteristics which academic and other critics of popular movements often invoke in their indictments.

The conception of rights which emerges here is not that which characterizes the liberal view. It does not refer to an extension of a right already ensured to others or the concrete enforcement of a formal and abstract right. It implies the creation, the invention of rights which emerges from concrete practice.[6] In this sense, the notion of citizenship is no longer confined to the access to previously defined rights, but it is a historical construction whose specificity arises from struggle itself. Such a citizenship from below is not a strategy of the dominant classes for the gradual political incorporation of excluded sectors, directed towards the promotion of social integration.[7] It requires the constituting of active social subjects, defining what they consider to be their rights, and struggling for their recognition.

In fact, in Latin-American societies, we can discern the initial stages in such a process: when people began to organize themselves in social movements they soon learnt that their first task was to affirm their right to have rights. This is what Dona Marlene expressed very clearly: 'We began to struggle for the right to the land. We didn't have this right to struggle for the right to the land. Because they thought we were taking land which wasn't ours, it belonged to the City Government.' She goes on, explaining it very carefully and spelling out a view of the state which is crucial to the conception of a new citizenship:

You have to look closely at the City Government: it owns nothing. Nothing. Neither the Mayor nor anybody there owns anything; when they enter there they do not become owners, they become employees of the people. Everybody has the right to claim what they want and they have the duty to answer if it is right, if it is wrong, but they must answer.... Because they [people in City Hall] didn't have anything. The strength they had came from the people, it was not theirs. You never saw a bird flying without its feathers; it needs the feathers to fly. And the feathers they have are not theirs. If they are up in those heights, who put them there? So I began to see this and then I began to lose any fear I had.

Such a view of state power is recurrent in Dona Marlene's account. Its main thrust certainly would sound familiar to analysts of democracy: all power comes from the people and in its name shall be exercised. Yet, beyond the notion that government must be accountable to the citizens who elected it and from whom it derives its power, there is also a conception of the people's own power. Relying again on references to simple facts of nature, a characteristic of popular discourse, D. Marlene talked about power emerging from popular struggle, embodying the dignity and strength of wild animals:

The most important thing I felt from all my struggle was remembering where I came from, where I was going, and where I arrived. Suddenly I became a wild animal [*uma fera*] . . . I used to think that the power was the wild animal. I had not yet discovered that we were the wild animal. The greatest wild animals are inside *us*, not in them. We used a new weapon and when you go that far, you realize that the wild animals are us, not them, nor the police!

Underlying the struggle is the view that the people are the ultimate source of power, but this is a potential still to be realized given the private appropriation of state power. The concrete relationship popular movements establish with the state is quite complex. As the state is obviously a fundamental instance in the recognition of rights, the struggle includes confrontation but also selective alliances and the search for support. Dona Marlene's memories are full of stories of confrontation, including the physical:

One day, they came in a jeep and brought the police along. They told me: 'Either you shut your mouth or you will be evicted.'

'I'd rather be evicted . . . And, I want to see the *macho* who is going to come here and remove my belongings! You will have to kill me. Then you would have to put me in a coffin and throw my children out in the street, and there are nine of them!'

We began to quarrel and as he [the City Inspector] got closer, I grabbed a piece of wood. Yes, I did! Do you think I would let that man get me? . . . I had to show him what I was made of . . . the determination I had! . . . When they saw that crowd [people from the neighbourhood had gathered in support], they got scared and dashed off in the jeep, saying that I wanted to smash it. I wasn't even close to it! . . . Then they threatened to kill me, I received death threats.

On Becoming a Citizen

At this point we were already in the Assembléia do Povo and the people there . . . told us that we should have an Associação [a formal neighbourhood organization] 'otherwise these people are going to kill you and throw your body somewhere far from here'. Then we decided to create the Associação and register it so I could be known and safe.

The dramatic narration of a crucial day in the struggle of the Assembléia illustrates the complexity of its members' relationship with the state. After convincing the Mayor to send the City Council the bill written by the movement, which would transform into law the right to land, they saw it voted down by the City Counsellors. That day represented almost two years of intense activity, during which the movement had explored several forms of struggle. Nevertheless, victory was hanging on a single word pronounced by twenty men:

We took the bill to the City Council and they kept promising they would vote on it and they didn't. We had to pressure them, it was a weapon we had. You have to demand what you need and what you believe in. It doesn't matter if they vote wrongly but you make your point clear . . . what you know from the struggle, what you know from living. We went there that night, 150 people. A lot of them still had their lunch pails, they had come straight from work. . . . Finally the vote was set for 12.30 a.m. because that's when the last buses depart. . . . We decided to stay there overnight. . . . When the voting finally started, they called the names of the Counsellors one by one and they stood up, saying 'No, no, no'. Only two or three voted in favour of our bill. One of them [an opponent] made a speech challenging the *favelados: Favelados* didn't have worker's identification cards [*carteira assinada*], *favelados* didn't have a place to live, *favelados* lived like rats. He spoke a lot. Listening to him made everybody sad. A woman started to cry. . . . Me, cry? No way I am going to cry here in front of these kinds of people! And I began to yell: 'Do you know why *favelados* are like this? Because you are nothing but thieves, wretches! When you are looking for votes you come with a straight face, just so you can be here tonight and betray everybody!' I started to call them names, I wanted to throw chairs at them but the chairs were all fastened to the floor! I wanted to break everything there that night. And I said, showing them my voter's card: 'Wait for us! Our active voice is here, this is how we will talk to you, with our vote, a vote of responsibility, a vote of struggle, a vote of knowledge! Because up to now our vote has been betrayed. We were deceived by false hopes. Nothing you promise when you look for votes ever happens!' . . . Then the police came. . . . That day I didn't feel afraid, I only felt outrage for having fought so hard, for having looked to the authorities, for their refusal to entertain a solution in accord with our struggle, and for punishing us the way they did.

This experience represented a turning-point in the movement: the *favelados* realized the importance of electing Counsellors committed to their struggle and to popular interests. The Assembléia then decided to nominate three of its participants as candidates in the forthcoming City Council election. They also decided to run under the newly formed Partido dos Trabalhadores. Such a decision expressed a significant rupture with old views on the nature of politics, like those D. Marlene expressed when referring to her experience in the countryside: 'Politics was always domination. Nobody could talk about politics because it was something belonging to those who were above us, those governing, not to us. We had to live dominated by the power and could say nothing.'

Party affiliation has always been seen in the literature as a problematic issue within popular movements. The main argument is that party affiliation can break up the hard-won unity of a movement and is usually avoided.[8] However, this does not appear to be a universal rule. It depends on the concrete options available and on the particular experience of each movement. The creation of the PT was a direct product of struggles of both social movements and trade unions. One can state that the very existence of the Assembléia do Povo, was crucial in determining the emergence and the shape of the party in Campinas. The connection between the Assembléia and the party was very clear to the great majority of the members, who had either participated in or supported the local organization of the PT. For them, at that particular moment, the new party represented the continuity of their own struggle and its extension into the institutional political level. Negative reaction from all the other parties, as evidenced by the famous City Council vote, only reinforced this choice. To Dona Marlene, one of the people chosen to run by the Assembléia, the party of affiliation was a clear option:

I agreed to run for Counsellor not because I was so interested in gaining the power, but to build the party.... because when we are in a struggle and I trust you, what I am doing you will do too, isn't it true? ... If I didn't win, somebody from the PT would win. It would help, the party was united.

Dona Marlene was not elected, although she won an impressive number of votes. The Assembléia did manage to get one of its three candidates elected: not surprisingly the only one who was not a *favelado*, a sociologist with close ties to the movement and a very active member of the party. The deeply rooted social authoritarianism of

Brazilian society, the generalized prejudice against *favelados*, which D. Marlene so frequently refers to, heavily discriminates against candidates from popular classes. Thus, to establish the *favelados*' right to have rights, their right to have a place to live, their right to participate in power, was not a struggle limited to their relationship with the state but implied a confrontation with society as a whole.

In a society in which inequality is so internalized as to constitute the cultural forms through which people relate to each other in everyday life, the notion of equal rights which characterizes the idea of citizenship has to confront the authoritarian culture which permeates all social relations. Class, race, and gender differences constitute the main bases for a social classification which has historically pervaded Brazilian culture, establishing different categories of people hierarchically ordered in their respective 'places' in society. Thus, transcending its original liberal framework, new citizenship is no longer a question confined to the relationship between the state and the individual; it points to a moral, intellectual, and cultural reform within civil society and the transformation of social practices. It also implies questioning the definition of what is considered to be the realm of politics and what is or is not relevant when we consider political transformations in society.

A *favelada*, daring to go out of her 'place' and to affirm her rights, Dona Marlene had to face multiple forms of social authoritarianism. Being a woman gave a wider scope to her battle; her fight for equal rights unfolded into a plural struggle. In this sense, the boundaries between public and private spheres of struggle became blurred, and different forms of unequal and hierarchical relations were confronted in the same process. In this sense, D. Marlene engendered her citizenship, politicizing her struggle as a woman. She recalls:

We asked for the installation of electric light. The inspector from the City Government came and told me: 'Go out with me and I will give you your lamp post.'

I looked him right in the eye and said: 'How many times did your wife go out with City Government Inspectors?!'

'What do you expect, living in a *favela* like this, what are you hoping for? There is nothing to build here, nothing, nothing. It doesn't matter if you go out with me or with somebody else, this is normal.'

'Do you know what? I don't trade myself for a lamp post, I don't trade my character for anything! I am poor but not because of my poverty will I act like a dog!'

'If you go out with me I'll help you, I'll arrange things for you at City Hall because they wanted to evict you.'

'They can come', I said, 'I'll call the newspapers, I'll make a fuss!'

Gender inequality and discrimination faced Dona Marlene very early and very closely. First, during her childhood, within her family:

I only went to school for a little while, just up to the second year of elementary school. There were usually no teachers then, my parents were poor and couldn't pay a teacher. We lived far out and there were no teachers at all. And there was something else. Girls didn't have to study; those who needed to study were the boys. Women couldn't study, men had to. The same thing with the vote: men had to vote, women couldn't. So, all this was my upbringing ... it was not an upbringing, it was domination. Parents dominated us in the way they educated us. And we had to obey because that was like a law. And this law was that you had to be quiet, not saying anything.

As she became involved in organizing, like most women who participate in popular movements, she had to face her husband's opposition:

Then I found that there was a group of people who met at Pio XII [a Catholic school] to talk about all that. So a woman friend of mine and I went there, in the evening so nobody would know where we were. My husband was very much against it [*contra, contra, contra, contra*]! He forbade me to go. I had to escape from the house in order to go. Finally ... he said he was going to lock me out of the house, he called me names, said I was the lowest of the low, you should have heard him!

'Nobody did anything so far. Are you the one who will do it?' he would say.

Oppressive gender relations had to be fought against within the movement itself:

Women were discriminated against in the movement as well. At the beginning, a lot of people thought of women as objects. People thought nobody would listen to a woman, the power wouldn't listen. Why a woman in the struggle, why not a man? Then we began to struggle and people saw the courage of women and began to believe in them. Like with me, when I was a candidate, people in the neighbourhood wouldn't vote for the party but they would vote for Marlene, a woman. They believed in me.

Dona Marlene later participated in women's groups. She was invited to speak at the University of Campinas and was a key person in the attempts made by the women's movement in the city to bridge the class divide and hold joint activities with poor women. But for D.

Marlene the struggle for rights as a *favelada* and as a woman has gone forward together. Her process of gaining autonomy and independence as a woman intertwined with her political trajectory:

I was married for 27 years, until my husband died in 1985. During my electoral campaign in 1982 he helped a lot. He didn't want it [the candidacy] but I had told him: 'Now I am the one who will control my life. If you like it, you like it, if you don't. . . . In spite of everything he didn't like, he never wanted to separate. He said he was going to struggle to be with me for the rest of his life. And so it happened.

Dona Marlene was President of her neighbourhood Associação until 1986, long after the Assembléia was dissolved:

We were able to get a lot done here in the neighbourhood; those three footbridges over the freeway . . . paved streets, the school, the day-care centre, a lot of houses, more than one hundred houses in an area expropriated by the City Government, without having to invade [a common strategy of homeless people]. We got it legally but through our struggle. . . . As President of the Associação I did a fine job. . . . Because I didn't believe that the Power has power. The people have the power, in everything.

During our talk, she came back repeatedly to the issue of the seduction of 'the power': 'They offered me a lot of positions in the City Administration. . . . If I wanted a job, even if I didn't have the qualifications, "I would get that job." ' A number of her friends succumbed, including the woman friend with whom she had gone to City Hall that first time: 'She works at the City Health Centre. She got the job to keep her quiet. I told myself, I will not get into this, these people want to stop us. Enough of domination.'

Talking about what she had learnt during her struggle, Marlene emphasized:

I learned respect for the people, I learned to love human beings more. I believe that all are equal, what hurts you hurts me as well. Respect does wonderful things in the life of any human being. . . . But I also learned to discriminate against those who go along with the power. Those who go along with the power don't govern for the people, they govern for themselves.

Fear was another recurrent issue:

We the people, Brazilians, have to struggle on the basis of our rights. We do not need to be afraid. Let us suppose somebody is going to die in the family? It doesn't matter, all of us are going to die, but the important thing is that you are going to build a better world for those who are being born. It doesn't matter if

I'm going to die, if I stop living, if those who come next can benefit from what we are doing.

Asked if she was not afraid of speaking out in public, she told me in a passionate tone what made her lose that fear:

'Will you speak?' they asked me. Of course I will speak, my grief is here inside me, this pain in my chest, my feelings, my life! And our rights? We are equal, all of us have rights. It is not only me, it is not only half a dozen, all have equal rights. But rights are different. Rights are equal but they are very divided [meaning unequal but maybe also separate], the division is very big: power, money, beauty, houses. Whereas some have everything, others, nothing. And all are workers, salaries are very divided but all are professionals. You don't have to think that a bricklayer has to receive less than a teacher, a garbage collector less than a doctor. It's a profession! Ask a doctor if he can do the job of a bricklayer and he can't. Ask the bricklayer if he can do the doctor's job and he can't.

To reinforce this radical conception of equality, she clarified where it came from, contrasting it with the concrete reality of her people:

You look at the face of thousands and thousands of people and you feel the same needs; this is what is important. You are a part which is low, small, but you are the majority, suffering and trying to struggle. All of them bear the mark, this mark of those who suffer: *favelados* living in swamps, being despised for being *favelados*, poor, not having a scrap of clothing to wear, a decent pair of shoes; people who had the courage to put their feet on the ground, to cross the mud barefoot, to take a hoe, a trowel, and build a house, to take a sewing machine and sew, to take a bundle of clothes and wash. Knowing that this was important and knowing that they knew to define the laws which had to be made. This is what is important.

The contrast points to changes that still need to be made. But the knowledge acquired in the struggle, the knowledge necessary to affirm their rights as equal citizens, is assessed here, along with the courage to build a new reality from their own work and energy, as a crucial element in the *favelados'* struggle. In addition, knowledge stands for an affirmation of equality itself. The capacity to define laws, something which has belonged to 'the power' in 'those heights', belongs now to the *favelados*. They emerged from the sites reserved for them, on the periphery of the city. They became visible, reached downtown, City Hall, the City Council, they wrote a bill and pressured City Counsellors for its approval. Their struggle for the land reaffirmed a conception of the world brought from the countryside, reinvented within the urban context. Such a struggle is not over, but they have affirmed their rights and become citizens.

Emphasizing the constitution of active, autonomous subjects and the socialization of politics, the building of new citizenship points towards the socialization of power underlying a radical conception of democracy. As a political strategy, the conception of citizenship may be able to provide answers to the challenges left by the failure of political struggles and theoretical reasoning which were not able to account for and integrate the multiplicity of dimensions of human struggle for a better life in contemporary societies. In this sense, such a conception can constitute an elastic system of reference able to encompass different expressions and dimensions of inequality: economic, social, political, and cultural, providing a common basis for the articulation of the different interests around which different social sectors organize themselves. At the cultural level, it certainly confronts the idea of social places by emphasizing the right to be equal. On the other hand, and at the same time—and this is decisive in the case of women, homosexuals, and blacks—it also implies the right to be different and the idea that difference shall not constitute a basis for inequality.

As a historical construction, a result of concrete struggle, the contents of citizenship are not pre-defined, but are open and dynamic. In this sense, becoming a citizen, contrary to liberal understanding, does not mean merely membership in an already given political system. Most importantly, what is at stake here, as the struggle of the *favelados* and Dona Marlene points out, is the right to define what we want to be members of, that is to say, the invention of a new society.

Notes

1. I refer throughout to 'Dona Marlene' or 'D. Marlene' because 'Dona', the Portuguese form of respect, was the name by which she was called by people in the movement.
2. The Assembléia do Povo has been the object of three academic studies: Maria José Taube, *De Migrantes a Favelados* (Campinas, 1986); Doraci Alves Lopes, 'O movimento da Assembléia do Povo e a crítica da marginalidade', unpublished Master's Thesis in Sociology, UNICAMP (Campinas, 1988); José Antonio Trasferetti, 'Deus da Vida—Vida do Povo: A Espiritualidade dos militantes da Assembléia do Povo', unpublished Master's Thesis in Moral Theology, Faculdade de Teologia Nossa Senhora da Assunção (São Paulo, 1987).
3. There is a retrospective logic 'that organizes the events recounted and gives them meaning according to the subject's overall perception of his past life' (Nathan Wachtel, 'Introduction', in *History and Anthropology*, 2 (1986), 210). For a similar finding and interpretation, see Bela Feldman-Bianco, 'Multiple Layers of Time and

Space: The Construction of Class, Ethnicity and Nationalism among Portuguese Immigrants', in N. Schiller, L. Basch, and C. Blanc-Szanton (eds.), *Towards a Transnational Perspective on Migration* (New York, 1992), 159.
4. Taube, *De migrantes a favelados*, 82.
5. 'The guarantee of land to live on' refers to the main claim of the *favelado* movement. It was later formalized in a bill sent to City Council, giving the *favelados* a piece of city land where they could live on (but not sell or rent) for a period of thirty years. The bill was voted down.
6. The 1988 Brazilian Constitution did not include the right to housing along others, such as the right to education, health, etc. More recent Municipal Constitutions have included such a right, as, for instance that of Porto Alegre, capital of the state of Rio Grande do Sul, governed by the Partido dos Trabalhadores.
7. For a similar view and a critique of different views of citizenship, see Bryan S. Turner, 'Outline of a Theory of Citizenship', *Sociology*, 24: 2 (1990), 189–207; and Antje Wiener, 'Citizenship—New Dynamics of an Old Concept. A Comparative Perspective', mimeo. paper presented at the XVII International Congress of the Latin American Studies Association, Los Angeles, Calif., 1992.
8. See, for instance, Eunice Durham, 'A Construção da Cidadania', *Novos Estudos Cebrap*, 10 (1984).

6

Identity, Racism, and Multiculturalism

Chinese-Australian Responses

JANIS WILTON

In 1903 the editorial in a small rural newspaper in northern New South Wales, Australia, railed against Chinese storekeepers in the region:

> We are opposed to Chinese and other coloured aliens in every shape and form. As believers in the policy of protection, we contend that foreign goods should be excluded; and with them, foreign labor of the cheap and undesirable class.[1]

The editorial was part of a state-wide campaign against the incursion of Chinese settlers into the business centres of rural towns and villages. The Chinese were accused of employing cheap labour, competing unfairly, living in unhealthy conditions, and sending all their profits home to China. They were also regarded as socially and culturally unacceptable. A columnist in another local newspaper from northern New South Wales explained:

> God and Nature made different races . . . [and] those of the so-called undesirable races who have settled in our land . . . never cease to be socially . . . ones who live outside the pale of our life. The 'bar sinister' is ever writ large upon all our intercourse with these people—and so it should be.[2]

This 1903 campaign summed up contemporary Australian attitudes. The Chinese were seen as a threat to the economic and cultural well-being of the Australian-born, and they were despised as inferior.[3]

Racism was well established. It underpinned the 1901 Immigration Restriction Act which, as much as any legislation, heralded the creation of the federation of Australia. This Act was directed particularly at the Chinese. It declared that anyone, including non-Europeans, seeking to enter Australia could only do so if they passed a dictation test in a European language! The clear intention was to prevent the permanent settlement of Chinese in Australia.[4]

It was against this background that a number of Chinese elected and managed to go on living and working in Australia, and to sponsor family members and fellow-villagers to come to Australia.[5] They and their descendants have experienced first-hand the racism which structured so much of Australian thinking and behaviour in the first half of the twentieth century, and which ensured that 'being Chinese' meant at best being labelled as exotic and inscrutable and, at worst, as inferior and threatening.

Since the Second World War and especially since the late 1960s, Australian attitudes at the official level have changed. This change has seen a move in government policy from racism through assimilation to multiculturalism. It is, of course, an uneven move. Racism and assimilation still thrive in Australia even among officials vested with the responsibility of promoting multiculturalism. Yet, Australia of the 1990s and beyond is lauded as a society which thrives on its cultural diversity, which strives to correct injustices and inequalities experienced by ethnic minorities, and which aims to achieve all this within a framework of economic well-being and growth.[6] Under the banner of multiculturalism, Chinese-Australians, along with Australians from other cultural backgrounds, are officially applauded and welcomed as valued citizens. Their achievements, contributions, and revived public interest in the Chinese part of their heritage are acclaimed as evidence of the 'success' of multiculturalism. Their existence under the hyphenated identity of being Chinese-Australian is encouraged. Policy change is seen implicitly as a way of constructing a new identity and future for Australia, and for those Australians who had previously found themselves on the margin. Is it working?

An analysis of the remembered experiences of a group of Chinese-Australians who were born during the first half of this century either in China or in Australia and who lived in the New England region of northern New South Wales offers an effective method for exploring aspects of the nature of the identities being constructed in multicultural Australia. These Chinese-Australians grew up and worked under the old racist policies, and they have experienced the official change from racism to multiculturalism. To date I have worked with fifty-one interviewees who have offered their own experiences as well as those passed on from earlier generations.[7] Complemented by family and business papers, memorabilia and photographs, and by archival records, the story which is emerging reveals that the legacy of a racist past is still structuring the process of remembering, and that elements of that racist past still exist and thrive in contemporary Australian society. There are silences, gaps, and lost or hidden traditions which can at least be partly attributed to surviving in a racist Australia, and there is evidence that Chinese-Australians themselves have absorbed and maintained some of the values and attitudes underpinning that racism. Equally apparent is an increasing willingness to explore and reclaim some of these silences, gaps, and lost or hidden traditions in the new and more secure climate of a multicultural Australia. However, a simple explanation which sees this change as a reflection of a clear and clean move from racism to multiculturalism denies the complexity of the memories and experiences offered by Chinese-Australians, and the failure of a multicultural Australia to rid itself completely of a racist past.

Despite the abundance of evidence pointing to a racism which reduced the Chinese in Australia to second- or even third-class citizens during the first half of the twentieth century, racism is not a topic which readily surfaces in oral-history interviews with Chinese-Australians. Other researchers have found this, and it also applies to those offering recollections of life in New England.[8]

Why is there this silence? Chinese-Australians participating in the present project offer some of the answers. In the first instance, they locate racism as something which, if it existed, belonged to their past and has little bearing on their present: 'Things have changed now.' They have compartmentalized their lives. What was, is no longer. What was must not be allowed to impinge on the present, especially when that present is about achievements and social acceptance.

For some participants, racism was experienced by their parents not by them. This is particularly the case for those born in Australia and who grew up there before and during the Second World War. It was their parents who, they declare, experienced the brunt of racist discrimination. Through establishing respectable business profiles in small country towns and through taking care to behave in a way acceptable to the local community, parents helped to deflect discrimination from their children. As one man whose father owned the general store in a small country town explained:

my father was the type of person that was a real gentlemanly type. Everyone who met him used to like him. I think he made things a lot easier because of the type of person he was . . . so there wasn't much racism directed at us at all. . . . Really, we had more people showing us good will than ill will. We were fortunate really. . . . You see, people used to think Chinese were dirty, untidy, or even immoral. The usual stereotype of Chinese in those days, and we were completely different. . . . We lived in probably one of the best houses . . . in the town.

Parents wanted their children to succeed in a culturally alien environment, and many focused on ensuring that they learnt the skills of survival even to the detriment of appreciating anything about their Chinese heritage. One woman who grew up in north Queensland in the 1930s recalled:

Dad was well into the Australian way of living and we all spoke . . . English . . . and we had a white housekeeper. . . . He always said, you have to learn Australian, you have to learn how to become a good Australian. And we were so busy trying to become good Australians that we forgot . . . that we were Chinese.

Children were also taught to be discreet:

I learnt from my father that when people are nasty, be nice to them.

I've learnt the best way to live is not to be outrageous. I remember what Pop used to say: 'They'll kiss your feet in the store but ignore you on Central Railway.'

Chinese try to suppress unpleasant things; they just don't talk about them.

As a part of this process, it was unlikely that grandparents and parents would imbue their descendents with anecdotes and evidence of discrimination. It was also unlikely that children and grandchildren would ask. Chinese tradition dictated that respect for elders meant not asking questions and, anyway, elders were usually too busy and children too disinterested:

He wasn't very talkative, Dad. No. I don't suppose there's any special reason. I don't suppose as children we asked him much. You know [about] what he did as a child.

Dad'd go away to work before we got up, more or less, and then he came home late, when . . . we were ready to go to bed. In those days we didn't have a great deal of communication with the parents. . . . We never ever spoke of what he used to do in his younger days.

The silences about racism are also shaped by the participants' ties to specific small, rural towns where, it seems, as the twentieth century progressed and the number of Chinese dwindled, the pervasiveness of overt racism was softened. This was aided by the business profiles of those Chinese who stayed: many became local businessmen who offered services and employment to the local non-Chinese community. Some of their children and grandchildren have continued to provide those services and forms of employment; others have moved on to professional occupations often still based in the same country towns. It would seem that the unspoken pressure here is to refrain from making comments which could reflect negatively on town, neighbours, or clients, and which could have repercussions on what is now regarded as acceptance and respect from the local community.

Another underlying pressure, only obliquely referred to by participants, is a reluctance to have experiences of discrimination recorded as the mainstay of their stories. As Australian oral historian Morag Loh, who has worked extensively with Chinese-Australians in other parts of the country, has observed: 'To go into an archive with tales of humiliation is to have those humiliations live forever: who would want that?'[9] This was expressed slightly differently by one participant in the present study when recalling her childhood in 1920s north Queensland: 'I often used to say how they [Australian children] made us seem so bad that you were ashamed to be Chinese. Really. I was ashamed to be a Chinese kid when I was going to school. What we suffered from the Australian kids.'

Shame and humiliation are not sentiments and experiences easily passed on. Rather, the story which Chinese-Australians want recorded is the story of their contributions and achievements. They focus on family and family achievements, on acceptance and participation in their local communities, and on Chinese traditions, lost and found. Their willingness now, to participate in a project which presents their perspectives on their lives, might be part of a desire to correct impressions that racism has been the dominant element shaping past and present experiences. This project—like other similar projects focusing on aspects of the Chinese-Australian experience[10]—provides an opportunity to display the contributions and success of Chinese-Australians, and to reinstate the significance of a Chinese heritage and identity not only for Chinese-Australians but for Australians generally.

Ironically, imbedded in the focus on achievements and contributions is a further possible factor shaping the silence about racism. These Chinese-Australians have succeeded only too well by Australian standards and, in succeeding, have absorbed some of the values and attitudes of 'white' Australia.

Underlying most family histories provided by participants is the image of Australia as the lucky country where anyone and everyone could 'have a go'. The accounts offered are primarily migrant success stories. The pattern becomes repetitive. Grandfathers and fathers came to Australia without money and without their women. They worked long and hard first as unskilled labourers, then moving into stores. Slowly they became partners in those stores, then owners. They built the stores into thriving concerns able to support an ever increasing number of family members—some from China, some born in Australia. Children were sent to Australian schools. The older ones worked in the family businesses. The younger children often went on to further education. By the third generation, tertiary qualifications and jobs in the professions are commonplace. Participants proudly list the number of doctors, accountants, teachers, solicitors, and other professionals in the family.[11] Upward social mobility has overlain or even overpowered the need to acknowledge or analyse racism in the past or in the present. On the surface, ethnicity and racial tension have succumbed to the desire and the proven ability to succeed in the lucky country.

Social success is also measured in Australian assimilationist terms. Participants are concerned to point to their and their predecessors' acceptance by their local Australian communities. They point to their reputations and records as business people willing to give credit and assist local farmers through the hard times of drought and depression. They supported and financed local sporting teams. They joined and participated in local service clubs, and they contributed to local charities. By the 1940s children were well enough accepted to be made school captains, and to lead local sporting teams. Today, for those still living in New England, the same commitment to local organizations remains, and they are proud and gratified by the support from community members for their families and their businesses. This was brought home to one Chinese-Australian family in the late 1970s when their store burnt down. Members of the town's service clubs and the community generally helped with the clean up:

One evening three hundred men turned up on the store site and within four hours had cleared away all the charred remains. This sort of rejuvenated all of us, particularly myself, in saying well this is where our future is. So we didn't have any hesitation about whether we would rebuild.[12]

Participants also point to intermarriage as an indicator of the extent to which Chinese-Australians have adapted to their Australian environment. They explain that for the older generations, intermarriage was out of the question. Chinese should always marry Chinese. That was one way to ensure the passing on of Chinese beliefs and values. That was also one way of surviving in an alien society by staying together. But things have now changed and family members have had to accept change, at least on the surface:

My father was pretty strict and the irony is that, in the family, there are two mixed marriages and two divorces. Pop never said a word. He obviously didn't like it but he never said a word. . . . Although I do recall him talking to me before I married. He used to talk to me as a third person, and he said to me, in that way, that I should not marry out.

During those years, looking back about the best part of sixty years or so, it was the usual thing to try and marry someone of your own race, but gradually it came out of that. It was shown by my family. All my children have married Australians, everyone of them. And then the grandchildren have married Australians, and it will go on you see.

The full extent of the submergence of difference within the upbringing, experiences, and outlooks which emphasized values recognized as particularly Australian, is well illustrated by one man who vividly recalled his response to being asked by a new acquaintance 'Where are you from?': 'I answered, "Tarragindi",[13] thinking he was asking where I lived. Then I realized he thought I was born overseas. See, I forget. I forget that I look Chinese and that some Australians think this means I've come from overseas.' The recollection highlights how well some Chinese-Australians identify as Australians. It also highlights how some non-Chinese-Australians believe that all people who 'look Chinese' cannot possibly be Australian-born. It points to the complexity of surviving in a racist and assimilationist environment. Essentially, the emphasis on assimilation in pre-1960s Australia helped channel Chinese-Australian efforts into upward social mobility and local community acceptance. The Chinese-Australians in this project have certainly succeeded in gaining some of the status and rewards defined within these Australian parameters. The reality of the heritage of racism, however, has helped ensure that Chinese-Australians continue to perceive themselves or at least be perceived as different. Some of this perception of difference may be simply a feature of actually being different; some may be related to pervading past and present stereotypes. But, by and large, the perception of difference was submerged during the assimilationist era and was replaced by an emphasis on success in particularly Australian terms.

Success, achievements, and contributions of individuals and their families provide one core of the memories offered by this group of Chinese-Australians. This is what they want remembered and passed on. Their telling is shaped by the terms and values learnt from a racist and assimilationist Australia but that does not negate their importance. Rather, it signifies that remembering is at least partly structured by the racism which so many participants want, at the very most, only as the background of their story.

All this apparent absorption and expression of Australian values also needs to be offset by another core element in the memories offered by Chinese-Australians, namely the evidence of the survival and adaptation of a Chinese heritage despite Australian lives. The survival has been threatened by the impact of decades of keeping it quiet or, at least, keeping it private because it was not acceptable publicly to reveal old-world traditions in new Australia. But the evidence is there as participants recall the regularity of visits paid to China before the Communist Revolution, and the revitalization of these visits in the 1980s. It is also evident in the networking which they explain found employment for family and clan members, in the family nature of the businesses established in Australia, and in the enduring support for and pride in family members' achievements. It is apparent in their accounts of continued celebrations of Chinese festivals, and in the maintenance of family records and memorabilia linking Australian lives to a past in China. It is also evident in the interest among participants and their families to explore, document, and present their Chinese heritage.

In the past fifteen years, some individuals have reclaimed their Chinese family names.[14] A number of the families and clans have had family and shop reunions as a means of maintaining and celebrating family links and histories. There is a recognition that living in Australia has put at risk Chinese heritages. As a third-generation Chinese-Australian explained when exhorting younger members of her clan to join a reunion: 'As successive generations live in Australia, we adopt a Western lifestyle while losing our Chinese background. It is up to us to learn and record our Chinese culture and family history before any more is lost.'[15] Another participant who still lives in New England observed that celebrating Chinese New Year with other Chinese-Australian families in the area, was one way of ensuring that younger family members 'could appreciate Chinese traditions a little'. A similar impetus lay behind visiting China: 'The boys became more aware after that trip about China and its customs'. This interest and activity in maintaining or at least reconstructing a Chinese past reflects a wider concern among Chinese in Australia to own, talk, and write about Chinese ancestry. Why has this happened?

An answer which would please governments bent on proving the worth of legislation which applauds cultural diversity as a national strength, and which promotes multicultural policies to ensure that cultural diversity and social equity go hand in hand, would be to point to the conscious move from racism to multiculturalism. However, the answer would be too glib. Certainly, there is an element of a more tolerant and supportive environment legitimizing and assisting the efforts of individuals, families, and communities to claim and assert their different cultural heritages. It is a changing climate recognized by Chinese-Australians themselves:

In the old days, when we were quite small, people hated you because you were Chinese. They were not only not friendly, they really had a hate for you. . . . it wasn't good to speak another language . . . outside. You just wouldn't. Nowadays, tradition, culture has changed and is becoming more broad-minded. So you wish you had that second language.

The changes, in many ways, reached their climax in the 1988 bicentennial of white settlement in Australia. Cultural diversity was trumpeted as one of the country's great achievements. Government funding poured into projects concerned to expose and applaud the experiences and contributions of ethnic communities.[16] It became acceptable, if not laudable—at least on an official level—to claim and assert publicly a non-English-speaking heritage.

However, an appeal to changing values and policies is not adequate in explaining a renewed interest in a Chinese heritage. There are other factors which can be found in the explanations and memories offered by participants. These memories provide evidence that, despite the success of policies of racism and assimilation in directing attention to issues of class and social mobility and away from ethnicity in defining the place of long-settled Chinese-Australians, ethnicity and cultural heritage have remained at the core of concerns about identity. It is just that their public surfacing and exploration had to wait for a convergence of a variety of factors, only one of which is the official flagging and promoting of multiculturalism.

The majority of participants have retired from full-time paid work, and all are over 50 years of age. Like most people at this stage of life, they have the time and are willing to look back, remember, and evaluate. They are also willing to talk about some things which, in earlier years, would have remained unsaid. As one man observed of his 90-year-old father:

> his memory has many closed cabinets which are only slowly being opened. He has locked away aspects of the past until some trigger causes the door to open. . . . It is only in the last ten to fifteen years that Dad has started to talk about his Chinese past—triggered by us eating Chinese food, and by the growing acceptance around this table of the Chinese part of the family story and heritage.

The triggers are also working now partly because many of those who could be hurt by particular memories have died. The reluctance to accuse family, neighbours, and business colleagues of the racist or discriminatory behaviour which forced a Chinese heritage underground, has receded as those family members, neighbours, and business colleagues have died.

There is also a desire to investigate and reconstruct the record which earlier generations were unable and perhaps unwilling to leave. One woman expressed this through her frustration at not knowing enough about her parents' and grandparents' experiences:

> See things are so sketchy because . . . there's nobody to tell us all this . . . the older brothers and sisters were not much older than my father, and the grandparents went back to China to die. . . . and, as children, we were so busy trying to become good Australians that we forgot . . . that we were Chinese . . . And now it's going full circle. Now you want to know who your ancestors are.

What little this woman knows about her family history, she wants saved and is willing to put down her own experiences so that later generations may have access to some of their heritage. Her memories, and those of other Chinese-Australians, are invited into the open partly by the concern that what little remains of their Chinese and Australian histories may die with them.

Memories have also been jogged by the opening up of China in the 1980s. For Chinese-Australians the links to China, broken and unbroken, are very important. Traditionally Chinese emigrated in order to return home and, even when they settled overseas, lengthy and regular visits to China were characteristic. This certainly applied to Chinese-Australians from New England. Their experiences in the first half of the century were regularly punctuated by visits to family in China, by prolonged stays in Hong Kong for Australian-born children

Identity, Racism, and Multiculturalism

to gain a Chinese education, and by sojourns in search of remedies for ill health.

Through their visits to China, Chinese-Australians certainly kept alive their exposure to Chinese traditions and practices. The links were made stronger by correspondence and by sending remittances home. The prospect of returning to live there was kept open as an alternative if life in Australia proved unfruitful. However, the Sino-Japanese War of the 1930s coupled with the Communist Revolution of the late 1940s put an end to the escape dream of settling back in China: 'My mother . . . thought she might go back after the war then, of course, Communism came and took over and they forgot about it. It wasn't good [there].'

The removal of the option of returning home either permanently or for prolonged visits meant that attention had to be focused more seriously on Australia. Family and future had greater and more secure prospects there. Contact with China during the period of tough Communist rule was sporadic and limited. Visits were not encouraged. Emigration could only be achieved illegally. The letters home became scattered, and the letters from China, when they did arrive, mainly confirmed fears about the privations being suffered there.[17] For those who had witnessed this China, the memories were of persecution, poverty, and denial of opportunities. By contrast, life in Australia seemed genuinely golden and Australian racism a small irritant. The earlier visits to a pre-war and pre-Communist China became a nostalgic memory.[18]

A change came in the 1980s with the 'freeing up' of China. There was renewed interest in visits to home villages and contact with relatives was re-established. Of the fifty-one participants so far involved in this project, fifteen have visited China in the past decade and, of these fifteen, five have been more than once. For those who had spent part of their childhood and earlier lives in China, these 1980s' visits renewed and built on memories. They have photographs and are able to identify what has and what has not changed. They go on to remember incidents connected with particular places. Their memories assist in bolstering the significance and closeness of a Chinese heritage:

Now that [showing a photo from a 1985 visit] is the home of our uncle, my father's younger brother. When we entered that the first time [in 1911] we saw a huge wooden object in the corner, this corner. It happened to be a coffin. I don't think my aunty was alive. It had to be uncle waiting for his death. . . . The house was still there when I went back in 1985. By my 1989 visit it had been demolished.

It was all such a pleasure and curiosity to see [the home village]. I knew that the river was there . . . and I said 'Where's the hoi?' 'Hoi' is the river. 'Over there,' they said. It is interesting how some of the words came back to me. And that was the village dialect. I think if I went back for six months it'd come back very, very quickly.

For first-time visitors to ancestral villages, the experience has stimulated further the interest in their Chinese pasts which lured them to visit in the first place. They marvel at the difference and familiarity of family homes, villages, and members previously known only through stories and letters:

The family home was bigger than expected. I was impressed by the mosaic tiles on the floor, all the different colours; by the sliding bars which could lock across the front doors and, if moved, could trigger alarms in the house.

A chappy that lives here [in Sydney] . . . gave me a letter and diagram on where to find my Dad's house. So when we got to the village the bus man went to the headquarters of that area and asked, and this gentleman walked us right to the house. . . . It was so exciting. There were two doors . . . We went into that house and then into that house. My sister remembered it. She'd lived there for a week when she was thirteen . . . and then we met this man who lives there. He's somehow related. My sister remembered him too. When they saw each other they remembered each other's names. I couldn't get over that. . . . They couldn't speak English, and none of us could remember Chinese too well except my sister—all of a sudden the Chinese came back to her.

The easing of Chinese emigration restrictions from the mid-1980s has also meant that, among the Chinese immigrants coming to Australia there have also been clan and family members providing links to a more recent Chinese heritage. The approaching change in the status of Hong Kong is similarly inspiring further family members to relocate to Australia.[19] These renewed and new links to China become an important factor in revitalizing and reshaping concepts of the Chinese part of a Chinese-Australian identity.

Another important factor is the audience this group of Chinese-Australians is addressing. They are not remembering and talking in a vacuum. Their recorded memories are being prompted by two types of listeners with different purposes and methods but sharing a willingness to listen and to hear what is being said.

The first audience consists of younger family members who are showing a deep concern and interest to learn about the pasts of parents and other ancestors. Some have actively encouraged the process. One participant has twice taken his father, then well into his eighties, to visit China. These were the first visits since he had been there as a child in 1911. The same man has actively encouraged his father to put on public record for the first time his quite clear experiences of racism. Another participant has set about pulling together records and memorabilia from the over 300 members of his clan, and another has become the memory and archives for her extended family.

The other listeners to whom participants are responding are outsiders—in this case, myself, as a female academic who lives and works in the rural region in New South Wales to which they have ties. I carry with me the disadvantages of an outsider—I have to learn the taboos and territory, I have to gain acceptance. But I also carry the advantages of an outsider. I am a symbol—and hopefully more than a symbol—that, finally, some Anglo-Australians are showing a serious interest in the Chinese-Australian experience, and are attempting to understand and evaluate that experience from the perspective of Chinese-Australians themselves. As one participant observed: 'It's great that someone from outside is finally taking a notice of all this.'

The change in official stance in Australia from racism through assimilation to multiculturalism has had an impact on the identity and self-definition of ethnic minorities. However, as analysed through the recorded life stories and oral histories of a specific group of Chinese-Australians, it is an impact which defies a simple linear explanation of positive change. Rather, the racism and assimilation which provided one of the backgrounds for early lives in Australia has, in some ways, been internalized and has re-emerged both as a denial of its impact and as praise for specifically Australian achievements. Class and social mobility attempt to replace ethnicity as defining characteristics but, it is an uneasy and only partial attempt made more difficult in a climate in which racism and assimilation survive despite government policies to the contrary. The sanctioning of cultural diversity under the era of multiculturalism has made it possible to express and explore in a public forum what was previously a private, hidden or suppressed interest and concern in a Chinese heritage and identity. Importantly, however, it is not multiculturalism alone which has made this possible. It has taken a coming together of a variety of factors. The age of participants, the breaking and re-creating of links to China, and the nature of listeners have also played their part.

Ultimately, an analysis of the move from racism to multiculturalism in Australia as experienced by members of a minority group raises difficult questions about the nature of emerging Australian identities. The simple and proud acclaim offered by 1990s' governments for their achievement of cultural and social equity for all ethnic minority groups in this extremely culturally diverse society is far too superficial. It denies the continuing influence of racism and assimilation both in overt forms and in their internalization among some ethnic community members. It also denies that factors other than changes in government policy have condoned and encouraged a more public face for the development of diverse cultural identities.

As well, a focus primarily on analysing the impact of changes in official policy and attitudes can result in a very blinkered view of the emerging histories, experiences, and identities of ethnic minorities in Australia. The focus on policy and its implications is extremely important for exposing the failings of Australian society and its power-brokers, and for recognizing that the heritage of a racist past haunts in many and devious ways. But this must be balanced by the emphases offered by members of ethnic minority groups themselves. These emphases can differ. In the case of the particular group of Chinese-Australians whose oral histories and life stories have been analysed here, rather than concentrating on how badly they were treated, they point to their successes and contributions, their family and community lives, their settlement in Australia, and their changing traditions. Their memories and memorabilia highlight the complex, diverse, and rich nature of their experiences, and there is a danger of losing this complexity, diversity, and richness if attention is concentrated solely on the impact of government policies and Australian attitudes.

Notes

This chapter has emerged from an ongoing research project which is recording, analysing, and presenting the oral history of the Chinese in twentieth-century New England, Australia. Particular thanks to Helen Andreoni, Anne-Katrin Eckermann, and Joseph Eisenberg for their helpful and critical comments.

1. *Inverell Times*, 30 Dec. 1903.
2. *Glen Innes Guardian*, 23 Sept. 1904. For an overview of the 1903-4 campaign against Chinese storekeepers, see C. Y. Yong, *The New Gold Mountain* (Adelaide, 1977), 70-7.

3. The analysis and evaluation of racist legislation and attitudes has, until recently, dominated the study of the Chinese in Australia. See J. Cushman, 'A "Colonial Casualty": The Chinese Community in Australian Historiography', *Asian Studies Association of Australia Review*, 7: 3 (1984), 100–13; and Min-Hsi Chan, 'The Chinese in Australia', in P. Hanks and A. Perry (eds.), *Working Papers on Migrant and Intercultural Studies*, Monash University, Melbourne, 12 (1988), 51–8.
4. There have been a number of detailed and early studies of the relevant immigration legislation. See, for example, H. I. London, *Non-White Immigration and the 'White Australia Policy'* (Sydney, 1970); and A. C. Palfreeman, *The Administration of the White Australia Policy* (Melbourne, 1967). See also Yong, *The New Gold Mountain*, for an account of the Chinese community's response to the legislation.
5. The number of Chinese in Australia reached a peak in the 1880s and 1890s when it is estimated that there were over 50,000. By 1901 there were approximately 33,000 Chinese in Australia. This included about 3,000 people classed as 'half-caste'. By 1947 there were approximately 12,500 Chinese recorded as still in Australia. These included new arrivals. For further details, see C. Y. Choi, *Chinese Migration and Settlement in Australia* (Sydney 1975), 42–6.
6. For an analysis of the move from racism to multiculturalism in Australia, see J. Wilton and R. Bosworth, *Old Worlds and New Australia* (Melbourne, 1984), esp. ch. 6. For a different approach, see S. Castles et al., *Mistaken Identity* (Sydney, 1989). For a broader understanding of racism and multiculturalism in Australia as they have affected ethnic minorities and Aboriginals, see K. McConnochie, D. Hollinsworth, and J. Petman, *Race and Racism in Australia* (Sydney, 1988). For a specific analysis of the survival of racism and assimilation, see Helen Andreoni, *'Outside the Gum Tree': The Visual Arts in Multicultural Australia* (Sydney, 1992, chs. 2–7.
7. Of the fifty-one participants so far contributing to the project, six came to Australia before 1939, one after 1945, the remaining forty-four are Australian-born Chinese. All were born between 1901 and 1939; twenty-five are male and twenty-six are female. All spent more than ten years Australian living and/or working in New England. Twelve have spent their entire Australian lives in New England. Four of the Australian-born participants spent a good part of their childhood and adolescence in China, and twelve paid lengthy visits (of one year or more) to China during the first four decades of the century.
8. For a discussion of these findings, see my earlier article, 'Remembering Racism', *Oral History Association of Australia Journal*, 13 (1991), 32–3.
9. Letter from Morag Loh, 15 Apr. 1991, quoted in ibid. 37.
10. See e.g. the work of Anne Atkinson in Perth, Diana Giese in Darwin, Morag Loh in Melbourne, and Cathy May in north Queensland. See also Eric Rolls, *Sojourners* (St Lucia, 1992).
11. Janis Wilton, *Hong Yuen: A Country Store and Its People* (Armidale, 1988), provides a clear example of this emphasis on the migrant success story. In a more detailed analysis of this generational social mobility, some attention will need to be paid to the cost of this 'success' as outlined by W.-M. Hurh and K.-C. Kim, 'The "Success" Image of Asian Americans', *Ethnic and Racial Studies*, 12: 4 (1989), 512–37.
12. Quoted in Wilton, *Hong Yuen*, 26.
13. Tarragindi is a suburb of Brisbane, capital city of the state of Queensland.
14. In Australia, as in North America, Chinese family names became lost as officialdom ethnocentrically assumed that a person's last name was their family name when in Chinese tradition, the first name is the family name. For example, Louie Mew Ping, Louie Mew Fay, and Louie Mew Lun were all brothers. Their family name was Louie. In Australia they became known as George Ping (Kee), Harry Fay, and Ernest Lun.

15. *Kwan Reunion Newsletter*, 2 (1986), 4.
16. For example, the end result of one bicentennial funded project was the hefty and informative, J. Jupp (ed.), *The Australian People: An Encyclopedia of the Nation, Its People, and Their Origins* (Sydney, 1988).
17. One participant in the project has provided her father's correspondence file dating back to the 1920s. It includes many letters from family and contacts in China. Those from the 1940s and early 1950s consist primarily of news about how grim life was in Chungsan following first Japanese occupation and then Communist rule.
18. Y.-F. Woon, 'Social Discontinuities in North American Chinese Communities', *Canadian Review of Sociology and Anthropology*, 15: 4 (1978), 443–51, makes similar observations about the different memories of home villages held by pre-1923 and post-1947 arrivals.
19. For an overview of changes in legislation since the 1960s, and the subsequent increased immigration of Chinese from China and elsewhere, see Hanks and Perry (eds.), *Working Papers*, 1–23.

7
Ethiopian Jews Encounter Israel
Narratives of Migration and the Problem of Identity

GADI BEN-EZER

The migration of black Ethiopian Jews to Israel since 1977 is a small yet dramatic movement, with unique features. It is interesting not only in its own right, but also because it shares, and often highlights, many features which are common to the migratory movements typical throughout the world in the later twentieth century. It is a migration from the South to the North (the Third World to the West), of black people into a predominantly white society; a movement primarily of the young and the fit, inspired by a utopian dream of life fulfilment; a dream sorely tested, if not shattered, by the experience of arrival in the 'promised land'. The migration dream of Ethiopian Jews has, as we shall see, exceptionally deep roots in their traditional culture, but their heightened expectations make the parallels in experience with migrants inspired by more typical secular dreams of particular interest.

This essay draws on the findings of an oral-history project which I carried out from 1986–8, collecting accounts of the migration of Ethiopian Jews and their encounter with Israel. Forty adolescents and young adults were interviewed within the tradition of the narrative interview, for between one and nine hours, in one to three sessions. All were at least one year in Israel at the time. In addition to the elicited open-ended story, they were also asked a set of specific questions on topics related to their experience of the journey and the encounter with Israel. The essay also draws on my experience working for ten years with Ethiopian Jews as a clinical and community psychologist, primarily in Israel, but including visits to Ethiopia.

There are altogether some 50,000 Ethiopian Jews now in Israel. Most are young: 80 per cent were under 35, and 60 per cent under 18 years of age at the time of their arrival. Geographically, the migration began with Jews from the Tigre region on the north side of the highland plateau. The contiguous Jewish population from the Gonder region, the largest group in the community, and the smaller group from the Wolkite area to the north-west, then followed. Between 1977 and 1984, in the first stage, roughly 8,000 immigrants reached Israel through the Sudan (although only 2,000 of them between 1977–82). Then between November 1984 and January 1985 another 8,000 were airlifted from the refugee camps in the Sudan, most in what became known as 'Operation Moses'. My interviewees all came to Israel during these years. Subsequently immigration almost completely ceased until 1990–1, after Ethiopia and Israel resumed diplomatic relations and a second airlift operation was undertaken. In particular, in May 1991 about 14,500 Jews were flown from Addis Ababa, where they had been trapped as refugees for a long period.

The migration stories which I collected yield many themes, but my focus here is on that of identity. I shall explore how the myth of a future migration, seen as 'a return', which had become embedded in traditional Ethiopian Jewish culture, was fundamental to the migrants' subjectivity and their sense of identity. It both motivated them to set out on their migration and sustained them through an exceptionally traumatic journey. But equally, once they had reached Israel, it became a major source for difficulties, contention, and even disillusionment.

Let us begin with the longer historical background. It is not clear either how or exactly when the Ethiopian Jewish community originated. There are at least five current hypotheses. At any rate, the Jewish traveller Eldad Ha-Dani who journeyed in the Middle East and North Africa in the ninth century certainly reported of Jews living in Ethiopia, although some details of his stories may be suspect.[1] According to Ethiopian traditions, a legendary Jewish queen named Judith (or Gudit) led a war of the southern peoples against the Axumite Kingdom in the ninth century, leading to its final collapse.[2] From the ninth to the fourteenth centuries, Jews seem to have controlled the Gonder/Semien region in Ethiopia, having a kind of Autonomy or a Kingdom. This Kingdom was finally abolished in 1632 after three centuries of intermittent war between the Jewish Kingdom and the Ethiopian Emperors.[3] During these years, the Jews turned from 'Beta Israel', literally—the House of Israel, into 'Falashas' or 'Falassin': that is, the people without the right to land (literally: exiles).[4] The term 'Falassi' was first used in the chronicles of the fifteenth century, when the

Christian Emperor Yeshag, after defeating the Jews and burning their villages, declared that only those Jews who converted by baptismal immersion to Christianity would have the right to own and inherit land. The others became Falassi.[5]

After losing their rights to land, Ethiopian Jewish men became the builders and women the ornamental craftworkers for the palaces and castles that were built by the new rulers of the Gonder region. Subsequently, during the period of the rule of princes, the Jews underwent a further deterioration in status, the men becoming blacksmiths and the women potters.[6] Holding these 'professions', they became essential to the Ethiopian economy, yet at the same time marginal in their social status. Their expertise made them essential: the men were almost the only blacksmiths in the region, producing all of its ploughs, sickles, knives, spades, and other tools, as well as instruments for religious purposes; and in modern times they also became experts in the repair of weapons. Jewish women came to be specialists in making clay pots for cooking, storage, and carrying water. These were made through highly skilled techniques, which included burning the material, and at times customizing each water pot to the size and strength of its carrier, hence needing great skill in its making. Other clay and silt tools had also become part of Ethiopian Jewish women's special expertise. Despite being essential to the economy, the Jews had become socially marginalized. According to Ethiopian (Amhara) traditional beliefs, people who worked with fire or made things out of earthy material, were of the lowest social status. Furthermore, these people were called 'budda' and were believed to be able to control Satanic powers. They were thought to have acquired the power of the 'evil eye', able to turn at night into the Spotted Hyena and consume the soul of another person. Therefore, often when a Christian died or was about to die, Jewish neighbours were blamed, persecuted, and even killed as an act of 'preventive medicine' or 'in return', as a 'justified' revenge.

In the late nineteenth century, a new era opened in the relations between Ethiopian Jews and other Jewish communities in the world. In 1867 the French Jewish professor of the Sorbonne, Yoseph Halevi, visited them and thereafter became dedicated to their cause. Nevertheless, it took another forty years or so—and the loss of half of the community in the Moslem invasion, the Ethiopian famine, and the epidemics, all between 1885–95—until Halevi's student, Professor Jaque Faitelovitch, had succeeded, in a lifetime project, in making most of the Jewish communities in the world aware of the existence of Ethiopian Jews and of their plight.

Nevertheless, even with the founding of the state of Israel in 1946, and the implementation of the policy of the ingathering of the exiles from around the world, no Ethiopian Jew arrived in Israel before the late 1970s on an immigration scheme. The main reason for this 'delay' was that doubt was cast on the authenticity of their Jewish identity. Consequently, they were not entitled to become Israeli citizens under the Law of Return. Only in 1975 were they recognized as Jews by the main religious authorities. It was then that the immigration process began.

The migration dream of return from long exile to Israel, to 'Yerussalem' as they called it, was fundamental to traditional Ethiopian Jewish society. In the migration stories I collected, the dream comes out clearly as a cross-generational message which was kept so much 'alive' that it served as a blueprint for action. Ethiopian Jews believed, moreover, that 'the time will arrive' for migration to take place, and that various signs would point out the ripeness of time. Apparently, this was a powerful concept which determined the moment of migration.

As far back as 1862, a distinguished Ethiopian Jew, called Abba Mahari, announced that the time had indeed arrived, meaning to go to Jerusalem. Thousands of Jews gathered around him in the Gonder region, and started the long march towards Jerusalem, in the direction of the Red Sea. The attempt failed. Most of the migrants died on the way, in the mountains and desert. Some continued until they arrived at a big river, probably in the Tigre area, where Abba Mahari, like Moses, pointed his walking stick towards the river waiting for God to part it so that the Jewish people could cross. When this did not happen, the remaining survivors turned and walked back to their villages.[7] This story shows the power and the vividness of the dream to get to Jerusalem, and the readiness of Ethiopian Jews to leave everything behind and go at once, 'when the time comes'. One of my interviewees, Daniel, aged 16, clearly describes the ancient dream and concept of 'the time will arrive':

It is known, to the one who is in exile, the land of Israel . . . Jerusalem, this is the most beautiful country in the world . . . Our parents had told us that way, so we accepted this thing, and *it was in our blood* . . .

At home, at celebrations, everywhere, everybody would say: 'Soon the time will arrive, to ascend, to *walk* to Israel.' This word, to ascend, is how we say it now; but to *walk* to Israel, they would always speak about *walking* to Israel, always!

Shmuel describes how the dream was kept alive in his family. When he and his father were ploughing their field together, his father would tell him: 'You know my son, the land that we are ploughing is not our land. *Our* land is far away, in Yerussalem.'

Shauil, aged 17, of the Wolkite area, tells of the ways in which the message of the dream was transmitted in the villages:

Especially in the remote villages, like my own, where there was no communication, and nobody came who had been to Israel, no one reached us, nobody from Israel . . . everything was through the stories that the older people used to tell from the Bible, and legends that were passed on. And also the true story that we were told, that Israel is a land of milk and honey . . .

In the village, no one had ever been to a Western country: no one had ever travelled even within Ethiopia, to Addis Ababa, or to Asmara, any place relatively more developed from the technological point of view. They were all villagers, telling these wonderful legendary stories, so that . . . we expected that all the people in Israel were religious people . . . this is *Jerusalem* [stressing the word] . . .

Once it happened that I heard on the news, and I told them, that there was a city called Tel Aviv, and that I had heard that it was the largest in Israel. They [the older people] said to me: 'What? How come?? Jerusalem is the largest!' And the name 'Israel' was not familiar, but Zion or Jerusalem . . .

And the grown-ups, the parents, always used to give us a blessing, if we did some favour [service for them]. Instead of saying 'Thank you', or something like that, or giving sweets, [smiles compassionately]—not many sweets to give—they would then say to us: 'May you reach the country', 'to your country', 'to Zion', or something like that.

The crucial role of the old dream in the decision to set out on the journey finds a special expression in Shlomo's story. He explains how the current events in Ethiopia, as well as the proposed direction of the Jewish migration through the Sudan, finally convinced him that the story was true, that the time *had* indeed arrived:

When the elders talked, I liked to listen, to get close to their feet and listen to what they said. . . . They used to say that in Ethiopia, a very formidable war would take place: there would be a Gog and Magog, meaning one shall eat the other, there would be a civil war, and there would emerge people that can judge near a tree, yes, as if their office is in the tree, under a big tree, there they shall carry out justice; so as [the elders] used to say—a war *did* actually happen, all kinds of underground groups came about in Ethiopia, and father fought against son. This had come true, and those who administered justice, they were actually representatives of the villages, selected by the underground, and they were judging under a tree, judging people. All these things had actually taken place. So the elders also said: 'At that time the Jews will come out [of Ethiopia]. If they do not come out at that time, there is no chance that they will [ever] come out.' And they did not say 'by airplane we shall come out', [but], 'we shall come out through the Sudan'. I am quoting this as I have heard it with my own ears!

The role of these stories in providing a motivation for the migration thus emerges strongly from the personal accounts. There were of course, as Shlomo's version suggests, other more material factors in the timing: above all, the opening of the migration door on the Israeli side, but also pressures in Ethiopia itself. The country was already suffering a long-term economic decline, which was to culminate in the onset of disastrous famine conditions in the 1980s. Social marginality was another pressure. The advent in 1974 of a Marxist regime in Ethiopia led to an immediate improvement in the position of the Jewish community, for in the subsequent land redistribution they were given their first land rights for three centuries, and some were able to take advantage of this new opportunity. But at the same time the social upheavals brought by the new regime, with the threat of forced conscription of adolescents into the army and with its commitment to secular progress, highlighted the difficulties of a highly traditional religious minority: for example, there was no possibility for social advancement through a Jewish system of education. These material factors provided the context in which the dream came to be realized, but little is made of them in the migrants' stories. As Elazar summed it up, 'A feeling got hold of us, which called out, "Go! Go! These are God's words" . . . So we went!'

So a growing trickle of Ethiopian Jews started to flow towards the Sudan. Many of them knew that a rigorous journey awaited them, but only in general terms. The distance to the Sudan depended on the departure point, but often people were forced to trek back and forth over hundreds of miles of side paths. A typical journey lasted for three to five weeks. It was followed by a stay in a refugee camp in the Sudan for, on the average, one to two years.

Walking to the Sudan was no simple process. The country was divided by war and the travellers had to dodge the authorities, underground groups, and robbers. Often they could only risk moving at night. The demands of the journey are described by Ami, aged 13:

The first night wasn't hard. We walked slowly with the man who took us out. The second night was very hard. The guides met up with us . . . they wanted to walk quickly, because if the soldiers caught them, *chick-chack* they get a bullet in their head. It was very hard to keep up. You can get mixed up and get left behind, on the way, you can easily get lost. I thought, 'If we have to walk like that another night I can't go on' . . . When you walk like that at night, what can you see? You don't see and you're not familiar with the place. And that is the problem, that only the guides know the way. . . . So we walked all night.

Baruch, also 13, tells of other dangers:

Meanwhile, the army arrived in the area; staying there became dangerous. So we ran away to the forests. In Ethiopia it's forbidden to go from one district to another without a permit and we didn't have a permit. If we got caught, they wouldn't ask many questions and show too much interest: we would be handed over to the authorities, and whoever got hold of us would get all our possessions as a reward.

Ya'akov tells how he, his brother, and his cousin were close to reaching the Sudan, when the border guards discovered them. It was night. Ya'akov's cousin made a mistake and ran in the direction of the gun shots. Ya'akov's brother jumped into the strongly flowing border river and started to go under. Ya'akov hesitated for a moment and then jumped into the water and managed to save his brother from drowning and to heave him out of the current on the Sudanese side, while he himself was tossed about in the stormy water for some distance. After he landed on the bank of the Sudanese side, he searched for his brother, found him, and escaped with him to an unknown destination. Ya'akov's brother's shoes had been lost in the river, so they ran using one of Ya'akov's shoes for each of them, limping, oblivious to the thorns that tore their skins and the sharp stones that cut their feet. The border guards shot illuminating flares into the night sky in an attempt to locate them. Ya'akov narrates:

We just ran, ran, ran. Without knowing where the place was. We didn't know. If we had come to the border of the Sudan, they would have killed us. We ran away. . . . Our whole body was blood. . . . Then we came to where those people called Lehawi are. They are Sudanese who simply kill. Whoever they find they kill. Where they were, that's where he falls down, my brother. And I can't hear him because his throat is dry. So I say to him, 'I am all right. I'll grab your hand and I'll run.' . . . I tell him, 'We'll live. With God's help we'll live.

I'll just grab you and run.' Then he said to me again, 'Our cousin, we heard shots. For sure they killed him when he ran there. So we're going to die too!' Then I yelled at him, 'Let's go. I'll pull you!' Did I run.

In some areas there was little or no water. There was little medicine. People had to cross both malaria-infested land and desert areas. Ahuva, aged 16, narrates:

We walked at night.... But one time we ran out of malaria pills. And I caught malaria. My friends, the ones I went to school with, made a bed from tree branches and they took me on it in the mountains. It was very hard for them but they didn't say so. They tried to make me laugh, to cheer me up, so they kept saying: 'pretty soon we'll get to Yerussalem.'

Others were incarcerated, attacked by bandits, or—especially women or girls—raped or kidnapped. Many died: most of all in the refugee camps in the Sudan, where the community lost over 4,000 people, about one-fifth of its members. Crossing the Sudan indeed, was not the end of their sufferings, since the immediate transit to Israel which they were expecting failed to materialize.

Edna describes the conditions in the Um-Raquba refugee camp:

People would go to get water. We would wait in line for five hours until they brought the water. People were thirsty.... After that there were diseases and people were very sick. We waited for three months because my brother's wife got sick. Then she died in Um-Raquba, together with her three children. Also two of my brother's sons died. Altogether, seven people died of us, and my mother was very sick too. I thought that all of us were going to die. I did not believe that we would ever leave Sudan.

Some of the hardships in the camps were general, but others were more particularly connected with their Jewish identity and the fact that they were heading for Israel. Esther describes the problem of needing to maintain a Kosher diet:

They would bring us a cooked chicken, and you wanted so much to eat it, but it isn't yours. We didn't eat it. Well, I remember that every time they brought us food, people would hide the children. They didn't let us see, so that we wouldn't be tempted and eat. So they would take it and throw it in the toilet. Because the Gentiles used to check to see if we ate or not, because we told them that we were Gentiles. Until one day the toilets got clogged up, and they opened them and found all the bones and stuff.... They said, 'You are Jews!'... Well, afterwards there was trouble but somebody rescued us. A kind of representative, someone from Israel. He paid money on the side and got us out.

Enduring such a difficult journey clearly demanded tremendous willpower, energy, and coping abilities. Many researchers and practitioners have indicated that ideologically motivated people cope better with difficulties and stressful life events. In his book, *Man's Search for Meaning*, Victor Frankl describes how people with some reason to live—a cause to fight for, a political ideology, a vision of the world they wanted to achieve, or some other goal, fared better in Nazi concentration camps than those who had no such cause. The supportive and protective function of ideology is also illustrated by Bruno Bettleheim in *The Informed Heart*, and by Jerome Frank in *Persuasion and Healing*.[8] More recent research and observations in refugee camps in different parts of the world[9] has shown that adolescent refugees show less symptomatology when they belong to an ideological movement, and can explain to themselves why they are encountering hardships, in contrast to those merely trying to survive in the camps. It has also been argued that enduring pain and loss is facilitated when conceptualized as part of a group experience, in contrast to an individualized perception.[10]

It seems to me that for Ethiopian Jews on their journey, Jewish identity served as an ideology which played a crucial role in their ability to cope with the journey's hardships. Certainly the narratives I collected portray Ethiopian Jews as relying on their traditional culture when facing adverse conditions and traumatic events. They refer to leaning 'on the power of God', 'on His guidance and protection', and struggling to observe the Jewish religious laws. Moreover, during the journey an image developed, consolidated, and became a core symbol. The Ethiopian Jews perceived that they were re-living and re-experiencing the myth of the original Exodus of the Israelites out of Egypt.

Shaul describes a particularly moving experience, when he had already been some years in Israel, and was invited—though he was still very young—to lead the Passover ceremony for fellow-Ethiopian Jews who had just arrived. A major aspect of this ceremony is the reading of the Haggada, the mythical story of the Exodus of the Israelites. At one point every person present is asked to feel as if he or she were the one going out of Egypt. When Shaul reached that passage he said to them: 'I don't have to explain *to you* what it means to go out of Egypt.' He then continued: 'I saw in their faces the full agreement to that, that they really felt the Exodus out of Egypt. There was a lot of excitement and emotion on their faces.'

Other interviewees associated various experiences on their journey with those of the Israelites in the desert. Brehanu recalled:

When we went out of Ethiopia, the haste in which the food was prepared reminded me of my father's stories of how the Israelites prepared their Matzot [unleavened bread]. I said to my father: 'This is like the Exodus out of Egypt.' He replied: 'This is true, and it is good that you recalled. It is exactly the same.'

Marito, a 13-year-old girl, said they had been safe on their way 'because the clouds covered us. . . . It was summer then, a very strong summer, yet all the time that we walked, when we were out of the bush, we were covered by clouds so that the sun never touched us. We said: "God is making this happen." ' Safety from clouds is a theme in the original Exodus story: for example, God puts the cloud between the Israelites and the pursuing Egyptian army so they cannot find them, and the Israelites cross the Red Sea in safety.

The story of the Israelites' Exodus from Egypt to Israel is considered by many to be the central myth of the Jewish people, of their passage from slavery to freedom. The Israelites wandered for forty years in the desert, during which they encountered enemy attacks, hunger, thirst, and epidemics. According to the Bible this long period of wandering and suffering was designed by God as a test of faith, for all those who doubted God's power would perish in the desert. Some Bible scholars also interpret it as a transformation process from the set of mind of slaves to that of a free people. It was during that time that the Israelites 'encountered' God and became a people, His chosen people. In essence this is a story of becoming, and it is a process of selection of those who deserved to enter the land of God.

As in the ancient myth, Ethiopian Jews too, believed that their journey served as a process of selection. It ensured that only the righteous, those who are deserving, would enter the land of Israel. This belief seems to have developed on the way, in response to the suffering and misfortunes of the journey. They had set out with the utopian image of Israel handed down through generations: as 'a land of milk and honey', where only righteous people, black people dressed in white gowns, lived; a place where all troubles would come to an end.

They made better sense of the obstacles on their way, as well as of the harsh conditions and loss of life in the refugee camps in the Sudan in terms of a process of selection and purification. Since the right to enter Yerussalem was reserved for the righteous only, the hardships were seen as a system of selection through which the worthy cleansed themselves of sins, wrong-doings, and proved their righteousness. In my view the special place given to this aspect of the ancient myth derives from the central role of purity and impurity within Ethiopian Jewish culture. Purity/impurity rules played an important role and were, according to some researchers, one of the major characteristics separating Jews from the Christians in Ethiopia.[11] The rules affected everyday familial relationships. For example, a special hut was used by women during menstruation, separating them according to Biblical rules. And Jews returning to their village after contact with Christians or other non-Jews were expected to observe the *Attenkun* custom (literally meaning 'do-not-touch-me') of purification through immersion. Hence the Christians called the Jews 'the people who smell of water' or pejoratively, 'stink of water'.

Thus, Ethiopian Jews saw themselves, like the Israelites, as walking through an unknown land, facing obstacles, enemies, sickness, and death: but they too were on their way to becoming Israelis;[12] they believed they were led and guarded by God while going to His chosen land. They saw themselves as 'a drop, a stream or a river, on its way to the sea, where no one could then distinguish between river and sea'. In Israel, among fellow Jewish people, they would 'feel more complete'.

With such high expectations, what has been the reality of their encounter with Israeli society? It might be summed up precisely as a failure to feel that completeness, and instead, a continuing struggle to realize their identity.

Unlike many migrants from the Third World to the West, they came with official state support. The Israeli authorities had prepared absorption plans in various areas, which sought to avoid what are known in Israel as 'the mistakes of the 1950s'. That is, the rapid and massive secularization of traditional societies in accord with a 'melting pot' ideology. Thus Ethiopian Jews were put into special absorption centres for their first twelve to eighteen months. These were usually headed by a social worker. The objective was a gradual integration of Ethiopian Jews into Israeli society, as the period spent in the absorption centre would give sufficient time for learning the new language, finding a permanent place to live and a proper job, and most of all, finding their way in Israeli culture and society. There were certainly some successes: notably through a number of educational-vocational projects in various parts of the country, designed specifically for the Ethiopian immigrants.

Unfortunately, however, due to housing shortages—partly created by unsuccessful governmental strategies—and certain bureaucratic conflicts, most Ethiopian Jews remained in absorption centres longer than intended. Thus, what was planned as a transient centre in many places turned into a permanent home. After being uprooted for so long, many Ethiopian immigrants were reluctant to move yet again, after having settled for two or three years in the absorption centre. Another problem in leaving ensued from the fact that the absorption centre in itself, as a 'total institution',[13] by taking care of all the immigrants' needs, made them fear the 'outside world', as they called it, where they had to fend for themselves. Many of them explicitly expressed their anxiety about leaving the all-embracing services of the absorption centres.

Most of the absorption centres were cheap apartment buildings in the most problematic areas of Israeli cities. The presence of the Ethiopian Jews for long periods of up to seven or eight years inevitably created social problems in itself. These areas already had their own difficulties, being mainly populated by Israelis of lower socio-economic status suffering from social marginality and the characteristic disadvantaged social services. The Ethiopian Jews were seen as competitors for limited resources—which made for a difficult start in social relations. In addition, finding employment was a major problem for Ethiopian Jews. Since 95 per cent came from agricultural backgrounds, few had a profession which they could immediately exercise; hence they found themselves very quickly with unskilled work, typically, in low status and underpaid jobs. Many found themselves living in areas where unemployment was already very high, and it was difficult to find a job at all.

Employment is a crucial factor in integration, since it determines whether a family can mount the resources needed to move to a neighbourhood where children can have better opportunities for education, and hence a chance for social mobility. It is equally important as a constituent of self-respect and the feeling of worth, which is so significant in times of migration; as well as a crucial ingredient in family cohesion.

An equally fundamental problem affecting most of the newcomers was the separation from their families, which were stranded in

Ethiopia. In January 1985 a leak to the press caused Operation Moses to come to a halt. An estimated 35,000 Jews were left in Ethiopia or were stuck somewhere along the way. In Israel some 1,500 Ethiopian children were unaccompanied by parents, who had been left behind. Many others were missing their relatives left in Ethiopia. Young people, themselves longing for their parents and struggling with their new conditions, had to become substitute parents to their brothers and sisters. The situation of the children influenced the entire Ethiopian community. It is not only that, cut off from their kin, they lacked completeness as families. But also in practical terms, young adults could not concentrate on their studies. Adolescents could not feel at rest knowing that their departure had left their parents more vulnerable and prone to harrassment in Ethiopia. And, decisions in Israel, such as choices of profession or marriage, were held back through waiting for the families to arrive. There were those who developed the Ethiopian syndrome of the *full abdomen*, whose 'stomach got filled up with troubles', which led them to stop eating. They had to be treated in hospitals, and some even committed suicide, stating a direct connection between their despair and their condition of familial separation.[14]

Another major problem for integration was skin colour. Being black in Israel aroused prejudices and various stereotypes as well as, on the psychological level, primitive fears of the strange and alien. David narrates: 'And this word "Kushi" ['black', as in biblical usage; but also connotes other meanings such as 'a slave'], when I first heard it I did not understand; and when I understood what it means, I couldn't believe it. Am I someone's slave? I was hurt.'

Another aspect of being black in Israel relates to the fact that in such a highly security-conscious society there is some suspicion and fear of anyone in the street who cannot be easily and straightforwardly identified and 'categorized' into one of the Israeli sub-groups or ethnic minorities. Such categorization makes it easier to identify who belongs to 'us' and who is part of 'them', the latter being Arabs who could be potential terrorists. Ethiopian Jews broke stereotypes and social categories in Israel in the 1980s, and it was not until the beginning of the 1990s that Israelis developed a clear social category of 'Ethiopian-black-Jewish-immigrant'. Only then did this particular suspicion and fear begin gradually to diminish.

Lastly, but perhaps most wounding of all, the Ethiopian Jews found the authenticity of their own Jewish identity itself under question. This doubt was carried over into the Israeli context. Religious authorities had declared, on the one hand, that there was no doubt that these were Jews (a declaration which was instrumental in bringing them to Israel, according to the Law of Return). Yet, on the other hand, the rabbinate demanded a process of 'symbolic conversion' to Judaism by Ethiopian Jews upon their arrival.

This decision of the rabbinate, and its line of reasoning, was unintelligible to Ethiopian Jews, as for many Israelis. A major conflict ensued, in which the whole issue of 'Who is a Jew?', and who is to decide on it in Israel, was rekindled. The 'dormant' issue of state and religion in Israel came into the public eye again, and the rabbinate came under unprecedented attack both in Israel and from Jewish leaders in the Diaspora. Basically, it was a struggle about the future of Israeli identity. Nevertheless, the decision remained unchanged, and Ethiopian Jews had to go through what was in their eyes a humiliating ceremony of symbolic conversion. Many of them refused. The doubt then remained.

Hence, reality shattered their specific dreams and expectations concerning Israel. A respectable elder of the community once shared with me his frustration at having to go through this symbolic ceremony. He said: 'We suffered so much on our way here and they question our Jewish identity!?'

Shlomo expressed vividly the frustration and disappointment of the 'rough face' shown to him at his journey's end:

When the airplane landed in Israel, the joy of it is beyond description. Suddenly you forget all the hardships you suffered, for a moment you put it aside, and . . . as if I was floating in the air out of happiness. Then they took us into the night, it was raining, and we saw the orange groves on our way, and we said to each other: 'Look. Here it is! The oranges. As we were told, the land of milk and honey! We are seeing it. It actually starts.' Then we arrived at the absorption centre, and relatives started visiting us, and we were so tired, and they would bring us the fruits of the country, and the joy was incredible . . .

And then, slowly, you start observing something strange . . . as if you were once in a place, [where] you had a certain dream, and now you encounter something, and your disappointment. For a moment it is hard to accept it, because . . . your expectations were different, your dreams were different, and then, all the hardships you went through in order to realize it, and for a moment, when you see that things are different than what you have expected, you turn to be . . . disappointed, asking yourself, 'Where did I actually arrive?' Because it is not the place. . . . There were in fact people who asked if they reached the right place . . . and 'Is it the place I dreamt of all my life?' . . .

Suddenly Shabbat arrived, and there were cars driving on a Shabbat. . . . And the bureaucracy . . . and when they used the word Kushi ['black'] . . . this was such an insult . . . and when people used it in a certain tone it would infuriate me, not only me but many of us felt: 'Did we arrive for this? Is this the reception we deserve? What we went through, what we suffered, no one asks, how many family members we have lost, no one asks, but instead, they say this word!' . . . And the problem with the rabbinate. . . . And people think that we had come because of hunger, which infuriates me! After all we have suffered because of our Jewishness on the journey.

Certainly this doubting of their Jewish identity has had a tremendous psychological effect upon the Ethiopian immigrants. It threatens to reframe[15] the events of the exodus, and to strip them of their meaning as part of a collective selection and purification process. Losses through death of a parent or a child can suddenly become meaningless, stripped of their previous significance.

Adaptation is in itself a stressful process which requires coping abilities and emotional resources. We may assume that Ethiopian Jews are helped in their present struggle for absorption by feeling that they are joining their fellow-Jews in Israel. Conversely, destabilizing their Jewish identity deprives them of that which, following Erik Erikson's theory,[16] is most needed as an integrating principle during the stress of resettlement. This is why the Ethiopian Jews responded with a social struggle in which they tried to remove this doubt, and to fight back at those in Israeli society who promoted it. During 1985 they staged a prolonged strike against the rabbinate. They involved the Prime Minister in this struggle and used their right to appeal to the Supreme Court and won their case. And for a period they insisted on continuing to have their own priests perform marriage ceremonies.

This struggle seems to be of importance if we look at it from yet another point of view: by struggling, they were compelled to address the question of what aspects of their original culture they wished to preserve, and what they were willing to give up. In that sense, paradoxically, the struggle against the religious authorities, and the heated dialogue with some sections of the Israeli public, launched them on an important process—a process which I would suggest, could be called 'becoming hyphenated'. Migrants, and sometimes refugees, if they stay long enough, do not go (as some would argue) through a total transformation into a newly created person, sometimes called an assimilated person, moulded anew in the model of the new (or host) society. Rather, they become hyphenated persons, people with a dual or even multiple sense of social identity, who are often referred to as Mexican-Americans, Italian-Americans, Chinese-English, or Bulgarian-Israelis. A veteran Ethiopian who came as an adolescent and had been for thirty years in Israel, once said to an interviewer who had asked him whether he was an Israeli in every sense: 'Of course, I belong to the process of the last thirty years. Yet, some basic things never change.' In these words, I believe, he meant that he is an Israeli of Ethiopian origin: an Ethiopian-Israeli.

A social dialogue is still taking place in Israel, in which different levels and segments of society interact with Ethiopian immigrants. We still do not know how this process will continue to unfold, and whether the kind of hyphenated identity that Ethiopian Jews will form will include seeds of future conflict and renewed marginalization, or the power of hope and integration which fired their journey.

Notes

This essay is part of a broader research project dealing with Ethiopian Jews' narratives of the journey and their relation to identity and to the encounter with Israel, summed up in a larger publication (forthcoming). This essay was made possible by a grant of the New-Land Foundation USA. I wish to thank Dr Albert Solnit and Dr Donald Cohen, former and present directors of Yale University Child Study Center, as well as to Gail Cohen for their essential support in the publication of my research. Special thanks are due to Professor Paul Thompson for his invaluable comments on a first version of this essay.

1. Abraham Epstein, *Eldad Ha-Dani: His Story and His Halakhot* (Pressburg, 1891) (Hebrew).
2. James Bruce, *Travels to Discover the Source of the Nile* (Edinburgh, 1790); Simon Messing, *The Story of the Falashas: 'Black Jews' of Ethiopia* (New York, 1982); Richard Pankhurst, *The Ethiopian Royal Chronicles* (London, 1967).
3. Messing, *Story*; David Kessler, *The Falashas: The Forgotten Jews of Ethiopia* (London, 1982); and Steven Kaplan, 'A Short History of Beta Israel', in *Beta Israel* (Tel Aviv, 1988) (Hebrew).
4. Most scholars, as well as the Ethiopian Jews themselves, refer to the fact that linguistically, this term is translated as 'exiles' and also connotes the meaning of 'invaders' or 'strangers'. While this meaning could have come from earlier times, either from their exile period from Israel or from the Axumite Kingdom (sixth century) as pointed out by Messing (*Story*, 13), its additional meaning relating to loss of the right for land might have appeared in the fifteenth century.
5. Taddese Tamrat, *Church and State in Ethiopia 1270–1527* (Oxford, 1972); Messing maintains that the term 'Falasha' was first used sometime earlier, during the reign of King Amda-Sion (1314–1344) (*Story*, 14).
6. Although they could not own land any more, many of the Jews maintained land-tenancy, supplementing it by the above-mentioned professions. Yet, they became *collectively* identified with the despised activities.
7. Shoshan Ben-Dor, 'The Journey to Eretz Israel: The story of Abba Mahari', *Pe'amim: Studies in the Cultural Heritage of Oriental Jewry*, 33 (1987), 5–31 (Hebrew).

8. Victor E. Frankl, *Man's Search for Meaning: An Introduction to Logotherapy* (Hebrew edition; Tel Aviv, 1970); Jerome D. Frank, *Persuasion and Healing* (Baltimore, 1961); Bruno Bettleheim, *The Informed Heart* (London, 1970).
9. Josephine Rynell, *Political Pawns: Refugees on the Thai-Kampuchean Border* (Refugee Studies Programmes; Oxford, 1989); Mary Dynes, Refugee Studies Programme, Oxford, personal communication, 1991; Raija-Leena Punamaki-Gitai, ' "Natural Healing Processes" and Experiences of Political Violence', paper presented at the III Annual Meeting of the International Research and Advisory Panel on Refugees and Other Displaced Persons, Refugee Studies Programme, Oxford University, 1992; D. Summerfield, paper presented to the Seminar on Psycho-Social Issues at the Refugee Studies Programme, University of Oxford, 1992; D. Summerfield and L. Toser, ' "Low Intensity" War and Mental Trauma in Nicaragua: A Study in a Rural Community', *Medicine and War*, 7 (1991), 84–99.
10. The effect of 'de-individualization' on coping is discussed by S. Buus and I. Agger, 'The Testimony-Method: The Use of Testimony as a Psychotherapeutic Tool in the Treatment of Traumatized Refugees in Denmark', *Refugee Participation Network*, 3 (1988), Refugee Studies Programme, University of Oxford; D. Blackwell, 'Testimony and Psychotherapy: A Reply to Buus and Agger', *Refugee Participation Network*, 6 (1990), Refugee Studies Programme, University of Oxford.
11. Yael Kahana, 'The Material Culture of Ethiopian Jews', in V. Netzer and H. Polani (eds.), *Agada Shel Aliya: The Jews of Ethiopia and Their Linguistic Absorption* (Jerusalem, 1987) (Hebrew); Emanuela Trevisan-Semi, 'The Beta Israel (Falashas): From Purity to Impurity', *Jewish Journal of Sociology*, 27: 2 (1985), 103–14. Purity/impurity rules exist in some other groups in Ethiopia, hence there is a question about its exclusiveness among Ethiopian Jews. Still the above researchers bring up the fact that they were the ones who were referred to as the people who smell of water, and to some unique practices. In any case, for our purposes, it is enough to know that such an element existed among them.
12. 'Israelis', here in the sense of natives, inhabitants of the land of Israel—Zion Yerussalem. As the original Israelites who were walking to the promised land, called Canaan then.
13. Erving Goffman, 'Characteristics of Total Institutions', Symposium on Preventive and Social Psychiatry, Washington DC, 1957.
14. An elaborate analysis of the effect of separation on mental health of Ethiopian children could be found in Gadi Ben-Ezer, 'Anorexia Nervosa or an Ethiopian Coping Style?', *Mind and Human Interaction* (special issue on Children in War), 2: 2 (1990), The Center for the Study of Mind and Human Interaction, University of Virginia, Charlottesville, Va. (An updated version in *Refugee Participation Network*, 12 (1992), Refugee Studies Programme, University of Oxford). The various physical, social, and psychological effects of separation on adaptation in Israel are mainly discussed in: Gadi Ben-Ezer, *As Light within a Clay Pot: Migration and Absorption of Ethiopian Jews* (Hebrew: K'mo Or Ba'kad) (Jerusalem, 1992); Rivka Hanegbi, 'The Cognitive Map of Ethiopian Jews', in Netzer and Polani (eds.), *Agada*; Gadi Ben-Ezer, 'Unaccompanied Ethiopian Children in Israel: Their Psychological Condition', position paper of *Defence for Children International-Israeli Section* (Jerusalem, 1987).
15. P. Watzlawick, J. Weakland, R. Fisch, *Change: Principles of Problem Formation and Problem Resolution* (New York, 1974).
16. Erik H. Erikson, *Identity, Youth and Crisis* (New York, 1968).

8

Family and Identity

Barbadian Migrants to Britain

MARY CHAMBERLAIN

'Our family love to travel' Olive told me,

my grandfather was in Cuba and send for my two uncles. . . . He leave the girls . . . with his wife. Then after my mother could get grown up, then she went to Trinidad . . . and leave me very small, as a baby. . . . [My mother] was working in Trinidad. . . . Then she . . . went on to Panama and meet her husband there. He took her from Panama to Jamaica. . . . I come up to England, 1958.[1]

Between 1955 and 1966, over 27,000 Barbadians migrated to Britain.[2] It was the largest mass migration from the island since that to Panama in the first two decades of the twentieth century, when approximately 45,000 Barbadians migrated.[3] The decades in between saw a steady flow of Barbadians to destinations within the Caribbean and beyond, to North and South America. Fear of the consequences of unemployment, and the resulting claims for overpopulation, led the government of Barbados to play an active role in the twentieth century in securing outlets for employment abroad. As early as 1905, a recruitment office was established in Bridgetown to encourage the movement of labour to Panama. Similar offices were established throughout the 1930s and 1940s to recruit labour to the United States. In 1955 the government began a Sponsored Workers Scheme and appointed a Liaison Officer in London whose brief was to secure employment for Barbadians in Britain. 'The population pressure in Barbados is such', wrote the Liaison Officer in London to the Permanent Secretary of the Ministry of Transport and Labour 'that migration is the only solution.'[4]

This was in marked contrast to nineteenth-century government policy which, despite a high population density[5] and widespread poverty, perceived migration as a threat to the plantation economy and restricted it through legislation. Yet for the former slaves independence from plantation discipline was a vital post-Emancipation goal. Given the shortage of land and opportunity in nineteenth-century Barbados, migration was seen by them as a route towards achieving this end. Popular goals and government policy were directly opposed. Wherever possible, therefore, Barbadians left,[6] and returned. Within popular perception, such migrations appeared not only as sources of income, but also as assertions of independence, if not acts of defiance, or heroism (given the location of the island, and the dangers of sea travel).

By the end of the nineteenth century the government reversed its policy and encouraged migration.[7] Throughout the twentieth century Barbadians travelled. Panama and Cuba, Curaçao and Trinidad, America and Britain, each destination coinciding with demands for labour from overseas. Olive's story was one I was to hear repeated many times. Yet the significance of her story lies not in the locations described, nor in the brief history of migration which it encapsulates, but in the simple fact that hers was a *family* which 'love to travel'.

Two major themes—motive and identity—pervade British studies of post-war Caribbean migration. In the first instance, using governmental and official data, the motive is perceived to be rational and economic, driven by a broader dynamic conforming to 'safety valve' policies in the home country, and labour demand in Britain. In the second, the focus has passed beyond an initial concern with problems of adjustment and assimilation in the metropole into investigating alienation, deviance, and/or the development of cultural form. Few academic studies have used oral sources, and none have investigated migration using family histories as primary data. Indeed, most studies written from this metropolitan perspective have perceived migration from the Caribbean as a discrete and aberrant event, rather than part of the Caribbean's continuing history of mobility, and have conflated individual island cultures into a broad Caribbean experience.

Once, however, family histories are taken as a perspective, then the motives for migration, and questions of identity, become more complex, ambiguous, and culturally specific. The significance of the family has long preoccupied the social and behavioural sciences. The family is central in the process of socialization, in the creation of attitudes and culture, and for the understanding of behaviour and relationships. Although some historians have looked to demography to provide clues to shifting family structures over time, or to genealogy for tracing family allegiances and lineage, most historians have been slow to recognize the role of the family in the process of social change or stasis. Even oral historians use family detail as a mirror to reflect the mentalities of a period, rather than the tool to understanding how those mentalities have been constructed and shaped, transmitted and transformed. The emphasis, and the debate, has been around the substance of memory, rather than the historical *context* in which memory is formulated and reformulated.

It is this context which needs now to be examined, for what may appear to be an individual, economic motive in migration often involves a family history of social and geographic mobility; equally, what may appear as a response to structural forces and migration policies, may derive from, and conform to, a culture of migration which places not only a material but a symbolic value on the process itself. At the same time, questions of identity are not reduced to forms of cultural expression in the metropole, but shift into a more contradictory, and mobile set of allegiances in which, again, the family, as the generator and reflector of culture, plays a central role. This tips the analytical balance away from the host and into the home society. From this perspective, migration is seen as the norm, not a departure from it, and the image of the migrant searching for an identity—like Peter Pan, chasing a shadow—becomes irrelevant.

This essay arises from life-story interviews with fifty Barbadians, out of a projected sample of one hundred. To date, interviews have been conducted with two generations of family members, though the project will include third-generation family members. I contacted the majority of informants through members of the Barbados Association and conducted nineteen interviews with migrants resident in Britain, sixteen with their parents in Barbados, and fifteen with return migrants. Contact was made with the latter through Barbadian friendship networks in Britain. Of the group of migrants and return migrants, all but two had family members of previous generations migrate. Statistically this is not surprising given the high levels of migration from Barbados throughout the twentieth century.

It becomes immediately apparent, however, that most families will include a model for migration, which suggests that the motivation to move may well originate as much in the family as in the material and structural conditions surrounding departure. In this sample, migration is the rule, rather than the exception. What form the family model assumes may, however, be more ambiguous and will have a bearing on perception and attitudes to migration and identity. This essay attempts to explore questions of motive and identity by tracing a detailed lineage of migration within three families from the overall sample, and by focusing on two particular themes, the structure of families and models of migration.

One important characteristic of Barbadian families is the generational leap-frogging of childcare. Olive,[8] whose story began this essay, had been brought up, in her mother's absence (in Trinidad), by her maternal grandmother and great-grandmother. Lola, her great-grandmother, had also raised Olive's mother (whose father was away in Cuba, and whose mother had to work). When Olive migrated to Britain in 1956, she left three of her four children in the care of her mother, and the fourth, her son Jasper, in the care of her grandmother, whom, Jasper recalls, 'I loved ... dearly ... she was so much a part of me.... I sometimes believe that my great-grandmother is still looking after me.'[9]

'Our family,' Olive insists, was 'very, very close.'[10] 'A big, happy family,' according to Jasper,[11] in which family identity was the primary loyalty and where,

> family meant something. The family relationship was very strong. . . . . My grandfather had about three women . . . and this all became part of the family . . . because we all belonged to one person . . . my grandfather. . . . The outside[12] family and the inside family, all were family.[13]

As a result, 'relatives used to travel for miles to bring ... provisions'[14] to provide continuing support for each other. The family facilitated migration in other ways. Olive's grandfather, who migrated to Cuba, paid for the passage to Cuba for his sons. In the same way, when Olive's husband first went to Britain, it was her mother who provided the money for the passage. Throughout the travels of the family members, close contact and financial support was maintained. When Olive's uncles followed their father to Cuba, 'they send back (remittances) to their mum. (When) my mother went too, my mum send back to her mum, they're always sending. . . . My uncle came from Curaçao . . . and used to send out a lot of clothes . . . and everything you could think of.'[15] In the same way, when Olive's husband migrated, her mother (by then in Jamaica) used, as Jasper recalled, 'to send money for us ... maybe once every fortnight',[16] until his father was in a position to send money home.

In this family, the pattern of childcare and family support enabled the migration of three generations of its members. At the same time, migration assisted in the maintenance of the family back home. It was a

Family and Identity

reciprocal pattern, ensuring family loyalty and a continuing family identity across the generations and across the seas. It may account for the ultimate return of family members to Barbados, which in turn became a component of this family's model of migration. Olive's grandfather returned from Cuba. Her uncle returned from Curaçao. Olive and Jasper both returned in 1988 from Britain. Jasper's daughter, although born in Britain, has also returned to Barbados.

But there is another script which helps to account for this loyalty and identification. Both Olive and Jasper stress that they were not 'plantation people', that is, agricultural labourers. They may have worked *at* a plantation; they were not *of* the plantation. This pride of independence can be traced to Lola who, in the nineteenth century, succeeded in buying the family an acre of land from the plantation for ten dollars.

Until the twentieth century, the majority of black Barbadians were plantation labourers, governed by the Contract Law of 1840, which bound them to work exclusively for the plantation from whom a 'house spot' was rented. Since most of the land was under white ownership, and since black labourers had little money to buy land, the majority were forced to rent land (a house spot) from the plantation and became liable, therefore, under the Contract Law. The Contract Law, imposed after the abolition of slavery, was perceived as its successor,[17] and one of the major impediments to realizing, in material terms, the freedom promised by the (full) Emancipation of 1838. It was not repealed until 1937. The desire to be independent of the plantation was very strong, although until the first two decades of the twentieth century (and the money generated from the migration to Panama) relatively few could achieve it.[18] Lola, however, had raised sufficient money, by baking and selling bread, to buy the family both land and release from the Contract Law. Although the house no longer exists, Jasper remembers,

there is a corner ... known as Lola's Corner ... where she baked.... There's nothing there now, just the piece of land ... which has been handed down from the family, from Lola to her daughter, which was my great-grandmother, to my grandmother, to my mother, and I suppose my mother pass it on to me.[19]

Lola's independence, of which the land remains a potent symbol, provides a clue to the sense of pride and family identity. It pervades the accounts of her family, whether they were descendants by blood or marriage. Olive's grandfather returned from Cuba 'a wealthy man', a fisherman who owned three boats and was able to support 'his own family at home, plus his outside relationships'.[20] Olive's uncle returned from Curaçao and built a 'lovely bungalow'. It pervades also the choice of occupation. Lola was a baker. Olive's grandmother was a cook; her mother had a restaurant business in Jamaica. Jasper himself made his money from catering. 'Our family', as Olive says, 'belong to the kitchen'.[21]

The role of Lola was fundamental in the creation of family identity. There is a clear recollection of genealogy and a recognition of her role in differentiating and demarcating the family route away from direct dependence on the plantation. Lola's aspirations had become incorporated into a family dynamic and had generated a family loyalty which was as much a part of the family inheritance as Lola's corner. Jasper believed his great-grandmother's spirit lived in him. At the same time, the family permitted and encouraged migration, and the model of migration and successful return created in the family was one which supported and enhanced this dynamic. Although the decision to leave, made by different members of this family, may have been prompted by a simple and time-specific economic expedient, the movement contains within it a far more complex history of social mobility, and geographic migration, in which loyalty to and identity with the family and with Barbados were maintained and strengthened.

The model of migration offered in the second family is more ambivalent. Here, the theme which emerges is one of struggle and resistance, and a reshaping of the family migration model. It is a theme consistent through two generations, although it assumes a different form. Charles was born in 1913 in St George, Barbados. He has two children of whom Irene, the eldest, migrated to Britain in 1960.

Charles's father migrated to Panama before he was born. He sent no remittances and made no contact. Charles never knew his father. Although his mother remained in Barbados, Charles was raised by his maternal grandparents. One maternal uncle who had also gone to Panama did, however, send remittances which proved the leitmotif of Charles's life:

When I were at the age of 12 years old, my uncle ... said he want me to go to secondary school because the people in Panama who is educated gets the best job. ... My grandmother had a brother and he worked on an estate as the bookkeeper. The white half could work there.[22] ... So I was to go to

Combermere.[23] I had my money, my books, my khaki suit, everything ready. The money . . . that my uncle send to pay for the school fees, it was eight dollars and eight cents. I will never forget this as long as I live. . . . I was home on evening . . . and my grandmother sister came very dressed. Two sisters came, two aunts, and my grandmother get dress. I saw her boots, her umbrella, and they leave. I do not know where they were going. But the next thing I heard, my uncle that was the bookkeeper . . . they ship him to Canada. . . . My grandmother took the money, with my two aunts, and ship my uncle to Canada.[24]

This uncle had got 'heself in trouble', through gambling with 'all these white fellas'.[25] Unlike Olive's family, this model of migration is confusing. Charles's father migrates and abandons him. One uncle migrates and promises him a better future. Another uncle 'robs' him of that future, by himself leaving on the money destined for Charles's education. The story of the 'robbery' occurred within the first few minutes of the interview. It was all Charles wished to tell. The interview concluded:

I made a oath. . . . If I walk the road, pick paper bag, bottles and sell, my children got to get a secondary education. . . . I've made that vow, for what my family did me. . . . But my other two friends (who went to Combermere) . . . ent as successful as me. I came out successful. My children will get education. I have a roof over my head and I am not hungry . . . I don't owe nobody nothing. Nothing.[26]

How did that success come about? Charles himself migrated shortly after his marriage to Muriel in 1941. He went first to Trinidad, then to St Lucia. After the war, he migrated to America, then returned to St Lucia where he stayed until 1978 when he retired and came home to Barbados. Charles was a master tailor by trade. He secured work, however, as a clerk on the American bases in St Lucia, even though 'I were not educated . . . I didn't went to Combermere but . . . I was really bright, man.'[27] His wife helped him in his work. 'And I thank she. . . . First thing she made me do, bought a dictionary and I got . . . a small book . . . algebras, different arithmetic . . . how to make up accounts, reports, all different things.'[28]

He worked as a clerk all his life, supplementing his income with tailoring. On each migration, Charles insisted that his family accompany him. 'No where I go to live and . . . there's no way my family can't come. . . . I have seen too many homes broken up.'[29] It was a story which his daughter, Irene, reflected upon,

My mother said that when my father sent for her, everybody says 'You're not going to St Lucia?' They thought it was bush and forest and snakes and donkeys... They said... 'That's no place to take a child.' And so my father said, 'But now we're a family'... that's as he saw it, that we were a family and you don't split a family up.... He's always kept and maintained that.... They say black men don't have that kind of responsibility, the women are usually left to do everything... they blame slavery, they blame the... economic set up in the West Indies. Well, it certainly wasn't the case in my family. I don't know where my father got his ideas from.[30]

On one level, Charles's own migration enabled him to fulfil the oath he made for himself when 'robbed' of his education. Throughout his narrative, the notion of being 'robbed' was frequently portrayed. Migration became synonymous with theft and absence. His motivation appeared to be to restore what he perceived as a lost inheritance—of education, success, and family. Charles paid for his two children to go to secondary school. Both now have university degrees.

This was a family that was 'together', but where, because of migration, the extended family did not function in an active or supportive role. In order to understand Irene's motivation for migrating to England in 1960, we need also to look at her mother, Muriel. She came from a family who 'felt we was a different breed, more elaborate in that neighbourhood [in Barbados]'.[31] Muriel's grandfather owned a 'big, upstairs house. Thirty, forty acres of land. He was a rich man'.[32] Like Lola, in the first story, he had amassed his fortune and secured the family's independence. Unlike her, this was the result of remittances sent by his children who had migrated to Panama and the United States.

The family employed servants in the house and hired labour to work the land. Muriel passed through seventh standard at elementary school and was sent to learn dressmaking. She wanted to be a nurse,

I was very bright too... [but] I believe my parents were a bit... backward... not that they didn't have the money to pay.... They would look out for the boys more than the girls, because [they say] a woman role in the house.... If I had my life to live over... I would be a brilliant woman some part of the world.[33]

In St Lucia, Muriel and Charles had servants in the house and, like Muriel's mother, hired labour to work the land. She engaged in voluntary work. Her friends were 'doctors and lawyers'. She helped Charles become a white-collar worker. For her, migration created her family's wealth and enabled her to maintain her status. Her only regret was her lack of further education.

For their daughter, Irene, the perspective on migration synthesized the complexities of class and struggle which was her familial inheritance. According to Irene, her father, Charles, migrated 'because he married my mother. It sounds silly, but for some reason he wasn't accepted by the family. Then he thought he was going to . . . make a life for himself and come back to Barbados and . . . prove his worth, so to speak.'[34] Irene grew up in St Lucia,

> and that was awful. . . . St Lucians tended not to like the Barbadians very much. . . . It was always 'You're from Barbados, why don't you go back where you came from?' . . . I wanted to belong and to be accepted, so I learned to speak patois. . . . I joined the Catholic religion, all that.[35]

Irene felt an outsider in St Lucia, distanced by nationality, culture, and by class: 'I wouldn't say that we were wealthy, but . . . we had servants . . . and the best of everything . . . beautiful hand-made leather shoes . . . music lessons, all that sort of thing . . . and that created a lot of envy in people.'[36] She also felt an outsider in her own family in Barbados, 'I missed out on all this sort of grandma, granddad, aunts, uncles, cousins, all that sort of thing. . . . When I met them I always felt somehow an outsider.'[37] 'The whole thing came to a head for me', she explained, in 1956, when

> I won a scholarship to go to Puerto Rico to train as a nurse. . . . My father . . . thought it wasn't good enough . . . if you were privileged enough to go to a grammar school, well, they thought teaching, or working in a bank, anything like that would be better than nursing. Nursing . . . just didn't have that kind of status.[38]

The scholarship was subsequently withdrawn when it was discovered that Irene was not St Lucian. 'I realized, yes, I am a stranger.'[39] According to her father, she was 'robbed'. After this, Irene was sent to stay with an aunt in Barbados. She remained there for two years, then migrated to England, to train as a nurse, this time with her parents' support. Within a year of arriving in England, however, Irene gave up her training to marry. Her husband was Barbadian, but 'life was rough. . . . I was living in a working-class area, being a working-class mum with working-class children and had middle-class values and expectations. . . . That was an awful time in my life . . . a very big mistake.'[40]

At the time, class differences, she felt, were not important. 'This was

England, and we were both young. . . . In the West Indies, he didn't have the opportunity.'[41] Migration had been the source of the family's social mobility. For Irene, it resulted in downward mobility. 'I didn't even correspond with my parents. I felt such a failure.'[42] Irene struggled to complete her training and study for a degree. She divorced her husband and remarried. Her second husband had gone to Combermere.

For Charles, migration implied absence. For his wife, it implied mobility. For Irene, it implied class and cultural distance. Paradoxically, however, for all of them it also implied opportunity. Like her father, Irene had to struggle and, like her father, she had won against the odds. Moreover, she had become the professional woman her mother had aspired to. But if the models and, therefore, the motives were mixed, what of identity? Unlike Olive and Jasper, the wider family did not provide a custom-made identity. Education was a dynamic, but it was a recent one. Irene lived her life as an outsider—in St Lucia, with her family in Barbados, with her first husband in England. The identity originates in the act of migration itself, and in the success deriving from that. 'To get here,' Irene says, 'it's not been easy.' 'I have a roof over my head and I am not hungry,' Charles insists, 'I don't owe nobody nothing. Nothing.' Charles and his wife returned to Barbados. Irene and her husband have made plans to return.

The third family investigates the perspective of the young 'non-voluntary' migrant to Britain and the search for identity for her generation of Barbadians in Britain. Beulah came to Britain in 1960 as a child of ten. Her mother had migrated four years previously. Her great-great-uncle had migrated to Cuba in 1920. Beulah recalls how her great-grandmother (born in 1898) 'used to tell me . . . all these stories . . . about her brother who went to Cuba. She never saw him again and I always remember as a little girl thinking how sad this was. It was a memory that stayed with me, how sad it was that he went away and they never saw him again.'[43]

Beulah recounts that story. Her mother, Estella, does not mention it. Why this story assumes a prominence relates to Beulah's use of family and lineage in the formation of identity. Her uncle in Cuba functioned as a metaphor for loss of family and identification. Beulah considers herself to be 'culturally together', in contrast to the confused identities held by her British-born siblings. Unlike her siblings, Beulah's early and formative years were spent in Barbados with her great-grandmother. This provided her with an awareness of family which she considers missing in their childhood. At the same time, however, she has reconstructed her family as a conscious response to growing up black in Britain, and in direct contrast to her siblings who have constructed a 'pseudo-English' identity. As a result, she considers them unable to come to terms with being black in Britain, which has resulted in their alienated and alienating behaviour. Her great-great-uncle's disappearance has become a mechanism by which her position is justified, and that of her siblings explained.[44]

Beulah's mother, Estella, was born in 1930 but raised by her maternal grandmother, a plantation labourer. In 1950 Estella gave birth to Beulah. When she migrated to Britain in 1956, she left Beulah in the care of this grandmother. 'My first image' Beulah recalls, 'is of my great-grandmother'

> I went everywhere with [her] . . . to the fields, when she was hoeing. . . . She put me under a guava tree. . . . 'Bo-bo, sit there till I come back.' . . . And bed time . . . I would be washed, night dress on, and then I would sit on her lap . . . and we would talk . . . and as she talked, she would be rocking me and singing . . . she told me Nancy stories, which frightened me to death.[45]

Like Jasper, Beulah 'can feel her presence even now'. By contrast, her mother, 'was this woman who wafted in, smelling of perfume, with nail polish, wide skirts, thin waist, made a lot of noise in the house, laughing, and out she waft again. . . . My great-grandmother was everything to me.'[46] Beulah was an 'outside' child. Her father was,

> what they call the 'village ram'. . . . He was a bus driver and that time, in the fifties, if you were a bus driver, you had all the girls and the prestige. . . . I remember him taking me down to his family . . . and I used to feel like a little treasure. . . . My [paternal] grandmother . . . just showed me off.[47]

Why did Beulah's mother Estella migrate in 1956? She was living 'comfortable' on her earnings (as a dressmaker), her grandmother's support, and with maintenance from Beulah's father. She had no pressing economic motive for moving away. Everybody was leaving so 'I thought I'd go and have a try . . . I was young and free and happy. I was this pretty young girl in this lovely red coat.'[48] When she left Beulah with her grandmother, 'I never bothered about it, because I know she was in good hands, it was Granny who used to do all the work on Beulah. . . . So when I had to leave her, I just kiss her down the water front, I kissed them all and said goodbye, and I weren't no way guilty for leaving.'[49]

Like many, Estella planned to stay for a short time. Shortly after arriving in Britain, however, she married. Four years later, at age ten, Beulah came to Britain to live with her mother, her stepfather, and her British-born siblings. However, 'I've never recovered from the fact that she'd had other children. . . . I feel bereaved since she's had the other four children, and I still can't come to terms with sharing her.'[50]

Her relationship with her stepfather was fraught. Beulah describes him as a violent and selfish man. She had to 'mother her mother', and her half-siblings, protecting them against her stepfather. By contrast, 'I had a charmed upbringing . . . in the Caribbean.' By contrast, also, her own father is 'wonderful . . . I am', she says, 'eternally grateful to her [mother] for giving me him.'

These are important contrasts, ultimately shaping how she grew up and lived as a black woman, a Barbadian, in Britain. Her family loyalties became orientated towards the great-grandmother in Barbados, and her father, rather than her siblings in Britain, a circumstance which, 'worries me, because culturally the fact that you are all [from] the same mother, in the Caribbean . . . you're all one, doesn't matter who the father is, but I just can't love them.'[51]

Beulah analyses this in terms of her relationship with her stepfather and in terms of culture. The two are inseparable. Her British-born siblings, she argues, 'deny' everything. One sister holds to 'a fairy tale upbringing that she has fabricated for herself . . . to me that's a form of denial', refusing to confront what Beulah perceives to be the truth about their father or her parents' marriage. This same sister married an Englishman, and 'was super English . . . to the point when her first born child would look at my mother and scream. . . . If his white family picked him up, he laughed, and he would look at any of us and he would burst out in tears. . . . I feel that if his mother died, we would never see him again.'[52]

She gives further examples. What worries her, she says, 'is any person with a black skin who says there's no such thing as prejudice or racism. . . . In the Brixton riots, [my sister] blamed everybody with a black skin for the fact that they were rioting. Now, that worried me.'[53] One brother, 'is in many ways pseudo-English. . . . I worry about him, because culturally I'm very together and he isn't and I often wonder, if any of that falls apart, what will he have to fall back on?'[54]

Beulah's analysis of both her siblings' response and her own is clear. First, her siblings did not have a Caribbean upbringing, and could not share, therefore, in the experience of family. Beulah says she was her '[great] grandmother's child'; she still feels her 'presence'. Secondly, and importantly, although her siblings were born in the 1960s, neither her stepfather, nor her mother, were into this 'culture thing'. Beulah, on the other hand, was brought into an early awareness of race by her father who:

is what you would consider a true black man, black in complexion and black of mind. . . . He would always preach to us that you are as good, if not better, than anybody else you meet. . . . He would tell us that people were racist, but we were not to allow that to get in our way . . . we had to try and overcome whatever in our lives was an obstacle. . . . So consequently I grew up always with this . . . feeling of confidence in myself which the others haven't got, they don't have that at all, so they're not together.[55]

Third, as a result of her father, and his influence, Beulah acquired an awareness of family which articulated and made sense of her own experience.

My father's very strong on family. He would sit and talk to me about his parents and all my other family that I got in Barbados. . . . [So] . . . I've got roots that the children [her younger siblings] haven't got. . . . When I went to school we were taught to assimilate, to blend but because I had my father . . . I was able to keep my stability, so I can see that the other children are quite screwed up.[56]

Lineage and family offer scope for forging an identity. She argues it in her own case and sees a change in one of her sisters,

when we had the Brixton riots . . . it was like a turning-point in her life. She said to me, 'Do you know what? I was in Asda [a supermarket] yesterday, and I could feel everybody looking at me, as if to say, "you black bitch".' And I said to her, 'Good . . . now you know what it's all about.' . . . From then I've seen a change in her, in that this girl has since been to Barbados. . . . She'd turned up at her grandfather, her father's father. He didn't know she was coming. He recognized her, he embraced her, he kissed her. Everybody in the village came and they were just pleased that she was theirs. . . . That was one of the things that, well, be it her blackness, that she felt. She said she felt as if she belonged to the people of Barbados. . . . She's since applied to be registered as a citizen. . . . She's teaching black studies, so she's come a long way. . . . She has taught herself to make sweetbread, black cake, souse, cou-cou from a book.[57]

Clearly, Beulah's relationship with her stepfather and siblings may have contributed to a sense of exclusion. Like her great-uncle, though at a metaphoric level, they 'went away'. As a result, this intensified the need for Beulah to reconstruct, and emphasize, 'family'. On the other hand, the extended family commonly incorporates step-parents and half-siblings. Her experience is not atypical. Her half-sister has now taken a similar route in the construction of identity.

In many ways, the first-generation migrants to Britain—that of Estella and her cohort—retained a Barbadian identity. The generation born in Britain, or brought there as young children, have had to construct theirs. Loss of family, and with it identity, was the theme behind Beulah's story of her great-great-uncle; the importance of discovery pervades her narrative. Her two sons travel frequently to Barbados, as do her young grandsons. They stay with Estella's mother, or with her father, Conrad, who returned to Barbados in 1992. Beulah intends to return to Barbados. So do her children. Estella has remigrated to Canada though she, too, plans to return. Like Jasper's family, there are five clearly defined generations, of which the last three, reared or born in Britain, see their identity with their family across the ocean.

These three case-studies have been drawn from a wider sample. Although the details of family histories differ, nevertheless investigating family data across generations may provide new dimensions on migration, revealing the motives as complex, varied, even obscure, and implying that orthodox 'push–pull' explanation for migration, and models of migrant behaviour, may be inadequate in several fundamental ways. It suggests also how cultural values, created, absorbed, transmitted, and transformed at the macro level, may have their origins at a micro level within the family. The data argues strongly for the existence of a migration culture, which in the twentieth century ran parallel with government policy, though had developed in opposition to it in the nineteenth century. Parallelism should not be confused with conformity. This culture has several features which can be identified through family histories. Thus social and family structures enabled and encouraged migration. In the three studies presented here, the importance of grandparents in the raising of grandchildren is clear. The wider sample confirms the resilience, and the role, of the bifurcated family where examples are presented of first- and second-generation British-born children being sent home to grandparents or family in Barbados. The study also displays a degree of gender equality in terms of migration, often obscured by more conventional approaches to the subject. Moreover, the sense of identity generated by family links is an important determinant in out and return migration, and in the perceptions and awareness of the Barbadian community in Britain. It also suggests a link between identity, family, professional success, and migration goals. The motive for migration may therefore have more to do with maintenance of the family livelihood, and with the enhancement of status and experience, within a culture which prizes migration *per se*, and historically has perceived it as a statement of independence, than individual economic self-advancement. Indeed, for the most part in this sample, those who migrated were skilled, employed workers, not economically the most needy, for whom time spent abroad was conceived, and continues to be conceived, as temporary.

This essay has identified family models as an alternative, and primary, locus of migrant motivation, and transmitter of a migration culture, obscured in metropolitan based, and biased, studies of migration. The existence of such culture, and the importance of family, is supported by research elsewhere in the study, which reveals how this culture then transferred to Britain and enabled the development there of survival strategies, such as social networks ('the grapevine'), cultural tolerance, employment mobility and multiplicity, and exploitation of opportunity and reward. Such behaviour is often perceived as deviant. From a migrant perspective, it is logical and predicated upon an eventual return.

Notes

Grateful acknowledgements are due to the Nuffield Foundation whose grant enabled me to conduct this research.

1. B5/1/A/9,2. All quotations are from the Barbados Migration Project, tapes and transcripts deposited with the National Life Story Collection, National Sound Archive, British Library.
2. Compilation figures from Office of Population Census and Survey of England and Wales.
3. Exact figures are not available. These are quoted by Hilary Beckles, *A History of Barbados* (Cambridge, 1990).
4. 22 June 1960. L10/19 Vol. 1, Department of Archives, Barbados.
5. In 1844 the population of Barbados was 122,200 or 740 per square mile. By 1891 the population had increased to 182,900 or 1,096 per square mile. G. W. Roberts, 'Emigration from the Island of Barbados', *Social and Economic Studies*, 4 (1955). In 1871 the death rate for the Parish of St Philip, Barbados was 44.10 per 1,000 (*Report of the Barbados Emigration Commission* (1895), Department of Archives, Barbados).
6. Census returns from British West Indian territories in the nineteenth century indicate that, despite the restrictions on out migration, significant numbers of Barbadians had migrated—20,000 by 1866, mainly to British Guyana and Trinidad,

30,000 by 1891. The 1891 census for Trinidad records 14,000 resident Barbadians. They also indicate a high level of return migration (Department of Archives, Barbados).
7. The 1895 Barbados Emigration Commission suggested that willingness to migrate should be made a condition of Parish Relief. Although this was not implemented, the post of Superintendant of Emigration was created and merged with the Clerkship of the Poor Law Board (*Report of the Barbados Emigration Commission* (1895), Department of Archives, Barbados).
8. Pseudonyms have been used throughout this essay.
9. B9/1/A/12.
10. B5/1/A/3.
11. B9/1/A/2.
12. The terms 'outside' and 'inside' are commonly used to describe extra and intra-marital relationships and family.
13. B9/1/A/9.
14. B9/1/A/9-10.
15. B5/1/A/10-11.
16. B9/1/A/23.
17. See Mary Chamberlain, 'Renters and Farmers: The Barbadian Plantation Tenantry System 1917-1937', *Journal of Caribbean History*, 24: 2 (1990).
18. For a study of the economic and political implications of this, see Bonham Richardson, *Panama Money in Barbados 1900-1920* (Knoxville, Tenn., 1985).
19. B9/1/A/16.
20. B9/1/A/10.
21. B5/1/A/3.
22. A great-grandparent had been white. At that time, black Barbadians were not given management positions on the plantations. This uncle, however, was sufficiently light skinned to secure work as a plantation bookeeper.
23. Combermere was one of the leading secondary schools in Barbados. It was fee paying. Free secondary school education was not provided until 1962. Until then, the majority of black Barbadians had an elementary education only.
24. B3/1/A/3.
25. B3/1/A/4.
26. B3/1/B/17.
27. B3/1/A/8.
28. Ibid.
29. B3/1/A/10.
30. BB1/1/A/16.
31. B2/1/A/5.
32. B2/1/A/2.
33. B2/1/A/8-9.
34. BB1/1/A/3.
35. BB1/1/A/5.
36. BB1/1/A/7.
37. BB1/1/A/5.
38. BB1/1/A/10.
39. BB1/1/A/7.
40. BB1/1/B/34-7.
41. Ibid.
42. BB1/1/B/38.
43. BB50/1/B.
44. For an interesting discussion on the role of family myths, see John Byng-Hall interviewed by Paul Thompson, 'The Power of Family Myths', in R. Samuel and P. Thomson (eds.), *The Myths We Live By* (London, 1990).

45. BB50/1/A.
46. BB50/1/A.
47. BB50/1/B.
48. BB49/1/B.
49. Ibid.
50. BB50/1/A.
51. Ibid.
52. BB50/1/B.
53. Ibid.
54. BB50/2/A.
55. BB50/1/B.
56. Ibid.
57. BB50/2/A.

9

Puerto Rican Women

Migration and Changes in Gender Roles

Elizabeth Crespo

Cuando mi hija me dijo que se quería casar yo le dije, pero ¿cuál es el apuro? . . . When my daughter told me she wanted to get married I said, but what's the hurry? Look, you have to think this over well. You want to get married and I am not going to forbid it. But I want you to think about it because if I were you I would wait until I finished school. You only have two and a half years to go. After that you can marry anyone you please. If you graduate and have a career, look, you don't have to take anything from anybody. Your husband is not good for you? All you have to do is leave him. You won't have to go begging anyone for a bite of food. That was the advice I gave her.[1]

Throughout this century women have given this advice to their daughters and granddaughters: 'Estudia por si tu marido te sale un sinvergüenza' ('Study in case your husband turns out to be no good'). It has become a popular saying whose origins are in working-class women's culture and as such it is recognized by Puerto Rican women who usually have a personal story to tell when they hear this adage.

This advice contains both traditional and non-traditional ideas about women's roles in society. It is a statement about the importance of marriage as a woman's goal in life. At the same time it expresses the importance of education and the independence that it allows women. It is a message about the need to work outside the home to fulfil home-based responsibilities and in this way it supports women's conventional roles as mothers and caretakers. But simultaneously it also expresses a desire for personal independence, control over financial resources, greater freedom from childbearing, and liberation from domestic violence. Heterosexuality is the norm confirmed in this message, but at the same time the independence proposed sets the grounds for future generations of women to assert lesbian or bisexual sexuality.

'Estudia por si tu marido te sale un sinvergüenza' proposes an ideal situation, which is marriage, and an alternative, which is to be found in education. One of the facts this statement points to is that marriage is a way to survive. It is about economics; about providing for basic needs (food, clothing, and a place to live) for women and their children. Women are warned of the possibility that marriage will not be a viable means of subsistence because the husband might turn out to be no good. In that case, women should have an education that will allow them to survive without husbands.

A competing message that expresses a situation where women had fewer options outside marriage is 'Soporta aunque tu marido sea un perdido, porque te tiene bien' ('Put up with your husband's abuse, because he is a good provider'). As the first message, this one also assumes that men are the providers. However, contrary to the first statement, the possibility that husbands would not be able to support their families is not contemplated. Neither is the possibility of education as an avenue to economic independence. In this situation, women must put up with abuse.

Although it became increasingly possible to escape violence within marriage as education and paid labour became more accessible to Puerto Rican working-class women, the possibility of supporting a family without a husband did not eliminate the message that told women to put up with mistreatment. Change did not occur in a linear fashion nor was there necessarily a progression between generations. Some grandmothers born at the end of the nineteenth century were very aware of the need for education, while some young women today are still told to put up with their husbands.

In this essay I will examine the significance of 'Estudia por si tu marido te sale un sinvergüenza' in the light of women's struggles to survive. I will argue that women have been direct agents of change. They have not merely reacted to the political, social, and economic transformations that Puerto Rico has experienced as a US colony. Rather, they have defined new roles and identities for themselves as women, which have contributed to shape changes in paid labour, access to education, and the structures of marriage, family, and sexuality.

Patriarchy was the institution most obviously challenged as women gained the possibility of obtaining a livelihood without a husband. Moreover, class and racial structures were transformed as well. The dramatic increase in women's participation in the Island's economy as paid labourers was an important part of the transition to a system of production based on wage rather than servile labour which accelerated significantly after the US take-over in 1898. In their struggle for personal and financial freedom, women also opposed racial barriers that subjected them to physical and sexual violence and kept them in a subordinated position in the labour force.

As wage labourers, Puerto Rican women became part of a migrant labour force. Puerto Rican migration to the United States, which increased dramatically after the Second World War, placed Puerto Rican women in a new context where gender, skin colour, class, and ethnicity were defined by categories of 'otherness' that differed from those on the Island. The meanings of gender for Puerto Rican women in the United States were constructed in opposition to the norm of a white, married, suburban middle-class, English-speaking housewife who has a husband to support the family. While work outside the home and education were primary concerns for working-class Puerto Rican women, these women were perceived as uneducated, lacking ambition, destined for welfare or low-paying jobs, and irresponsible mothers with too many children. These perceptions made it more difficult for Puerto Rican women to get an education and find jobs. In this US context as well, 'Estudia por si tu marido te sale un sinvergüenza' was not only a message about financial self-sufficiency that presented the possibility of breaking with patriarchal barriers to equality, but one that also led working-class women to challenge structures of race and class that kept them subordinated.

Drawing on oral histories,[2] I explore the contradictory meanings of 'Estudia por si tu marido te sale un sinvergüenza' and some of the implications they have for analysing the changes in Puerto Rican women's roles and identities during this century in Puerto Rico and in the context of migration to the United States.

'Estudia por si tu marido te sale un sinvergüenza' broke with tradition. It expressed new ideas about the importance of education for women. Earlier generations were told that education was unnecessary and unfit for working-class women. During the sixteenth, seventeenth, and eighteenth centuries under the Spanish colonial regime, education for working-class women was mostly limited to practical and oral knowledge transmitted by older women in the home, based on skills related to their domestic duties. It was not until 1799 that the first four schools for girls were established in San Juan. During the nineteenth century the number of girls' schools increased, but they were located principally in urban areas and served mostly the wealthiest sectors of society.[3] Even so, my interviews indicate that some working-class women were able to go to school although only for a short time. They were soon pulled out of school to fulfil domestic duties in their own homes or work as domestic servants in the homes of others.

At the end of the nineteenth century, government and ecclesiastical authorities in Puerto Rico proposed education as a way to instil values of modesty and motherhood, which they thought were lacking because of the great number of consensual marriages.[4] Liberals argued that society would be more progressive and wise if it educated women, since women have the task of raising children. Feminists organized against the Spanish colonial regime for not providing educational opportunities for women.[5] After the United States' military invasion of Puerto Rico in 1898, and the decline of the landowning class (*hacendados*), many women from this class saw the need to acquire a profession that would allow them to make a living in the cities. At this time, education was increasingly stressed by governmental authorities for the entire population to create a more skilled workforce.[6] Education was also seen as a way in which Puerto Ricans could learn the values of the institutions established by the new colonial power.[7]

However, education was important for working-class mothers for reasons other than the ones stated above. Their reasons were related to basic conditions of survival. During the nineteenth century, women participated extensively in various economic activities including the production of goods and services for consumption in the home and non-wage agricultural labour. In 1899 only a small percentage of women (9.9) worked in what were categorized by the US Census as 'gainful occupations': occupations from which they earned money or an equivalent.[8] This suggests that at the end of the nineteenth century (when the grandmother's generation was born), working-class women's work was mainly part of a domestic unit where husbands were seen as the main source of livelihood. This changed as a result of the restructuring of the Island's economy during the twentieth century that increasingly displaced male workers while women became an important source of cheap labour.[9] As a result, many men were no longer fulfilling the role of primary providers. The succeeding generations of women increasingly saw the need to offer their daughters an important tool for survival: education.

The significance of this change in the value of education can be appreciated if we look at the statistics on women's levels of schooling.

These statistics indicate that the generation of women born between 1941 and 1955 was the first to go to school in a setting where the proportion of females enrolled equalled that of males. Before this, the percentage of males was always considerably higher. Census data on literacy indicates that starting with the generation of girls born between 1945 and 1950 literacy levels became for the first time higher for girls than for boys.[10]

This is quite a significant achievement. From the beginning of the twentieth century, the rapid growth of public schooling in Puerto Rico gave working-class women a greater opportunity to get an education. In 1952 the Island's Constitution made primary education compulsory. What role did women play in making this happen? When mothers began emphasizing the importance of education to their daughters, what were they in fact telling them?

Data obtained through my interviews indicates that during the twentieth century working-class women increasingly received advice from their mothers stressing the new importance that education was acquiring. This had a particular impact on the generation of women born approximately between 1940 and 1960. These statistics do not indicate merely that education was stressed for the population as a whole, and that as a consequence women's levels of education rose. I propose that the significance goes beyond this, and that education became a working-class women's issue. According to Ana, who belongs to this generation,

En casa siempre era que estudies, que estudies. . . . At home it was always that I should study, study, and go to college because it is the most important thing. It is the most important thing because we are women.[11]

From a feminist perspective the struggle for education was revolutionary and subversive and had a profound impact on creating and changing the structures of capitalism and patriarchy in Puerto Rico during this century. What did education and paid labour have to offer women? How did education and paid labour change women's situation within the household and their relations with men and children? In what ways did working-class women want these relations to change? In what ways did they want to transform their situation within society? If women had not seen something they could gain, the whole process would not have occurred the way it did.

These questions have many possible answers. Consuelo offers one answer when she tells the story of her mother and paternal grandmother. Consuelo's paternal grandmother who was born near 1900, wanted to work, handle her own money, and redefine her responsibilities in the home.

My [paternal] grandmother stopped going to school when she was in sixth grade to take care of her brothers and sisters because her mother was sick. She had lost her father by that time. She wanted to go to school and graduate, but she never fulfilled that dream. My grandmother was very interested in my education. She would take me to museums, the library, and shows.

My [paternal] grandfather had his own business in the house. My grandmother worked outside the home. She had a job, made her own money, and handled her own business. My grandmother was a seamstress specializing in fine needle work and was employed by a very small company for many, many years. My grandfather stayed home and cooked and cleaned because he had a business at home. My mother [the grandmother's daughter-in-law] didn't approve of that and neither did my father. My father told us that when he was a child he was embarrassed that his father was hanging out the laundry including his wife's underwear. Everybody would look at this man washing his wife's underwear. So as a child he resented that. It was very unusual at the time. The people that worked in the factory with my grandmother were family women who came home to do the cooking and cleaning and the taking care of children.

Because of this, my grandmother was criticized. I remember because my mother used to talk about it. 'You know they talk about your grandmother, how she gives all her responsibilities to Roberto [her husband], and she comes home and she just sits and she relaxes.' But my grandfather was agreeable with the arrangement.

I thought the arrangement was pretty good because they had what they needed. My grandmother was not as tired as my mother even though my mother was much younger. My mother was doing all the work, with the exception of what I could do after school. When my grandmother came home from work, the food was cooked, the house was cleaned, the shopping was done. So I thought that was a better arrangement. She had a lot of influence on me.[12]

What was different and unconventional about Consuelo's paternal grandmother was not that she worked outside the home, but that she did so even though she had a husband to sustain her. In a small municipality, such as the one she lived in, this was particularly unusual and she became the talk of the town. She handled her own money and, what was most unacceptable, came home from work to just sit and relax letting her husband do all the housework while she was away. Consuelo's paternal grandmother's experience suggests that two things women might have wanted from paid labour were personal and economic freedom, and this subverted patriarchal norms.

Other narratives show that Puerto Rican women made enormous efforts to pursue personal goals and experienced great hardships in obtaining what they wanted. Like Consuelo's grandmother, many other working-class women realized the importance of education. To achieve this goal many women of the mother's generation worked outside the home to supplement the family income, sometimes in spite of their husband's discomfort or outright opposition. By providing an alternative source of income to their husband's earnings, many women were able to guarantee that their children had clothes, and in particular shoes to go to school. This was Fela's experience whose advice to her daughter opened this essay. She describes her struggles as follows:

Mi familia era bien pobrecita y yo tuve que dejar de ir a la escuela porque no tenía zapatos. . . . My family was very poor and I had to leave school because I didn't have shoes. School was far away, you see, and I had to walk a long distance to get there. So I made it my purpose to make sure that I would earn money doing whatever, in the factory or making handicrafts to sell, so that my children would have clothes and shoes to go to school. . . . At first my husband was opposed but later saw that I was right.[13]

These personal struggles had a profound impact not only in shaping individual lives, but also a larger cumulative social effect in changing the conditions in which women negotiate their relations within the family, in the workplace and in society in general.

Consuelo's story is an example of the great lengths women of the granddaughter's generation went through to achieve personal goals and how this struggle challenged and changed conventional norms. Consuelo was born in 1940 in Puerto Rico. She wanted to study and she wanted to work. In spite of greater opportunities for women of her generation to get an education, it was not uncommon for husbands or parents to still disapprove of women's desire and efforts to get an education. There were also significant differences between small, rural towns and major cities. In rural towns such as the one she grew up in, patriarchal norms were more entrenched and educational opportunities fewer. Her mother did not want her daughter to leave home to go to college. She thought it was inappropriate for a girl to live outside the home if she was not married. She thought her daughter should get married and stay home taking care of children as she had. Consuelo's paternal grandmother in contrast, had always taken a special interest in her granddaughter's education and had herself claimed a significant degree of personal and economic independence, as we have seen. Consuelo describes her options: to stay home and either get married or become an old maid, or come to New York to live with an uncle.

Consuelo came to New York, but her uncle left for California a few weeks after she arrived so she lived alone for a time. Her parents viewed this as a very undesirable situation for her. The only way it would be acceptable for her to remain in New York was if she got married. Responding to this pressure, she did. Consuelo describes the obstacles she confronted in trying to get an education in the passage that follows.

My husband did not approve of me getting an education. His perception of a wife was the same as what his mother was to his father. She was a wife until she died. She never worked outside the house and she followed her husband around. Whenever he decided to move she would leave with him. And that was a conflict I had with my husband from the very beginning. Because even though I was not going to college at the time we got married, I was taking different kinds of courses in the adult education center. And he didn't like that.

At one point he took all the books and dumped them out of the window. He just took them and threw them out. He did this because he perceived that as a threat. He graduated from High School and didn't study after that.

But education was a number one issue for me that I just didn't give up, and it created more and more problems because I was working full time. I only took a couple of breaks from work when the children were born, and I was taking courses in the evening. But I still had to take care of the children, I still had to come in and cook.

So studying was very difficult. Sometimes I had to lock myself in the bathroom or get up at three o'clock in the morning to do the readings and the work. But if he saw me with anything that had to do with books he would get very violent. He would take the books and tear them up and really. . . . And then I met the woman that I'm living with now. And that was it. I decided this is it. This is it.[14]

Getting an education meant three times more work: at home, on the job, and in school. It was a breach of the responsibilities of a mother and a housewife. It was a threat to her husband's authority. It was a threat to the order that her husband had known in the family he had grown up in, and ultimately, to his masculinity. And it meant violence. When she left him because of this, it also meant that she lived under the threat of losing her children.

The new roles that Consuelo took on also challenged racist/sexist/classist stereotypes about Puerto Rican and poor women in the United

States. When Consuelo got divorced, her husband refused to give her money for child support arguing that she had deserted the family and neglected him by going to school instead of staying home and taking care of the children. The judge agreed with her husband and could not imagine why a woman like her (Puerto Rican with low income) would have any ambitions other than to be a housewife and have a husband to support her.

I went to court and the judge actually asked me, 'Why did you want to go to school? Why did you want to work? Why don't you go on welfare like everybody else?' Yes. He said that to me. 'Why do you want to work?'[15]

In the United States, Puerto Rican women faced a different racial and ethnic context than in Puerto Rico. This new social context added another dimension to who Consuelo was and what was expected of her. She was not only a working-class woman, she was also non-white. In this new setting her skin colour, ethnicity, and language put her in a category of 'otherness' she had not experienced on the Island. In Puerto Rico her light olive-toned skin, dark straight hair, and dark eyes did not make her a victim of racism. However in the United States, Consuelo's struggles to study and support her family on her own were hindered by racist/classist conceptions of what was considered appropriate behaviour for Puerto Rican migrant women in addition to the patriarchal norms her husband, mother, and father had tried to impose upon her.

As we have discussed in the previous pages, 'Estudia por si tu marido te sale un sinvergüenza' is a statement about the need for education and the possibility of supporting a family without a husband. The examples presented show how this subverted many patriarchal, racist, and classist notions about women's place in the home and in society. Nevertheless, many times the motivations and the framework that inspired the transgression were rooted in patriarchal values: education and financial independence were a way to fulfil conventional home-based responsibilities.

Economic autonomy offered women a certain degree of personal freedom as we have seen in the stories above. However, it was also necessary for survival. Women had to enter the paid workforce to ensure that their children would have clothes, a house, and enough to eat, as it became more difficult for men to fulfil their role as providers.

Agricultural work, the main source of employment for Puerto Rican men at the end of the nineteenth century was restructured during the first decades of the twentieth century and reduced drastically by 1960.[16] One of the principal results was large-scale unemployment and declining male labour-force participation rates. At the same time, manufacturing industries that employed many women grew. In 1899 only 15 per cent of women 16 years and older in Puerto Rico were in the labour force. By 1950 the proportion had more than doubled. During this period the increase in female labour-force participation compensated the decline in male labour-force participation. Furthermore, the women that came into the labour force in greatest numbers by far, were women of childbearing ages.[17] Considering the difficulties of combining child-rearing and work outside the home, these statistics suggest that many women became wage earners without a man in the household and that even in households with a man present, women's work was crucial to sustain the household.

As families migrated to New York in the first decades of this century, women also became wage workers in this new setting. Almost 35 per cent of the female migrant population was employed. Families also relied on women's work in the informal economy to complement low wages earned by men.[18]

After the Second World War, women and their families migrated to the United States in still greater numbers. In the United States women's work as wage earners became more important than in Puerto Rico. In 1950 female labour-force participation rates increased to 39 per cent in the United States, compared with 33 per cent for women in Puerto Rico. During the next decades, in New York, the state with the largest concentration of Puerto Ricans, labour-force participation rates declined for both men and women but dramatically more for men. In the other four states with the largest concentrations of Puerto Ricans, women's labour-force participation rates continued to increase.[19]

Given this historical panorama, the message older generations of women gave their daughters about the importance of being able to sustain themselves on their own broke with conventional norms because it made many women primary providers. Nevertheless, it had as well a conservative meaning and motivation. It was a message about fulfilling women's customary responsibilities of caring for children. To carry out these duties, women now had to work outside as well as in the home. Posed within traditional and contradictory frameworks, women were none the less redefining their own roles as well as men's within the family.

When mothers and grandmothers told their daughters to get an education, they were implying that daughters should wait until they finished school to get married and have children. Also implied was the possibility of a greater degree of freedom from childbearing. Some women were motivated by a desire to have more control over their own bodies. On the other hand, many of these women expressed that their motivations to have fewer children also arose within the more sanctioned framework of a desire to provide adequately for the children they already had. However, even when women's motivations may have been situated within the socially accepted framework of providing for children, the effects of their actions had subversive possibilities for themselves as well as for other generations. It gave women the possibility of creating other identities in addition to their identity as mothers.

But there is another part to the advice that women gave their daughters—'Estudia POR SI' . . . the part of the statement that said IF. Study IN CASE your husband turns out to be no good. And the IN CASE, was as powerful as the part of the advice that told daughters to study. Marriage remained the ideal. Marta, who was born in 1949 and raised in New York, describes her mother's message as follows:

My mother was against education because men did not like women who were smart and had their own opinions. She would hide my books because she said all I needed to learn was how to iron and clean so I would become a good wife. But at the same time my mother wanted me to be educated. Money was very scarce but my mother sent me to Catholic school, which was very expensive. The message was 'study, but don't study too much'. You need to go to school just in case your husband turns out to be no good so you can have something to fall back on.[20]

Part of the ideal marriage was virginity. A husband was entitled to return his wife to her parents' family if he discovered she was not a virgin. Women were considered men's property and this was established by a sexual act. This idea of women as property spilled over into all other areas of women's lives. Obedience to one's husband was something women learnt in church and at home, although according to most women no one ever talked about it.

In the interviews I conducted, most heterosexual women born between 1940 and 1960, openly challenged the idea of being a virgin when they got married. For lesbians who had discovered their sexuality at an early age, it was never an issue because they had defined their sexuality independently from men. On the contrary, the women from the mothers' generation expressed a strong opinion on the importance of virginity.

At the same time that mothers were saying study, create the possibility of being independent, they were also telling daughters that they were their husband's property and were expected to do as he said.

The marriage that mothers described to their daughters was an economic contract based on heterosexuality. Mothers told daughters that this was the place where love, companionship, passion, and security could be found even though many of them had not found this in their marriages. Consuelo, a lesbian who as we learnt earlier got married so that her family would let her stay in New York, recalls this:

If I had been told something else, I wouldn't have married. If I was told that it was okay to be a woman alone, to live in your own apartment, live with another woman or with somebody else who's not family, I wouldn't have married. Marriage was never a goal. Because I had all these crazy dreams when I was an adolescent; dreams of different things I wanted to explore. I wanted to travel all over the world. I wanted to get an education; those kinds of dreams. I never thought about marriage. It was social pressure.[21]

'Estudia por si tu marido te sale un sinvergüenza' is a conditional statement. It implies that marriage is the ideal. Study is something women should do just in case. To better understand this statement it is necessary to see that it has both subversive and conservative elements and that these are not juxtaposed. The subversive and the conservative are actually contained within each other. Many times the motivations and the framework that inspired the erosion of accepted norms were stated in terms of traditional patriarchal values: marriage, children, and motherhood.

The message broke with convention, but not in the sense of a conscious conspiracy to overthrow patriarchy. It was revolutionary in its effects. An education gave women the possibility of depending less on men's wages for their survival and that of their children. Financial self-sufficiency increased women's options and gave them a better position from which to negotiate their relations within society. Women's struggles for education and the ability to support a family without a husband also challenged structures of race and class that kept women subordinated.

As women increasingly worked outside the home for wages, they became part of an international migrant reserve labour force that supplied workers for the metropolis. The analysis of migration sheds further light on the complexity of the interrelationships between race, gender, ethnicity, and class. It shows that gender is constructed in relation to various systems of oppression that coexist and are defined through one another. As Puerto Rican working-class women moved to a different geographical and national context they were faced with new definitions of gender based on different perceptions of class, race, language, and ethnicity. These in turn became new elements in their struggles to define new social roles for themselves.

As a methodological tool, oral history puts the lives of individuals at the centre of our analysis. This offers a new perspective to historical enquiry which very often looks for change in large social structures and institutions. Through oral histories we can look at changes in personal lives as an important source of social transformation with a profound impact on society at large. As we look at the complexities that have shaped the lives of the women who tell us their stories, we acquire different perspectives and can pose new hypotheses about the forces that shape social change and the ways in which ideas about gender and sexuality are transmitted from one generation to another.

Notes

1. Fela, interview by author, Puerto Rico, 20 July 1992 (translated from Spanish).
2. Between 1990 and 1992 I recorded approximately 70 hours of interviews from 30 Puerto Rican women in Puerto Rico, New York, and New Jersey. These tapes are housed in my personal archives. The quotes presented from these interviews have been edited with two purposes in mind: to preserve the originality of thought and expression of the interviewee while creating a readable text. Spanish interviews have been translated to English. Because of space constraints I have not included the original Spanish text in the notes.
3. M. Rivera, 'El proceso educativo en Puerto Rico y la reproducción de la subordinación feminina', in Y. Azize (ed.), *La mujer en Puerto Rico: Ensayos de investigación* (Río Piedras, 1987), 113–137.
4. W. Ferree, I. Illich, and J. Fitzpatrick (eds.), *Spiritual Care of Puerto Rican Migrants* (México, 1970), 4/48–4/49.
5. I. Picó, 'Apuntes preliminares para el estudio de la mujer puertorriqueña y su participación en las luchas sociales de principios del siglo XX', in E. Acosta-Belén (ed.), *La Mujer en la sociedad puertorriqueña* (Río Piedras, 1980), 23–40.
6. Rivera, 'El proceso educativo en Puerto Rico'.
7. A. Negrón de Montilla, *La americanización de Puerto Rico y el sistema de instrucción pública 1900–1930* (Río Piedras, 1977).
8. Rivera, 'Incorporación de las mujeres al mercado de trabajo en el desarrollo del capitalismo', in Acosta-Belén (ed.), *La mujer en la sociedad puertorriqueña*, 41–66.

9. See History Task Force-Centro de Estudios Puertorriqueños, *Labor Migration under Capitalism* (New York, 1979).
10. J. L. Vázquez Calzada, *La población de Puerto Rico y su trayectoria histórica* (Río Piedras, 1988), 72–3.
11. Ana, interview by author, Puerto Rico, 4 Apr. 1991 (translated from Spanish).
12. Consuelo, interview by author, New York, 10 Mar. 1991.
13. Fela, interview by author, Puerto Rico, 20 July 1992 (translated from Spanish).
14. Consuelo, interview by author, New York, 10 Mar. 1991.
15. Ibid.
16. At the end of the nineteenth century, 97% of Puerto Rican men over the age of 16 in Puerto Rico were in the labour force. In 1920, this dropped to 89%, and in 1960, when many of our 1940s generation of women were at the marrying age, it dropped to 76%. Between 1940 and 1960 the unemployment rate among men fluctuated between 12% and 16% rising to 27% in the early 1980s. Vázquez Calzada, *La población de Puerto Rico*, 81, 88.
17. Ibid. 81–2.
18. V. Sánchez Korrol, *From Colonia to Community: The History of Puerto Ricans in New York City, 1917–1948* (Westport, Conn., 1983), 90–108.
19. Vázquez Calzada, *La población de Puerto Rico*, 81; R. Santana Cooney and A. Colón, 'Work and Family: The Recent Struggle of Puerto Rican Females', in C. Rodríguez, O. Alers, and V. Sánchez Korrol (eds.), *The Puerto Rican Struggle: Essays on Survival in the US* (New York, 1980), 62; V. Ortiz, 'Changes in the Characteristics of Puerto Rican Migrants from 1955 to 1980', *International Migration Review*, 20 (1986), 622.
20. Marta, interview by author, New York, 17 Mar. 1991.
21. Consuelo, interview by author, New York, 10 Mar. 1991.

10

Identity and Gender in the Mexican-American *Testimonio*

The Life and Narrative of Frances Esquivel Tywoniak

MARIO T. GARCÍA

> 'We tell ourselves stories of our past, make fictions or stories of it, and these narrations *become* the past, the only part of our lives that is not submerged.'
>
> (Carolyn G. Heilbrun, *Writing a Woman's Life*)

Recent Chicana and Latina texts rewrite the traditional Latina narrative by focusing on women as subjects, as historical agents, and by imagining a new future for women. Their subjects in different ways challenge the traditional Latino model for women's proper sphere. Rather than accepting what Shari Benstock terms the 'private self' as representing the world of women, the new Latina writers project themselves and their subjects into the public world as well.[1] While the private may not always be political, it is certainly not divorced from women's public roles and their public aspirations. In effect, as Carolyn Heilbrun suggests about other transgressive writers, who dare to cross previously closed borders concerning identity and self-representation, these Latina writers reject womanhood—at least as defined in traditional patriarchal terms—and instead rewrite the definition of being a woman. They dare, to use Heilbrun's term, to be 'ambiguous women'.[2]

The conflict between the private and the public in a Mexican-American context, and the attempt to merge the two is one of the dominant themes that emerges from a recent oral-history project that I am conducting. In 1990 after completing another oral-history project concerning Bert Corona, a long-time Mexican-American activist in Los Angeles,[3] I embarked on a second *testimonio*. *Testimonio* is a Latin-American genre of autobiographical texts that are the result of oral-history projects usually involving academic scholars or journalists, on the one hand, and grass-roots activists, on the other. While the *testimonio* has been recently recognized as a new and more populist genre in Latin-American literature, in fact its roots lie deeper in the oral traditions of Latin-American culture. Moreover, *testimonios* are not only literary texts. They are first and foremost part of political struggles. Perhaps the best known *testimonio* is *I . . . Rigoberta Menchú: An Indian Woman in Guatemala* co-produced by the anthropologist Elisabeth Burgos-Debray and the indigenous activist and Nobel Peace Prize winner, Rigoberta Menchú.[4]

My current testimonial project involves the aunt of a former student at the University of California, Santa Barbara. Unlike the Corona text which is similar to the Latin American *testimonio* in that it is overtly political and centred on Corona's participation and leadership in the Mexican-American community's struggle against injustice and discrimination, Frances Esquivel Tywoniak's narrative is not. Her life, unlike Corona's, is not a political one, at least not in the traditional sense. Her *testimonio* is an attempt to redefine and to rewrite Latina lives in order to assert what Mary Mason refers to as 'the other voice'.[5] In this effort both gender and ethnicity along with race and class are linked together, although in a state of tension, in order to re-create not only a new woman but a new Latina. Yet this rewriting or self-inscription is not an attempt to create an essentialist notion of a Latina woman.

What I conclude, for example, in examining Corona's life is that his sense of ethnic, racial, class, and gender identity is multiple. Corona's ethnic self is the result, not of some inherent essence of being Mexican, but the result of a variety of historical, ethnic, cultural, class, ideological, and personal influences on his life. His sense of ethnicity is not determined by just one of these influences at one particular juncture of his life, but by multiple ones throughout his life. Corona's ethnic self is a good example of the argument put forth by Werner Sollors and others that ethnicity is a constantly changing variable.[6] It is not something fixed in time. Instead it is invented and reinvented. One finds in Corona's narrative multiple or polyphonic voices negotiating a particular concept of ethnic identity. The same can be said of the narrative of Frances Esquivel Tywoniak, or Fran as I shall refer to her in this essay.[7]

I believe that for Mexican-Americans ethnic identity has not been a singular experience, but a multi-faceted one. Like for other American ethnic groups, identity represents a dialogic relationship. That is, the experience involves a historical and ethnic dialogue at least at three levels: one, a dialogue with the dominant culture framed by what we refer to as Anglo-American society; two, a dialogue with other marginalized ethnic/racialized minorities; and, three, a dialogue within the Mexican-American community itself.

The intersections of these dialogic relationships have resulted in a Mexican-American *heteroglossia*, to adopt a term from the Russian literary critic, Mikhail Bakhtin. There is not one Mexican-American world but many. Heteroglossia implies the presence of a multiplicity of voices in a literary text. I use the concept here to suggest that in the actual social relationships lived by Mexican-Americans there exists a multiplicity of voices and subjects rather than one voice and one unified subject. From this perspective, identity, both individual and social, is multiple rather than singular. In response to the unified masculine subject proposed by the Chicano Movement of the late 1960s and early 1970s, for example, new Chicana writers of the 1980s, such as Gloria Anzaldúa, Cherríe Moraga, and Sandra Cisneros propose a complex, multi-faceted subject constructed at the intersection of ethnicity, race, gender, class, and sexuality.

Moreover, experiences such as the Mexican-American one suggest that the process of 'imagining community', to use Benedict Anderson's term,[8] in a multi-ethnic society such as the United States has been limited to only white ethnic groups. In contrast, a critical multicultural approach interprets issues of national identity both dialectically and dialogically to propose, not only a synthesis of national expression, but the persistence and validation of ethnic and cultural difference.

From this perspective, I want to analyse in this essay the multiple influences on the gender and ethnic identity of the young Fran Esquivel.

Born in 1931, Fran Esquivel's early childhood to age 6 was set in south-eastern New Mexico. In 1938 her parents and their three children joined the Dust-Bowl Migration to California to seek a better life during the Great Depression. Fran's *testimonio* is largely her memories of coming of age in the rural and semi-rural environment of California's San Joaquín Valley. There Fran confronted who she was and what she wanted to be. Developing as an excellent student in her high school years, Fran was one of the few Mexican-American women in the late 1940s who was able to attend college. In 1949 she received a scholarship to the University of California–Berkeley and graduated in

1953 with a degree in languages. She doesn't recall ever encountering another Mexican-American, male or female, at Berkeley during her undergraduate years. After graduation, and after marrying and having her first child, Fran went on to become a successful teacher and school administrator in the Bay Area. She retired in 1992 after serving almost forty years in the San Francisco school district.[9]

Although raised largely in the San Joaquín Valley of California, the context of Fran's earlier life in New Mexico was extremely important. Her New Mexico experience unconsciously fixed in her mind a sense of ethnic community based on the extended family or what Albert Stone terms the 'immediate community'.[10] This community was centred around her maternal grandparents whose roots in New Mexico went back several generations. Shepherds, the Flores family struggled to retain their lands and their way of life despite the dislocations of the Great Depression. Fran recalls a closely knit extended family where aunts, uncles, and cousins lived in close proximity and all interacted as one family. Later in California, when she struggled with her self-identity as a Mexican-American female, Fran carried with her and came to appreciate her New Mexican background. Returning years later to New Mexico as a mature adult, she was moved by the warmth and familiarity with which her relatives, particularly her aunts, welcomed her back. 'When I returned to New Mexico for a visit for the first time in almost forty years,' she notes, 'my aunts greeted me as if I had never been away. "Our own daughter," they declared, is "one of ours" [*una de las nuestras*].'

Like most other Mexican-Americans, and indeed most other ethnic Americans, Fran grew up with ambivalence concerning her ethnic identity. She experienced what W. E. B. DuBois observed of Afro-Americans: the sense of a dual consciousness—of being part of an ethnic/racial minority and of being American.[11] Not that this duality is always conscious, but anyone who has grown up in a racialized environment can attest, I believe, to this sense of duality. Fran experienced these tensions. She aspired to become 'American', but at the same time sensed that she was really not 'American'. Part of her struggle consisted of wanting to be seen as her own singular self and not just reflecting a self-representation shaped from the outside by Anglo-Americans who stereotype Mexicans.

Yet she was also part of a family and part of other cultural constructs that she recognized even though she was partly alienated from it. As she in time confronted these tensions and attempted, consciously and

Identity and Gender

unconsciously, to negotiate ethnic, gender, class, and cultural border crossings between competing forces, Fran reclaimed and reinvented her New Mexican identity. It is these historical memories that provide her with what Doris Sommer and other critics refer to as the 'plural self' or the 'collective self'.[12] For it was the New Mexican memories that reawakened in her the strength of family and of community. The New Mexican collective self helped to balance the alienated sense of individuality that gnawed at her during her coming of age years.

Carolyn Heilbrun notes that most women, unlike men, have only been able to write about themselves in relationship to other individuals. Heilbrun suggests that this represents an expression of women's sense of inferiority and dependence in comparison to men.[13] Yet, I would disagree and instead suggest that Heilbrun's contention is a culturally biased one. In a different cultural context, women writing about their relationship to others, especially regarding family, may be more of an expression of what is referred to as the collective self or 'collective identity'.

Hence, in Fran's narrative her memories of her early New Mexico childhood, for example, create a historical context to the personal struggle she later engaged in. That is, her attempt to participate in the debate over the proper role for women and the issue of private versus public is not divorced from a Mexican-American context. Her individual struggle and quest is also an ethnic one. Her attempt to resolve the gender and ethnic ambivalences she felt are not separated from her sense of ethnic loyalty and ethnic community. For Fran, rewriting a woman's life is also rewriting the meaning of being Mexican-American or Latina.

Within her extended family, Fran recalls a strong sense of what she calls a 'quiet love'. Family members were not particularly or overtly affectionate. Yet she remembers a pervasive sense of solidarity that permeated family relationships. Since her maternal grandfather, the patriarch of the family, died one year after Fran was born, the extended family revolved around her grandmother as the matriarch. Fran's sense of gender identity within a Mexican-American context was partly shaped by the memories of her grandmother:

My grandmother I remember very well. She was a very tiny, tiny lady with very dark wavy hair and very green eyes. She had a very positive presence. I've always wondered how she could have had all those children beginning at age 15 when she married my grandfather and at the same time worked tirelessly on the ranch. I have a memory of her as a partner to her husband. This memory or what I was told about her has influenced my own thinking. As I see today the concern over the role of working women, I recall that in my grandmother's days women also worked. Perhaps not for an outside wage, but as working partners with their husbands in the home and, as in the case of my grandmother, on the ranch.

This sense of a woman's role of being a partner rather than a subordinate wife, whether really true for her grandmother or not, is an image that influenced Fran's own interpretation of the concept of womanhood and marriage. It was her grandmother's image as partner that became one of Fran's models.

Of course, her relationship with her mother helped frame part of Fran's New Mexican collective self as well as part of her gender and ethnic identity. What she draws from the memories of her mother in New Mexico is an appreciation of the importance of obtaining an education. Her mother struggled for what little formal education she acquired. Fran recalls her mother telling her that she attended a segregated school of Hispanics (Mexican-Americans in New Mexico) and that this school only provided a third-grade education. Despite her limited schooling, Fran's mother always supported education for her children and encouraged it. While her mother was not prepared to break with traditional Hispanic gender roles that largely relegated women to being wives and mothers and as secondary bread-winners, still Fran's mother aspired to more for her daughters. In her own way, her mother surreptitiously aided Fran's rejection of this structured gender role.

Fran also discerns from these particular New Mexican memories the beginnings of bilingual influences within her family partly initiated by her mother. Even though Fran lived in a largely Spanish-speaking world in New Mexico, some English was incorporated into daily life. Her mother had learnt English at school and Fran recalls that her mother read to her in English from a Sears Roebuck or Montgomery Ward catalogue while looking for items to order.

But Fran's early identification with her family was not limited to her mother's side. She was also deeply influenced by her relationship with her father. Her father represented a sense of family and ethnic community, but was also a symbol of what she later sought to reject— the patriarchal culture. This was a tension that Fran negotiated over time, not outside her family cultural environment but within it. In New Mexico her father represented an outsider. He was the 'Mexican' of the family. He had been born in northern Mexico and had first migrated to work in Texas. He then went to south-eastern New Mexico where he worked as a labourer and where he met his future wife and became integrated into the New Mexican extended family.

Additionally, Fran's father represented another ethnic and cultural influence. His Mexican and south-western cultural baggage merged with Fran's mother's south-eastern New Mexican influences. In particular, Fran recalls the strong Mexican Catholicism centred on the cult of the *Virgen de Guadalupe* that her father introduced into the family. Her father was more religious and devout than her mother:

He was devoted to the *Virgen de Guadalupe*. He did the novena in early December around the feast day of the *Virgen*. He introduced the devotion to the *Virgen* to my mother's family and we did the novena. I can remember kneeling what seemed to me an eternity. My family set up an elaborate altar to the *Virgen* and many people joined us for the nine days of the novena. To me religion in New Mexico was my father's dramatic devotion to the *Virgen* and to Christ. Not so much God. It was Jesus Christ and the *Virgen*. I learned a lot from my father about the *Virgen* and about humility. That was an important message.

Fran's father was, in fact, part of a wider Mexican and southwestern cultural tradition growing within the region of south-eastern New Mexico. Migrant workers from Texas found employment on the land owned or leased by Fran's family. She particularly recalls these workers in the evenings sitting around their automobiles and listening to a Spanish-language radio station that played Mexican and border *ranchero* music, especially the songs of the legendary Lydia Mendoza. Fran's father, like some of the other *mexicanos*, would bring out a guitar and sing *rancheras*. This was a man's cultural world, but Fran as a child recalls being allowed some access to it.

What Fran's early childhood in New Mexico provided, even after her family migrated to California, was a sense of roots, of a physical space that she knew she belonged to in some way. For Fran, going back, going home, would not be to Mexico or some other southwestern location, but to the rural plains of south-eastern New Mexico. This sense of place and of identifying with others from New Mexico provided Fran with a certain distance from other Mexican-Americans in the San Joaquín Valley and underscored the great regional diversity among Mexican-Americans. Fran recalls that in California her mother would often recognize other people or neighbours. '*Es de Nuevo Mexico*,' her mother would say:

There was that identification with people from New Mexico. I guess patterning myself after that, I still do that myself. I feel affinity with people from New Mexico. So this identification has been meaningful. It has been an integral part of me.

If Fran's New Mexican experience has meant anything it is that it has served to reinforce, perhaps unconsciously during her coming of age years, a sense of collective selfhood despite whatever competing acculturating tensions that were associated with her relationship to family, particularly to her parents. Family provided Fran with support which helped her to negotiate her self-identity.

My early childhood in New Mexico had a profound influence on me that I didn't know for some time and didn't appreciate until much later. I think the influence was that there was 100 per cent family support. Even in the worst of times, I have known that I always had family support. It was a given. In retrospect, I was one of many yet I was also made to feel that I was important.

Fran's gender and ethnic self is further shaped by class forces that dislocated her family as small ranchers and farmers in New Mexico during the Great Depression and their migration to California in the late 1930s to begin life anew as migrant agricultural workers. Fran's father instead of helping to manage the Flores ranch in New Mexico now reverted back to being strictly a labourer in the California fields. In California Fran underwent important changes regarding gender and ethnic identity during her coming of age years in Visalia. This section focuses on Fran's experiences between the ages of 10 and 14— her age of puberty and of youthful adolescence.

During this period, she began to recognize the 'double consciousness' referred to by DuBois. Fran sensed being 'other' but at the same time did not want to be seen as 'other'. She also experienced the dilemma, shared by many other ethnic subjects, over which personal strategy of self-identity to pursue. Fran's dual consciousness or what she now refers to as 'parallelism'—the growing divide between home and school environments, between Mexican- and Anglo-American worlds—is manifested in different ways during these years.

Fran recalls that around age 10 she began to feel tensions over what seemed to her to be an abyss between her Spanish at home and her English at school. Like most other Mexican-Americans, and indeed other ethnic Americans, Fran's English-language experiences in school meant that she was becoming more proficient and functional among her peers in English. She began to undergo what Richard

Rodríguez suggests is the sense that Spanish in a Mexican-American cultural context represents a 'private language' whereas English symbolizes the 'public language'.[14] Rodríguez's assertion can and has been criticized with some justification, for it is too rigidly polarized. In an increasingly Spanish-speaking environment like California, Spanish and English can be both private and public.

Nevertheless, for a young adolescent girl this was not as clear. Hence, Fran's sense of language separation was then as real as it was for Rodríguez. Fran's growing alienation from Spanish interacted with her own growing struggle against family control, especially the control of her strict father. Speaking English outside the home, but—more importantly—attempting surreptitiously to integrate it at home, represented for Fran, as she later acknowledged, part of her adolescent rebellion:

Spanish became increasingly burdensome as a responsibility because of what I believe was my natural orientation to oppose parental authority. Language was tied to parental authority because my father was adamant about the use of Spanish in my early years.

At the same time that the division of language was framed in youthful rebellion against parental authority, it also reflected a growing recognition on Fran's part that Spanish (a metaphor for family and culture) represented the 'other'. Previously, Spanish stood for security and familiarity; now it became an embarrassing symbol for parental culture which was perceived by the Anglo-American world as foreign. This is a damaging experience too often repeated in ethnic America:

I started dealing with the fact that my parents were perceived as foreign and didn't function fully in English. I became very conscious of the fact that the world of school was a separate world within which my parents didn't function.

Yet while Fran perceived school and family to be completely separate cultural spheres, she also experienced alienation from her English-speaking school environment. While at one level she may have sought assimilation, at another she struggled against it, or at least for a bridge between two cultures. She recalls, for example, that the stories she read in school seemed totally unreal and foreign to her.

My life was not in the books. My experiences were not in the books. I was not in the books. I remember *Heidi of the Mountain* and detesting that story vehemently. It was a book read to our class over a period of weeks when I was in grade three or four. Even though I had grown up with animals, I couldn't identify with Heidi. We had no goats when we were growing up and worse I couldn't image any little girl being so interested in goats and climbing up hills in Switzerland or wherever it was, a land that seemed so alien to my experiences. I had no clue what the story was about and I could have cared less. I remember deliberately not listening and instead occupying my mind in observing the teacher's behaviour and the behaviour of other pupils. The teacher was oblivious to my existence as a person. I hated Heidi and I didn't want to hear about Heidi and I hated this teacher droning on and on about Heidi.

Finding alienation both at home and at school, Fran attempted to create a separate consciousness for herself: something that was neither home nor school, but in reality some of both. This constituted what Gloria Anzalidúa refers to as a border area or *la frontera*—a space, territorial but also symbolic and cultural, where Chicanos (Mexican-Americans) invent something uniquely their own.[15]

We're talking about those early years and my guess is that about this time I started what ultimately would become somewhat more pronounced later, which is a realization that I was dealing with separate worlds in my life. My world at home, my world at school, and my world in my head.

Fran's struggle to create a more autonomous self-identity, or what Heilbrun terms a 'quest plot',[16] is related to both gender and ethnicity and is influenced by class position and race structure. Fran's efforts to understand herself as a young woman and as a Mexican-American were affected by the distinct social structure in the San Joaquín Valley in which Mexican-Americans were relegated to menial positions as farm labourers and segregated in a Mexican-American cultural world. Fran's attempts at self-representation, for example, through physical appearance, specifically forms of dress, reveal the intersections of gender, ethnicity, race, and class.

Fran perceived at first that there seemed to be only two basic models of appearance: an Anglo- and a Mexican-American one. Initially, she believed that she really had little choice. The Anglo-American model was inaccessible. Fran was not an Anglo-American and didn't deceive herself into thinking that she was. Even if she believed she could transform herself through appearance into an Anglo-American she could not. If not her clothes, then her bronze skin and dark hair signified her Mexican ancestry. While issues of both racial and ethnic differences existed as ambivalent factors in Fran's early life, she was still subject to the racialized system that Anglo-Americans have imposed on Mexicans since the United States' seizure of Mexico's

Identity and Gender

northern frontier, including California, in the mid-nineteenth century.

More basically as a member of a poor family, Fran could not afford to purchase the type of clothes worn by her Anglo-American peers. Hence, for better or for worse, there was only one model that she could relate to or transform, the Mexican-American model.

I was aware that Mexicans were different in appearance from Anglos and my models in terms of physical appearance were from the Mexican community. These were the only models I knew. There was no reason for me to look elsewhere for models. As soon as I became aware of the outside world, I could see that relative to the Anglo community, I was different in appearance and that was a source of extreme discomfort and anguish because I couldn't match that model, that hairdo, and that type of clothing.

While at one level, Fran lamented that she could not become an Anglo-American through appearance, there was also a sense of rejecting this appearance and of choosing one that reflected more of herself. She rejected the Anglo-American model because she perceived it as too babyish and immature. Fran recalls that she was already physically developed as a young woman, even before becoming a teenager, and that she opted for the more mature style of the *pachuca* look of the 1940s. This decision was also influenced by her recollection that, unlike the Anglo-American community, in the Mexican-American one there seemed to be no real childhood or adolescent stage:

It was babyhood and then adult-type behaviour including self-adornment through hairdo, earrings, facial make-up, and clothes. The Anglo kids maintained a more youthful look, a look that was more in the direction of children's clothing that barrio kids considered to be wimpy, in contrast to their effort to appear more adult-like.

Rejecting the Anglo-American look, Fran instead adopted a modified barrio look consisting of a scaled-down bouffant hairdo accompanied by a tight skirt and a sweater that, according to Fran, 'revealed the emerging young girl versus the baby—the Anglo kid with a loose-fitting dress and straight hair with little barrettes—the smockey child look'. Fran doesn't recall wearing much lipstick, but notes that many Mexican-American girls her age did and in some cases they wore a great deal of it.

Yet Fran's ethnic and gender look was really an ambiguous one. By her junior high school years the ambivalence about herself and her relationship to both the Anglo- and Mexican-American worlds led her to adopt a more 'mainstream', and less of a barrio look. In this period, Fran appears to have consciously made the decision that, if she were to have a future outside of the traditional and prescribed role for Mexican-American women like her mother, it had to be separate and apart from the barrio. There was no future for her there. This decision was accompanied by a change in her appearance. It was not so much that Fran opted to become an 'Anglo', but that she attempted to design a strategy that would empower her as both a young woman and as a person of Mexican descent.

But to undergo this change brought her into direct confrontation with some of her Mexican-American peers—specifically the *pachucas* of this era. *Pachucos* and *pachucas* (male and female) were Mexican-Americans who, not unlike Fran, expressed ambivalences concerning both Anglo- and Mexican-American cultures and in response rebelled against both in the hope of creating their own cultural and stylistic space. Yet for them, unlike for Fran, this space was to be within the barrio and not outside of it. Fran did not essentially reject the barrio. She was partly a product of it, but she believed that to remain within the barrio would doom her to a fate not unlike that of her mother and of other women in her family and outside of it.

What was at work here was, I believe, an integrationist strategy, not of an 'Uncle Tom' or 'Tio Taco' variety, but one with oppositional connotations. Fran's personal strategy was similar to the political strategy of integration pursued by what I have labelled the Mexican-American Generation. Groups such as the League of United Latin-American Citizens (LULAC), the American GI Forum, and more radical ones such as the National Spanish-Speaking People's Congress advocated integration—not assimilation—as a viable way to break down discriminatory barriers erected against Mexican-Americans. While Fran's strategy was not political *per se*, nevertheless it possessed the same basic understanding that one viable option for Mexican-Americans to achieve equal opportunities lay in an integrationist philosophy.[17]

This strategy was also a gender-based one. For Fran, liberation from the traditional role for Mexican-American women could only come by altering gender expectations and moving in the direction of new cultural fronts: education and professional careers.

To achieve her integrationist goal, Fran modelled her appearance to reflect a more 'mainstream look'. 'I began to choose clothing that I thought made me look good even if the clothes were different from the clothes worn in the barrio.' Skirts and blouses along with Spaulding white bucks—the Anglo bobby-sox look—made up Fran's junior high school and high school wardrobe. Yet, as Fran explains it, this was not a totally mainstream look, since she retained a modified stacked hairdo and never was able to afford the cashmere sweaters favoured by the Anglo girls. Opposed to this was the *pachuca* look, adopted by other Mexican-American girls. It consisted of a short and tight black skirt, a baggy sweater, high-top shoes, and black bobby-socks. The *pachucas* wore their hair in exaggerated bouffant styles. Lipstick and cosmetics added to the statement.

Dressed differently from the *pachucas*, Fran recalls tense encounters with them, especially after school and on the way home. She remembers being taunted and she engaged in what was called 'mad-dogging', the exchange of hostile looks. According to Fran, *pachucas* in Visalia had a reputation for violence, but she never engaged in physical conflict with them. Fran believes that what was involved here was a dual form of assertiveness that possessed different objectives. The *pachucas* of Fran's era authored their lives in one particular way, a defiant way, but it was not Fran's way. For Fran, the *pachucas* embodied the worst aspects of the barrio, those aspects that Fran believed promoted conformity and an inward-looking perspective, one that frowned on those who desired mobility out of the barrio.

Fran explains how she could not accept this. She says she saw this mode of thinking as reinforcing—at least for her—the traditional expectations of Mexican-American women. For Fran, the struggle against dominant female gender roles required an integrationist strategy and perspective that was not accommodationist, but oppositional—oppositional to the limitations imposed within Mexican-American culture on women, and oppositional to the discriminatory attitudes and practices of Anglo society against Mexican-Americans, both men and women.

Fran did not see herself as wanting to become an Anglo. But she recognized that, in order to achieve success in school and career mobility, she would have to make personal and cultural choices. It likewise involved differentiating herself from those other Mexican-American students who—for whatever reasons—chose not to share her aspirations. Fran concentrated at first on stylistic choices, but, in fact, she was also making a statement regarding social class. Fran's aspirations to make something of herself beyond the farmworker/barrio experiences of her parents and her Mexican-American peers contained a desire to escape her working-class position and to achieve middle-class status. She recalls that these were not easy choices. They were the result of ambivalences, insecurities, and tensions of her youth, which followed her into her high school years:

> I was a successful student in high school, but during those years I was having a difficult time defining myself. Every success in school increasingly separated me from other Hispanic students and, I felt, from Hispanic culture. Being an academically successful student meant that I had to accept being 'different'. My school friends increasingly became other academically successful girls.
>
> I knew that there were many places in town where Mexicans were not welcome, and I knew that in town job opportunities for Mexicans were almost non-existent. But I also knew I had tenacity and the ability to succeed.

To Fran, the barrio represented not a romanticized haven, but a closed environment with limited opportunities. Unlike New Mexico, which to Fran was defined by a sense of community, the Visalia barrio remained an uncertain place. For Mexican-American young women, even for those with some education and some hopes of a better life, the opportunities for mobility in the barrio were limited due to racial/ethnic/gender discrimination. The best one could aspire to was a job as a store clerk or a bank cashier; even this depended, as Fran recalls, on the shade of your skin:

> I think that at that early age, I began to understand that Visalia was a dead-end place in terms of opportunities for a person like me. I did not see myself in any sense tied to Visalia. I definitely knew that I would be going on in some fashion. Life was going on elsewhere for me. I think that as I was going through these years, comparing myself to others, I was acquiring a definite sense of 'I can do more—I can do better. There is more and I can reach out for more because there is more.'

Perhaps the experience that most tellingly and sensitively illustrates Fran's attempt to remake her life as a Mexican-American woman was her break with her barrio boyfriend, Peter Nava. Fran met Peter when she was in junior high school and he in high school. They dated for about a year and a half. Fran recalls Peter as a sensitive and caring individual—the antithesis of the traditional macho type. Peter never put any pressure, either of a social or sexual nature on Fran. Yet at a certain point Fran recognized that there was little if any point to their relationship. She wanted an education and some kind of career. Peter would not go to school beyond high school and seemed preordained to remain part of the Visalia barrio. Fran knew that if she stayed in Visalia her only future with Peter would be marriage and children. Fran believed that other Mexican-American girls would be content with this:

The girls I was surrounded by did not seem to be future-oriented. There was not much discussion of the future. I don't remember any discussion among the girls as to what tomorrow holds. I think that they accepted being in the barrio and that was it, and the expectation was that they would marry. I certainly don't remember talking about getting married or having babies or that sort of thing, or saying to Peter, 'Let's get married, let's have babies.' I think it was just kind of an accepted way of life: women as marriage partners or sex objects.

Fran ended her relationship with Peter as she entered high school. As she recalls she loved Peter, but she knew that the relationship had no future:

It was clear to me that going on to school meant changing my associations. I think I perceived that having a boyfriend meant getting married and I knew that that was not it for me at that time. I wasn't pro-marriage or against marriage. My family didn't talk about it, but it became crystal clear to me that marriage was not for me at that time. Peter and I couldn't continue seeing each other, caring for each other as much as we did, and not consider marriage. We both understood this without talking about it publicly. I was young and I had my schooling to attend to. We were physically attracted to each other, but that was all it could be.

Frances Esquivel Tywoniak's *testimonio* is much more involved and complex than I can portray in this short space. The multiple influences on her coming of age identity were to be compounded in young adulthood, especially after her marriage to Ed Tywoniak, a man of Polish Jewish background whom she met as a student at the University of California–Berkeley. But this later saga must be left to the full publication of Fran's *testimonio*. What I do want to conclude, based on the segments of her text that I have analysed here, is that Fran's narrative, what Bernice Johnson Reagon calls a 'cultural autobiography',[18] and that of other Latina and post-colonial ethnic women, represents a new form of authorship. This is an authorship that seeks to rewrite the very nature of both gender and ethnicity. To paraphrase, modify, and expand upon Heilbrun: 'I believe that [ethnic] women have long searched, and continue to search, for an identity "other" than their own. Caught in the conventions of their sex, they have sought an escape from [both] gender [and ethnicity].'[19] While these narratives are not or should never be whole or closed texts, they do reveal challenging efforts to engage in a dialogic relationship concerning gender and ethnicity. By constructing through oral narrative what amounts to an 'exemplary life', I believe Fran challenges us to dismantle the past and to reimagine the future based on the invention of an alternative, autonomous, and powerful self.

Notes

1. See Shari Benstock (ed.), *The Private Self: Theory and Practice of Women's Autobiographical Writings* (Chapel Hill, NC, 1988).
2. Carolyn G. Heilbrun, *Writing a Woman's Life* (New York, 1988).
3. Mario T. García, *Memories of Chicano History: The Life and Narrative of Bert Corona* (Berkeley and Los Angeles, forthcoming, 1994).
4. Rigoberta Menchú, *I . . . Rigoberta Menchú: An Indian Woman in Guatemala*, ed. Elisabeth Burgos-Debray, trans. by Ann Wright (London, 1984).
5. Mary G. Mason, 'The Other Voice: Autobiographies of Women Writers', in Bella Brodzki and Celeste Schenck (eds.), *Life/Lines: Theorizing Women's Autobiography* (Ithaca, NY, 1988).
6. Werner Sollors, *Beyond Ethnicity: Consent and Descent in American Culture* (Cambridge, Mass., 1986).
7. I borrow the concept of polyphonic voices from the Russian literary critic Mikhail Bakhtin. See Katerina Clark and Michael Holquist, *Mikhail Bakhtin* (Cambridge, Mass., 1984).
8. Benedict Anderson, *Imagined Communities: Reflections on the Origin and Spread of Nationalism* (London, 1983).
9. The oral-history interviews which form the basis of Frances Esquivel Tywoniak's narrative were conducted during the summers of 1990 and 1991. At this time, both the audio tapes and the transcripts remain in the possession of the author.
10. As quoted in Carolyn G. Heilbrun, 'Non-Autobiographies of "Privileged" Women: England and America', in Brodzki and Schenck (eds.), *Life/Lines*, 62.
11. W. E. B. DuBois, *The Souls of Black Folk* (Chicago, 1903).
12. See Doris Sommer, ' "Not Just a Personal Story": Women's *Testimonio* and the Plural Self', in Brodzki and Schenck (eds.), *Life/Lines*, 107–30.
13. Heilbrun, *Woman's Life*, 24.
14. Richard Rodríguez, *Hunger of Memory: The Education of Richard Rodríguez* (Boston, 1982).
15. See Gloria Anzaldúa, *Borderlands/La Frontera: The New Mestiza* (San Francisco, 1987).
16. Heilbrun, *Woman's Life*, 48.
17. See Mario T. García, *Mexican Americans: Leadership, Ideology, and Identity, 1930–1960* (New Haven, Conn., 1989); Richard A. García, *Rise of the Mexican-American Middle Class: San Antonio, 1929–1941* (College Station, Tex., 1990).
18. As quoted in Susan Stanford Friedman, 'Women's Autobiographical Selves: Theory and Practice', in Benstock, (ed.), *The Private Self*, 43.
19. Heilbrun, *Women's Life*, 111–12.

11

Central American Refugee Testimonies and Performed Life Histories in the Sanctuary Movement

William Westerman

> To testify is to bear witness, to tell what you have seen or felt. A religious experience, perhaps, or a crime. Then to come forward and speak. To deliver the word.

December 1987. We are standing in the Cathedral of San Salvador, El Salvador, tape recorders in hand. There are around two hundred people occupying the Cathedral, just dispersed with tear gas and rubber hoses from the National Ministry of Justice. Young men are taking off their shirts to allow witnesses to photograph the red welts on their backs from the beatings. Scattered among the people in the church, at the doors, in the pews, and before us, dressed in black, their heads covered by white scarves, are the women of COMADRES, the Committee of Mothers and Relatives of Political Prisoners, Disappeared, and Assassinated of El Salvador. They are standing on the front steps of the Cathedral with banners and megaphones, telling all of San Salvador of the injustices they have witnessed. They are blocking the doors, making sure only those who bring no harm can enter. Who are you, they ask us. A North American delegation. Come on in.

One woman stands before us, and our tape recorders and cameras. She tells us why she is there, about the demonstration violently disrupted by the police. She tells us that a 22-year-old baker had been found dead just several days earlier. He had been held for a brief time in one of the political prisons. They found his corpse, the body mutilated, the skin peeled back in strips from his arms and his thighs, burns from a live wire tied around his tongue. She and the other women of COMADRES were protesting at the Justice Department to demand why.

She asks if we would like to hear her personal testimony. Yes, we tell her, shaking, while our eyes check the doors guarded by the other women for security. She gives us her testimony, and tells us about those in her family she has lost to the death squads, the police, and the government. A daughter. A son. A grandchild. She will go on fighting, speaking out, she says, until the end, until she finds justice, because she has nothing else left to live for. Only a hope that one day there will be justice, one day she might not live to see. Still, she speaks.

Most of us North Americans in the Cathedral that day had previously heard these stories, these testimonies, but without having been to Central America. Since 1980 we had been hearing these accounts across the United States, in churches and synagogues, schools and union halls. They had been brought north to us, on foot, by bus, by plane, by hundreds of thousands of refugees from El Salvador and Guatemala. In the words of one Arizona priest, in 1980 for the first time,

Not only were there people who came here [to the church] daily for food, for handouts, that were stranded, but there were a new breed of people who came and not only were without food and clothing, but had a story to tell. And it was that story of horror, of terror, from not Mexico but from El Salvador, and from Guatemala, that demanded a new pastoral response.[1]

They came by the thousands: as many as 750,000 fleeing death squads and war in El Salvador which left over 75,000 dead; fleeing massacres, assassinations, torture and repression, hunger and disease in Guatemala, which left at least 30,000 dead as well as up to another 70,000–100,000 'disappeared', killed and buried in clandestine cemeteries.

All the refugees came with stories, histories of why they left and how they arrived. But a select few, at least a thousand, came forward in some way, and began to tell their life stories in public, to North Americans, as a way of informing the US (and Canadian) public about the repression in El Salvador and Guatemala, repression largely funded by our own US Government.

Most of those who came forward to speak during the years 1982 to 1987 were affiliated with the well-known Sanctuary movement, a loose conglomeration of over four hundred congregations which sponsored, transported, and provided legal, medical, and other assistance to Central American refugees, many of whom were undocumented.[2] Though protected by the Geneva Conventions ratified by the US Senate and the US Refugee Act of 1980, most were considered unwelcome by the Reagan and Bush administrations, under which fewer than 3 per cent could obtain political asylum.[3] Some refugees only spoke because they had to, to a judge or lawyer during deportation proceedings, if they got that far. But others, some associated with Sanctuary and some not, spoke out and continue to speak out in public, and these have included union leaders, students, human-rights workers, health workers, businesspeople, peasants. Many spoke out, in the hopes that, as one Salvadoran said to me, 'Once these people listen to us, I believe that they are not going to be the same anymore.'[4] In other words, they hoped that the US public would be moved to act and to question their own government, just as they had done in their home countries.

Those refugees who chose to go public were mostly between 18 and 35 years of age, reflecting in part the age of those who had been most involved politically. Rather than deliver a political 'analysis', the refugees usually delivered a life history in public, which they themselves referred to as 'testimony', a direct translation of the Spanish *testimonio*, or 'personal experience'. These testimonies, lasting between twenty and forty-five minutes in length, were delivered in Spanish, through an interpreter, or preferably in English, since translators became notorious for their errors or failure to capture subtle shades of meaning. English also became the language of choice because North American listeners were more inclined to pay attention and be directly affected by hearing a testimony in their own language. When Spanish was used, it was more formal than usual conversational Central American Spanish, with fewer colloquialisms and clearer pronunciation, both because this accommodated the translators, who often spoke Spanish as their second language, and because the testimony took on the nature of a formal oration.

Such testimony could be given in a variety of contexts, usually in religious settings. Most commonly the personal testimony was a formal component of the ceremony in which the refugee was welcomed into sanctuary. On those occasions, it might also have been released in written form. But testimony would also have been given in a variety of other situations: in private house meetings and gatherings, in elementary and secondary schools, at colleges and universities, in churches and synagogues, in union halls, in law offices, at governmental hearings, even at fashion shows, and on regional tours to areas where there were interested people, but no formal sanctuary communities. It could also have been given in the course of a formal interview with a reporter or with an ethnographer, as in my case as part of a long-term, field-based study.

We now can safely say that testimony was effective, because of the rapid growth in the Sanctuary movement and other Central American solidarity movements during the early 1980s. The Sanctuary movement in the south-west US actually grew out of the experience of listening to the stories of refugees just having crossed the border. A number of Sanctuary workers I interviewed remembered distinctly the first time they ever heard a refugee speak and could relate to me the story they heard. Word of mouth, personal visits, and refugee narratives were responsible for the participation of most of the active congregations. The Sanctuary movement might possibly have grown anyway had there not been personal testimony, but the success in converting the sceptical and the 'apolitical' to a politicized stance, as well as the involvement of the religious sector in the larger Central American solidarity movement, was largely due to the strength of a few individuals who learnt to speak out, to bear witness to the injustice they had known and were committed to end.

What emerged was an overall consistent traditional pattern to these narratives. Testimony was always in the first person, with episodes concerning third parties—children, siblings, parents—mentioned, but usually only in relation to the speaker. Most examples I heard and compared showed the same structure, including six definite sections: (1) introduction and background, (2) life and activity in the home country, (3) persecution, (4) escape, (5) exile, and (6) analysis and call to action.[5] This is the general chronological pattern, too. This structure was found to be most successful with North American audiences. While the structure seems intuitive, the choice of autobiography was instead cultural and practical, as Central Americans realized North Americans were much more willing to listen to personal experiences than political discussion. Fundamental parts of the story would not be omitted, but short episodes, details, and descriptions could be lengthened, shortened, or dropped altogether, depending on the audience. The important themes and episodes, according to one refugee, are those 'which are marked in your life'.[6]

Certain historical episodes (such as the military take-over of El Salvador's National University, the assassination and funeral of Archbishop Oscar Romero, or fleeing from aerial bombardments, to name a few) were part of the experience of so many people that they recurred as traditional motifs. Other, more personal episodes were of course unique to the teller, such as a story of capture and torture, but similar thematically to those told by others. Thus each testimony was personal, yet commented upon the larger social picture.

Rather than existing in isolation, these testimonies were each part of that larger mural of the recent history of Central America, and they corroborated one another by offering overlapping perspectives of the same historical event. Indeed, considerable interchange and story-sharing did go on among refugees in the United States. The structure of having two or more refugees in one evening's house or church meeting made such public interaction unavoidable, but also refugees worked together in human rights and church offices and socialized together, trading experiences informally and analysing speaking strategies more formally in business meetings. Discussions among refugees yielded pointers and suggestions, with less experienced speakers learning about form, and these same newer arrivals giving updates on recent political developments at home. Though individual experiences were often different, through refugee interactions testimonies became 'traditional' in their structure.

In the case of Central American refugee narratives, each story was the story of an individual, but only moved people to action when placed within the context of an entire nation of similar testimonies. Hearing one testimony was not sufficient. Nor was content alone the significant feature, and eventually it became important for North Americans not only to hear a variety of refugee testimonies but to visit Central America and hear the testimonies of those who had not left and who continued (and continue) to experience repression on a day-to-day basis while struggling for justice. And it became important for Central Americans in the United States to develop a speaking style that would engage listeners, without making an audience feel threatened or become bored. That meant concentrating on human, anecdotal narrative and removing political commentary that could be construed as inflammatory or accusatory.

More recent research, including a brief trip to El Salvador in 1987, made me aware that testimony in North America was merely that *testimonio* in Central America which had been brought north. In other words, the concept of testimony was not devised in and for the United States, though the idea of delivering testimony to North Americans *in their own country and language* was. As a verbal form conveying historical or eyewitness information, thousands of people continue to speak out in El Salvador and Guatemala, painting a canvas so large and complex that together it gives an oral historical portrait of a people at war, seeking justice.[7] What went on in the United States, the testimony from those who had left or escaped, was only a small part of a larger phenomenon.

Here is an example of personal testimony by Gregorio (pseudonym), from a personal interview in Philadelphia, Pennsylvania, 11 March 1986.[8] Gregorio begins his testimony by describing the day in June 1980 when the military took over the University, killed more than thirty students including some of his classmates, and prevented the remainder, including Gregorio himself, from continuing their student careers. (This section of his testimony has been omitted for reasons of space.) He continues:

And um, I was since '77, you know '78 was—we started to form our Christian base communities in my neighbourhood. So I was, I decided to, to do the social work you know, with the, through the diocese of San Salvador. And um, I was you know doing that and we were travelling the different count—you know to different provinces like uh you know, San Vicente, Morazán, Chalatenango. And um, we were bringing food, you know clothes, medicines, to the people, teaching, 'bout um, you know malnutritions things, I mean very, um, helps [or 'health'?], you know, education, things like that, and we were makin' a cam—uh, a liter—you know, literature [literacy] campaigns for the childrens.

Um, in my neighbourhood, there were a lot of shanty towns around—you know, in the areas, so we were you know, raising material aid for them in my neighbourhood, and we were you know, bringing to them.

Um, we get meetings every week, you know, sometimes in the church, in our parishes, in my neighbourhood, sometimes in houses. And um, a letter, you know, from the death squad, we received three letters, to our, you know, community, that was threaten us. They were saying, if we continue doing that work, um, we are going to get killed, you know, and they got the names of all of us and everything. And they say, you know we were trying to organize guerrillas in the neighbourhood [laughs] so we, we are laugh, you know and everything. We say that's ridiculous, you know.

So anyway we didn't get scared, they didn't scare to us, we continued doing the work. So, that, you know, that was before the, that was after the Monseñor Romero assassination, but two months after, that was in my neighbourhood, they—the death squad came and they disappeared two of my friends who I was working with, you know. And um, 'bout two weeks later we found the bodies, you know with, decapitated, they were with signs of torture and everything.

And, you know, I went to recognize these bodies with the workers of the Legal Aid office of the Diocese.

Testimonies and Performed Life Histories 173

And um, I started you know to be worried about, you know, to living in my house in the neighbourhood, or to live in other places. So, you know, that's my, my m—parents, they started to get worried and they say, 'You must live in other places 'cause otherwise they are going to kill you.' [clears throat]. And you know I started to living in, in parishes and, you know, other houses of friends. And um—but not in the neighbourhood.

And two months that, you know, later that happened with my friends, the army, they made a raid in the neighbourhood again, and they captured two of my other friends who, you know, were working the same thing. And um, we didn't found them, you know. So the mothers they still looking for them. I mean they are part of the Comité de Madres, you know, the mothers' committee the disappeared.

So umm, you know I was, I—I was continuing doing the work, so you know, I'd say I won't, I won't get back to my place you know, 'cause I know they are going to, you know, be after me. So that was, that is, you know something that, really, you know, scared me, you know. I knew that that was dangerous but that's the commitment what I got that was really straight.

Um, one time I was visiting to my parents in the neighbourhood, you know, and picking up personal stuff [clears throat].

And um, you know in, being in San Salvador, you know in El Salvador the— all the people recognize the death squad's, you know, cars. So you know, we know if they move in jeeps, or Cherokee Chief jeeps and things like that, you know, little, you know, pickups trucks.

So um I—I was getting off of my, you know, of my home, in the door of my, of my home. So in the street, you know about two blocks of distance there was a car, you know, a Cherokee Chief. They were, you know, trying to parking that. And then, you know when I saw them I jumped the front of my house. They saw me, you know, of course 'cause they made a couple shots. So I was you know, running away. I mean you know I, I knew that they were looking for me, but uh, thanks God I didn't get any shots [laughs softly]. That was the most important thing.

Um, I get back to you know to the place of where I was working in San Salvador, and I told the story to some friends, priests and things like that. They told me I have to leave as soon as possible, 'cause otherwise, you know, they are going to kill me, 'cause you know if they were looking for me at the house, they are follow my, you know, steps and the pli—the places where I am going to visit and everything [clears throat]. So that was, that's you know when, you know my parents they were in that time in the house, they heard the shots and everything, so they were very scared, they thought I was killed, things like that. So they knew the place where I was you know working in San Salvador so they visited me and they gave some money, in order to you know get off of the country. So they told me you know, it's very hard to you continue living here.

And um, I was talking with other, you know, with the friends who they told me to, if I wants to get some passport, to don't do it, 'cause that were dangerous too, 'cause the umm government offices they have a list, you know, of people they are involved in, you know, political organizations or human rights, um, groups. And uh, if they find me on the list they, you know, they are going to capture me immediately. So I decided to leave like a tourist, you know, from San Salvador to Guatemala. (The testimony continues with a discussion of the escape to the United States and his life and work here.)

Why did (and do) these people speak out, and why did they speak out in the form that they did, that is, telling their personal history? For one thing, these personal narratives were also religious testimony within the framework of the widely practised theology of liberation. This radical reinterpretation of official, standard religion emphasizes the liberation of the poor and oppressed from the repressive situations and societies in which they live. Developed at the grass-roots level since Pope John XXIII, and becoming widely practised in Latin America since 1972, it became closely linked with the liberation movements in Nicaragua, El Salvador, and Guatemala, and elsewhere in Latin America.[9] Liberation theology focuses on the active role of the community and the individual in ending the sinful state of oppression and violence perpetrated by the state and in building the Kingdom of God on earth. This religious interpretation is not limited to theory alone, but also demands action.

Testimony, then, became one such form of action. The conversion experience of liberation theology is known as 'conscientization': the process of becoming conscious of the often unjust political and social reality and its root causes. In bringing the message of liberation theology to North America, refugees had to first make North Americans aware of the social, economic, and political conditions in Latin America, as well as of the political reality in the United States and the role of the US Government in maintaining conditions as they are throughout Latin America.

Clearly, the personal testimony in this context was indeed religious, and one essential purpose of giving testimony was to bring about the conscientization in North Americans. Most of the refugee speakers were devoutly Roman Catholic, and many had backgrounds in the practice of liberation theology in the Christian base communities, the local study- or worship-groups through which the popular church is organized. Giving testimony and denouncing oppression is therefore one way of being a good Christian. The refugees asked North Americans for a similar conversion, such that US citizens would side not with the oppressors (the governments of the United States, El

Salvador, and Guatemala) but with the oppressed. The refugees asked for—and in many cases secured—a commitment to social change and social justice.

Also from liberation theology comes an idea central to testimony and crucial for its success: the creation of solidarity between North and Central Americans, between the middle and upper classes of the North, and the poor and oppressed of Latin America (as well as, I might add, the poor and oppressed in the North, too). The Central Americans were more than aware of the distance between the two cultures; that distance is in itself responsible for the problem of North American apathy and ignorance concerning the US Government's actions or its heavy involvement in Central American affairs (up to $1.5 million US tax dollars a day were spent in El Salvador alone for some years, for example, not to mention the deployment of US military advisers in combat, US funding of the Nicaraguan *contras*, and the militarization of Honduras). Refugee testimony was personal and included the essential function of conveying a part of the history that was not recorded in the official media of the state and dominant culture.

In order to achieve this awakening, intimacy needed to be created[10] and personal identification with the refugee became essential. The refugee had to present himself or herself as a complete, three-dimensional, feeling human being in order to show, quite simply, that the war and repression had very real victims. By performing their life histories, the refugees presented themselves as fully human; and as they described their pain and their experience they encouraged identification, sympathy, and empathy, leading, they hoped, to action on the part of the listeners. In the words of one Salvadoran in Philadelphia, 'The [North American] people, they can feel us, you know, they can—they can hear us, they can s[ee] us, they can *think* [of us] . . . human beings—we have been suffering that, that situation.'[11] Testimony was, in an oft-quoted phrase of Archbishop Oscar Romero, 'the voice of the voiceless', and in North America it had the additional feature of making the statistics human.

Intimacy and personal identification ideally led to more politicized solidarity, going beyond empathy to concrete work on behalf of the poor and oppressed. Paulo Freire, the Brazilian educator and theorist, writes that the:

oppressor is solidary with the oppressed only when he stops regarding the oppressed as an abstract category and sees them as persons who have been unjustly dealt with, deprived of their voice, cheated in the sale of their labor—when he stops making pious, sentimental, and individualistic gestures and risks an act of love.[12]

Speaking itself became one way to render the oppressed no longer as abstractions, but as representatives of all too real human suffering in Central America. Speaking, and committed listening, became one such risky act of love, a love which in the words of theologian Gustavo Gutiérrez, 'seeks also to liberate the oppressors from their own power, from their ambition, and from their selfishness . . . One loves the oppressors by liberating them from their inhuman condition as oppressors, by liberating them from themselves.'[13] Refugee testimony was a manifestation of this act of love, even when it involved disagreement or conflict.

The functions of testimony, then, were fourfold. First, speaking itself was a political act, an act of denouncing the injustice from which the refugees fled. It was also a religious act, a way of concretizing faith so that it transcended belief to include action as a manifestation of that belief. Thirdly, testimony created solidarity between the refugees and those representatives of a people whose government was held responsible for creating refugees in the first place, and in turn, that solidarity led to further political action by US citizens. And fourthly, there was and continues to be a therapeutic function, in the sense that speaking out is a way of making sense of a destructive, violent past, a past in which one often felt victim, and of triumphing over that experience, turning it into a motivation for living and working in the pursuit of certain social ideals. One Salvadoran told me that when he first entered this country he had hoped to remain anonymous, but his outlook changed after being encouraged to speak out. For him, it was a way of overcoming feelings of helplessness and depression.[14] I would also say that, significantly, testimony need not have been a spoken narrative. I have heard songs of personal experience, seen narrative embroidered tapestries from refugee camps, and have heard refugees mention 'testimony of life', that is, when one gives one's life for the purpose of social justice, as in the case of a martyred priest or nun.

Testimony can be visual too; one refugee asked me in Spanish (the first time I ever met him, in fact), 'You want my testimony? This is my testimony,' and he pulled up his sleeve to reveal a deep gouged out scar from a bullet wound in his shoulder, received, as I later found out, when he was taken out to a garbage dump with other prisoners, lined up and shot.

Testimonies and Performed Life Histories

Testimony is about people rising from a condition of being victims, objects of history, and taking charge of their history, becoming subjects, actors in it. History no longer makes them; they make it, write it, speak it. On one level, this concerns the everyday struggle to stay alive. But this also concerns at another level the role of the individual in history, and how all of us depict that experience in our narratives. Anthropologist Barbara Myerhoff, in describing a life-history class among elderly Jews in Los Angeles, commented that:

> Conditions sometimes make the members of a generational cohort acutely self-conscious, and then they become active participants in their own history; they provide their own sharp, insistent definitions of themselves, their own explanations for their past and their destiny. They are then knowing actors in a historical drama which they themselves script, rather than subjects in someone else's study.[15]

Becoming the subject, the 'active participant' in one's own history requires, according to Freire, questioning, speaking out, being critical of one's own life.[16] Freire has written, in his earlier *Pedagogy of the Oppressed* that:

> There is no true word that is not at the same time a praxis. Therefore, to speak a true word is to transform the world . . .
>
> Human existence cannot be silent, nor can it be nourished by false words, but only by true words, with which men transform the world. To exist, humanly, is to *name* the world, to change it. . . . Men are not built in silence, but in word, in work, in action-reflection.
>
> But while to say the true word—which is work, which is praxis—is to transform the world, saying that word is not the privilege of some few men, but the right of every man.[17]

Testimony was, and in Latin America continues to be, precisely this, the naming the world by denouncing the oppression, the beginning of dialogue between Central and North Americans, and the liberation of individuals, and eventually a people, through the process of becoming historical narrators, and thus actors. Testimony is a word that transforms, but moreover, a word that emerges from the critical examination of one's own life by those deeply involved in the shaping of history. To give testimony is to bear witness; it is to tell the unofficial story, to construct a history of people, of individual lives, a history not of those in power, but by those confronted by power, and becoming *em*powered.

Finally, at the risk of romanticizing refugee testimony, I would like to make the argument that this utilitarian speech was also a folk art form and that it subscribed to a traditional aesthetic which was both conscious and well defined. The terms 'art' and 'aesthetic' can be misleading, suggesting the creation of pleasure or beauty. But certainly folklorists recognize that not only can the utilitarian be art but functional qualities can also render something aesthetic. With folk art, the judgement of what is 'good' or 'aesthetic' often rests with the community itself, and this was very true of refugee testimony. Good testimony, as defined by the refugees, was that which was most effective in moving the audience to a new level of understanding or action. The good speaker, like a good story-teller, was responsive to the different interests of each audience. He or she would have prepared those topics to be emphasized and would have decided on the level of political analysis to be included, for example, concentrating on repression against workers in a talk to a labour union audience. What would make the content or structure 'good' was the effect the talk had on the audience, to move them, motivate them, make them reflect. The best testimony was that which was easy to understand, got the point across, and reached people on an emotional and moral as well as intellectual level. That required having an important story to tell, and understanding how to turn that personal experience into something that others—people who in this case were linguistically, culturally, politically, often religiously, and economically different—could appreciate. The testimony was more important than the abilities of the speaker, the process of subsequent action ultimately more important.

Unlike many forms of narrative story-telling, the goal was not to come up with, in folklorist Richard Bauman's words, 'artful texts, identified on independent formal grounds,'[18] though many testimonies were beautiful in the sense of being emotionally moving. But as this was a group of people speaking from a politically marginal position, most often in broken English or poorly translated Spanish, their materials were determined by necessity and their aesthetic ideals by political as well as cultural and religious factors. Without recognizing that, we might fail to appreciate what is good or beautiful—that is, artistic—in these narratives and might miss their message altogether. Furthermore, the performers could 'be both admired and feared—admired for their artistic skill and power and for the enhancement of experience they provide, feared because of the potential they represent for . . . transforming the *status quo*'.[19] That status quo could be of course political, but also personal, since the refugees implicitly (and sometimes explicitly, later) asked for commitment and action in everyday life that North Americans generally were unprepared—and may otherwise have felt unable—to give. Though in some ways this separated them from the North American population to whom they were talking, such narratives helped to establish them as representatives of the struggles for social justice that were being waged back in their countries of origin. Thus there was a tension between allying themselves with the North Americans with whom they had to, wanted to, work everyday, and remaining distinct, Salvadorans and Guatemalans with their own histories, identities, and experiences that were separate from those of their North American audiences.

In that context, inflammatory speeches which emphasized too much political analysis would have been threatening to a North American audience and were dismissed by refugees as ineffective. Often, it was the most personal, and most understated talks that had the most impact. John A. Robinson has noted that one possible motivation for telling a personal narrative is 'to instigate action . . . in a way that avoids preaching or invoking one or another type of authority'.[20] Such narratives can be one method of accomplishing this because the 'very typicality of an incident . . . recommends it for narration, rather than its remarkableness'. This may be particularly true when the action in the narrative is typical for the speaker, but not for the audience. Hence, 'commonplace activities may excite great interest in listeners who are unfamiliar with the sphere of life to be discussed'.[21] By personalizing the history of Central America, then, the refugees could offer authority without being seen as authoritarian. And, it was the unfortunately commonplace quality of the episodes which made testimony so effective. The atrocities and the poverty described are part of the everyday life of Central Americans. Thus a narrative told in an understated, almost offhand manner could actually be more effective than a fiery speech, since the content had not been presented as something remarkable. The implication was that the miserable situation was almost normal, but still not acceptable. If it were not seen as normal, such acts of violence and oppression would seem isolated and would to some extent not be cause for such alarm or concentrated political activity in response.

We can also therefore begin to understand these refugees as historical actors by looking further at the genre of performed life history. The life histories became powerful tools in the construction of a more just society when wielded by devoted performers skilled in their use. As Myerhoff notes, such actors ' "make" themselves . . . an activity which is not inevitable or automatic but reserved for special people and special circumstances'.[22] If, in Dell Hymes's words, the acceptance of responsibility determines a 'breakthrough into performance', then testimony was an example of performance *par excellence*. They accepted—even grabbed—responsibility 'not only for knowledge but also for performance . . . [in order] to shape history'[23] and not only for verbal performance but for historical performance as well. By being witnesses from Central America, they earned the right to be authentic speakers, the right to take on that responsibility. Their tradition demanded of its bearers careful attention to an aesthetic, sensitivity to an audience, the memory of the past, a view to the future, and considerable bravery just to assume the responsibilities of performance.

Notes

An earlier version of this essay was delivered at the annual meeting of the Oral History Association in Baltimore, on 14 Oct. 1988, and other portions were given at the annual meeting of the American Folklore Society in Baltimore, on 23 Oct. 1986. My greatest gratitude to the many Salvadorans and Guatemalans and Sanctuary workers who have welcomed me into their communities and shared so much insight with me. I hope someday their contributions can be acknowledged more publicly. Additionally, for earlier readings of this work and encouragement to publish it, I would like to thank Dell Hymes, Virginia Hymes, Don Yoder, Margaret Mills, Leonard Norman Primiano, Norma Stoltz Chinchilla, and Joel Gardner.

1. Interview with Fr Matthews (pseudonym), Nogales, Arizona, 2 Aug. 1986. Because of the legal history of the Sanctuary movement and people involved in it, although some people were willing to allow me to use their names, I have made the choice—preferring to err on the side of safety—to use pseudonyms.
2. By 1988 the structure of personal testimony began to change, at least outside the south-western, border areas of the country. The focus shifted away from 'protecting the refugee' to defending the right of the civilians, and especially the displaced, back home. As interest in the Sanctuary movement waned (some congregations remained active into the 1990s), the focus on publicly performed life stories faded too.
3. For the best summary of the legality of Salvadoran and Guatemalan refugees, see Ignatius Bau, *This Ground is Holy* (Mahwah, NJ, 1985), 39–56. Since then, further legal decisions showed that the United States, through the Immigration and Naturalization Service (INS) denied the civil rights of Salvadoran refugees in this country. But it remained extremely difficult for Salvadorans and Guatemalans to obtain political asylum, as the State Department deemed them economic, not political, refugees, much as the State Department more recently considered Haitian refugees after the overthrow of President Aristide.
4. Interview with Diego (pseudonym), Los Angeles, California, 11 Aug. 1986.
5. Which could really be two sections, depending on the individual. In order to determine exactly, it would be necessary to examine linguistic and paralinguistic

markers, such as particles and pauses, to see exactly how each speaker structured the narrative and where the 'sections' were divided. The outline I have provided above refers primarily to a plot structure, rather than a linguistic one.

6. A comment made to me by Gregorio (pseudonym), a Salvadoran in Philadelphia, in 1986.
7. Collections and examples include Manlio Argueta, *One Day of Life*, trans. by Bill Brow (New York, 1983; orig. published 1980), the testimony of a Salvadoran peasant woman in novel form; Alfonso Hernández, *León de Piedra* (El Salvador, 1981); Maria López Vigil (ed.), *Marxismo y cristianismo en Morazán: Testimonio del Padre Rogelio* (El Salvador, 1987); examples published in Renny Golden and Michael McConnell, *Sanctuary: The New Underground Railroad* (Maryknoll, NY, 1986); Rigoberta Menchú, *I . . . Rigoberta Menchú*, ed. by Elisabeth Burgos-Debray, trans. by Ann Wright (London, 1984); and Victor Montejo, *Testimony: Death of a Guatemalan Village*, trans. by Victor Perera (Willimantic, Conn., 1987).
8. For space reasons this passage is not arranged ethnopoetically according to the styles adopted by Dell Hymes and Dennis Tedlock to reflect linguistic patterning and pause. All particles have been left in, however.
9. Two of the best introductions to liberation theology in Latin-American politics are Phillip Berryman, *The Religious Roots of Rebellion* (Maryknoll, NY, 1984); and Penny Lernoux, *Cry of the People* (New York, 1980).
10. Part of this process, then, is what Sandra K. Dolby-Stahl calls the creation of intimacy. 'The higher the percentage of "private" folklore embedded in a story, the more likely the creation of intimacy is a major motivation for the storytelling' ('A Literary-Folkloristic Methodology for the Study of Meaning in Personal Narrative', *Journal of Folklore Research*, 22 (1985), 47–8). The motivations for creating the intimacy in this case are significant. In order to overcome the cultural, linguistic, historical, and political differences, some sense of a 'shared inner life' between Central and North Americans had to be created.
11. Gregorio, 1986.
12. Paulo Freire, *Pedagogy of the Oppressed*, trans. by Myra Bergman Ramos (New York, 1970; first published 1968), 34–5.
13. Gustavo Gutiérrez, *A Theology of Liberation*, trans. by Sister Caridad Inda and John Eagleson (Maryknoll, NY, 1973; first published 1971), 275–6.
14. Personal interview with Diego, Los Angeles, 11 Aug. 1986. His experience was by no means unique. See also Inger Agger and Søren Buus Jensen, 'Testimony as Ritual and Evidence in Psychotherapy for Political Refugees', *Journal of Traumatic Stress*, 3 (1990), 115–30; and Ana Julia Cienfuegos and Cristina Monelli, 'The Testimony of Political Repression as a Therapeutic Instrument', *American Journal of Orthopsychiatry*, 53 (1983), 43–51.
15. Barbara Myerhoff, 'Telling One's Story', *Center Magazine*, 13: 2 (Feb. 1980), 22.
16. Paulo Freire, *The Politics of Education*, trans. by Donaldo Macedo and Loretta Slover (South Hadley, Mass., 1985), 199.
17. Freire, *Pedagogy*, 75–6.
18. Richard Bauman, 'Verbal Art as Performance', *American Anthropologist*, 77 (1975), 293.
19. Ibid. 305.
20. John A. Robinson, 'Personal Narratives Reconsidered', *Journal of American Folklore*, 94 (1981), 61.
21. Ibid. 62.
22. Myerhoff, 'Telling', 22.
23. Dell Hymes, *'In Vain I Tried to Tell You'* (Philadelphia, 1981), 134.

12

Between Identities

HOMI BHABHA interviewed by PAUL THOMPSON

Homi Bhabha is an Indian academic and cultural critic who has written and taught widely on colonial and post-colonial issues in the arts. He is editor of *Nation and Narration* (London, 1990) and author of *The Location of Culture* (London, 1993). He lives in London, where this edited interview was recorded in June 1993. He was asked at the start to recount his own story and the experiences and influences which led him to his present interests and perspectives.

I was born in India, in Bombay. And I belonged to a small community of Parsees, a largely urban community of Persian migrants who'd come to India in the seventh century. This minority community is not very well known, generally, and is very small, but has a very distinctive flavour, or style, rather than a distinctive tradition. And there is something about belonging to a community with a style or a flavour, rather than a tradition of tablets, which has a rather contemporary feel about it. Because the essentialist model of identity seems, in some way, now *passé*: identities are much more performative, and you construct a sense of identity.

Let me first say what the Parsees didn't have. The Parsees don't have a great Parsee literature. They don't have a great Parsee art. But amongst the Indian communities, they formed a very early Westernized bourgeois class, much earlier than Hindus or Muslims. Parsees were the middle men between the British and the Indians. Although conversion is not permitted and intermarriage not encouraged, they were not restricted by prescriptive or prohibitive codes or caste regulations, such as the Hindus were, or in different ways the Muslims. So they had a kind of cosmopolitan feel about them, they were freer to circulate, and they became the conduits for certain kinds of British communication. But despite that bourgeois history, unlike the Jews, they did not produce great works of art or high culture. What they did produce was a very advanced commercial, banking, and professional class that serviced both the British and the Indians. They were great industrialists, great bankers, doctors, lawyers. So they were part of the mid- to late nineteenth-century, early twentieth-century modernization of India. But with a handful of exceptions, they did not play great political roles. I think, as a minority, they wanted to tread easily and cover themselves. So no great politicians, no great artists, no great musicians. Of course, there's Zubin Mehta. There are no great writers of a recognizably Parsee tradition, except now, there's a certain currency of Parsee writing, part of the post-colonial moment. So, none of that.

Then, what is their style? Well, they had a particular family form, a particular kind of humour and self-irony. They had a very distinctive cuisine, something quite strangely delicious, with synthetic borrowings from a number of Persian and Indian sources, but somehow distinctive. Their lifestyle was, you know, very 'post-modern'. In my grandparents' house, if I think about it, or my parents' house, even as it is today, they will have borrowings from Bauhaus, from 1950s and 1960s European style, 1920s chrome and art deco, art nouveau, a number of citations, and yet in the midst of all that, you will have the prayer table, showing signs of the very strong ancestor worship within the Parsee tradition. My mother is a devotee of the French language and culture, and yet will pray regularly, say her Parsee prayers, and very regularly will speak in French with her colleagues, in Gujerati for the family charities that she deals with, so it's a multi-vocal culture. And it's a culture whose authenticity, whose scriptural authenticity, whether it was books or great religious texts, was always under question. So, to find one's identity in that particular Parsee culture, within the wider landscape of India, which is very culturally differentiated, was a very interesting position to have.

Migration is also part of this culture: both as the myth and historical reality of Parsees. Indeed, the fable of Parsee migration is actually folded in with a whole question mark around the purity and cultural authenticity of the Parsees. The Parsees were supposed to have migrated from Persia, and they came by sea, we are told, and they brought with them the fire, which is a great symbol of the Zoroastrian faith. They brought the fire. They were persecuted by the Muslims, and brought the fire with them, and settled on the west coast of India, where they built their fire temples. They first settled into rural peasant communities. So that's the story. Now purity is a very significant principle of Parsee life. Parsees cannot marry out of the community,

Between Identities

and if you do marry out of the community, there's a question about whether your children can belong. This whole 'ethic' of purity has been very preciously guarded. The myth of migration, however, says that only Parsee men came on the boat, guarding the sacred fire. Well, if only Parsee men came on the boat, guarding the sacred fire, how come that—you know, there are not that many Parsees, but there are 15,000! What happened? So that's why I say that the very primal myth of Parsee migration is at once a myth of purity and a myth of miscegenation. And I rather like this ambiguity, this ambivalence towards the whole question of what it means to be a Parsee.

Later on, Parsees migrated, in the late eighteenth century, to the city, and now in India, they are largely an urban community. Abroad too: there are now Parsee settlements in Toronto, in Sydney, in London. This migration has been not necessarily of educated Parsees. Clearly the impetus must have come from Parsees either sent abroad for education, who then brought their families, or Parsees who were fairly educated and decided to relocate. But my great-grandfather on my mother's side, later ran a stevedore's business in the docks, actually pawned his wife's jewellery, or so the family story has it, and took a ship and came to England and made contacts. And then he returned to India to establish himself in the port of Bombay. Now, his name was Dhubash and in the early sections of Conrad's *Lord Jim*, there is a little cameo where this chattering stevedore, Parsee Dhubash is mentioned, who comes to the ship while the trial of Jim is going on, drinks tea, and brings all the portside gossip. In fact, I did a talk called 'Bombay Mix' for the BBC, on 'Southern Voices', and a talk about this particular mix of the Parsee community. Parsees are rather like 'Bombay Mix' from the health food shops, you know! Rather like that!

In fact, it is a very interesting question, the nature of Parsee migration. Clearly, the upper echelons of the Parsees were Westernized, and many of them were as colonial as Colonel Blimp. So while the British were there, and after they left, some of them came to England to go to university or to college. They were reasonably wealthy, and they decided that you ought to be in the authentic place, so they came, lived here, and went to the Army and Navy Stores, or Fortnum and Masons, and thought that they were really in touch with God and reality! But, so there was clearly that class. Later, however, there were Parsees who went on Scholarships, boys more than girls, obviously, or Parsees who went to qualify, and then decided to stay on, and to bring their families over. Our accountant in Princeton came from a very repressive lower-middle class, Bombay suburban community, and she married somebody who brought her over to the States. The marriage broke up, but she put herself through university, doing evening classes, qualified, found her freedom, and then slowly pulled, brought her brothers and sisters, and settled them, and gave them educational opportunities, but also gave them too a sense of a more liberated life. So there is that whole lower-middle class Parsee.

And then you say, 'What about working-class Parsees?' Well, there are working-class Parsees, by objective criteria, but they're not working class in the sense of being part of the labour process, factory workers. The poorer Parsees are protected by large charities; so those who would slip into an Indian working class are preserved as a peculiarly protected lower-middle class, people who work in clerical jobs fostered by Parsee industrialists. Lower-middle-class Parsees have a reputation for honesty and meticulousness, they speak English, and Hindi, and Gujerati. In the prime localities of Bombay now, you have these large, substantial housing estates for poorer Parsees, supported by charities. All this is reminiscent of Victorian philanthropy, but some of the poorer Parsees have become richer Parsees: through migration, either going to the Middle East, or their children going abroad. Those who remain at the lower end of the economic scale area are a depressed and demoralized community.

My own family maintain their base in Bombay, but continue to visit Britain for education or vacations. My father was trained as a lawyer entirely in India. He did come to chambers here in the early 1950s, when some new death duties legislation was introduced in India, very much of the English model, and he joined chambers here in Lincoln's Inn. In my immediate family, only my sister and I have been here for most of our university education. I did my English degree first in Bombay, and then came to Oxford. My sister did exactly the same but read history. And both of us have ended up living here. But in my immediate family, that's it. And if you take a slightly large concentric survey, then my mother's sister, and her husband and daughter, and now granddaughter, moved to England in the 1950s, and they're settled here. My mother's brother sent his son to public school, but the son has now returned to India. His daughter is here, went to Cambridge, and now is training to be a solicitor. So, yes, there's that kind of coming and going: interestingly, more on my mother's side, really, than on my father's side. Although I have cousins in California who are the children of my father's eldest sister.

My own choice of English as my subject was due, I think, almost entirely to the influence of my mother. My earliest memories of my mother are redolent with her love of books and reading and writing. She had a very rudimentary formal education, but is a considerable autodidact, and has this great desire and thirst for poetry and art and culture, and languages. A thirst that is all the sharper because she didn't get it; she was very wealthy, it's not that she was deprived, but her life circumstances were such that she married early and left university. Our home was full of the most interesting books. She used to subscribe—I'm now talking about the 1960s and early 1970s—to the *Paris Review*, the *London* Magazine, the *New York Review*, the *New York Times Book Review*, the *Listener*, the *TLS*. Very Anglocentric in that way. I remember she would read poems to me that neither she nor I, for different reasons, could fully grasp, but just the, the tenor and the sound were as seductive to her as they are to me. I frequently read things where I'm compelled by the structure of the language, the tone, the sound. So I think there's no doubt about it, that it was my mother's love of literature which was communicated to me.

My first degree at Bombay was at Elphinstone College, the college named after Lord Elphinstone, and we were taught largely by people who had either been to Oxford or Cambridge, or people who had regretted that they had never been to Oxford and displayed even greater signs of what it might have been to have participated in the myth of Oxford! But it was a very good traditional education, as I think about it. We had a succession of influential teachers—because academic conditions in India—the pressures, library resources, were not really conducive, in the Eng. Lit. field, to major writing projects. I have to say this has really now changed to a great extent.

It was a great experience to go to college in Bombay, one that I fought to have, because my mother was very keen that I should come to England, and go to public school, and then do Oxford entrance. And I felt I really wanted to experience the city as a young adult. And it is a very fascinating city. I now feel, in retrospect, that those were even more important years than I thought at the time. At their best, colonial or post-colonial cities have a mixture of cultures, a cosmopolitanism: an ability to cite and quote and relocate, repeat and revise cultural styles, traditions and identities, which is quite remarkable. I say 'at their best' because you also have the spectacle of those same Indian cities ripped apart by communal riots between Hindus and Muslims.

But I think that must not be allowed to obscure the fact that there is a very particular kind of colonial and post-colonial modernity, an ethic of cultural tolerance, of the survival of various cultures, coming together in a rich intersection, which is quite unique. And, sometimes, when you are in the midst of what are considered to be great Western metropolitan centres, and you hear, as we did the other day, the Member of Parliament, Winston Churchill, trying to revive Enoch Powell's 'rivers of blood' prophecy, claiming that, now, the centres of most British cities were overrun by immigrants, there was no little private place in which you could be British any longer—then you may think that there is another history of communal living, which is to be learnt from the former colonial cities. The pity is that nationalistically minded indigenous intellectuals want to disavow that rich mixture of styles, traditions, periods, time-frames. On the other hand, Western metropolitan cultural critics persist in avoiding aesthetic criteria adequate to this contemporary cultural hybridity and will always portray that kind of cultural practice or product as, somehow, second-rate imitations. And I think the limitation is theirs. It's a limitation in their critical thinking really.

I myself never studied 'colonial' or Third World literature in a formal sense. In India, the option didn't arise. We were put through an Oxford-style Middle English to Modern English course of studies. Certainly, at Oxford in the early 1970s there was no option to work on any colonial or post-colonial writers. Of course, you could work on Kipling or on Forster. But I may even have been the first person to write an M.Phil. dissertation on V. S. Naipaul. I may have been. Of course, in Leeds you had the School of Commonwealth Literature, producing the *Journal of Commonwealth Literature*, and Wally Soyinka and Edward Braithwaite were students there. So I never really studied colonial literature, in a formal sense.

But I remember reading Naipaul, it must have been *A House for Mr Biswas*, and some of the earlier short stories. And experiencing such an authentic echo through the work, through the representation of these Indian migrants who went to the Caribbean as indentured labourers, and re-created something which was partly Indian, and partly Caribbean, and partly American. The attempt, in those conditions, to relate to Dickens or the movies of Humphrey Bogart, to attempt to live the pious verities of Samuel Smiles, to confront that condition of cultural imposition and cultural deprivation at the same time, and to produce a sense of self-reliance . . . Biswas tries to build his own house, which, of course, he can never quite achieve; every house he builds is not the appropriate house. So that uncanny story from the post-colonial moment really echoed with me. And I felt that if the Enlightenment could produce one great narrative of culture, or the age of Empire, or the age of industry, then I felt, certainly in my own little patch, that there was another theme. And that was the theme of the poignancy and the poetry of these partial identifications, this culture of relocation and migration—these hybrid cultural moments. I felt that there was a great theme there for the late-modern age.

I remember, very clearly, that summer in Oxford in which I sat, trying to write about some of these things, and felt quite paralysed, because there wasn't a critical culture that I felt I could identify with. Much Commonwealth literature was a sort of a descriptive, illustrative content-based study, and my feeling was that the key was not merely in the sociological or the historical verities of that literature, but it had to do with the very form in which one constructs one's identity, through these partial identifications. That was really the important thing. I felt that, in some way, I would have to construct the critical method with which I would then have to work.

At this point, I should mention two other influences. The first is of my wife, Jackie, whom I met and married while I was in Oxford. Her family has another story of migration. She was born in India too. But her parents were part of the German Jewish diaspora who escaped to Bombay, made a life there for almost two decades, and then left to settle in Milan in the early 1960s. Jackie grew up in Italy, and then came to an English boarding-school as a teenager. After we met she worked as a social researcher in an Asian community in Birmingham, and then trained as a lawyer, specializing in immigration and refugee law. So I have gained new perspectives through her.

The second is the influence of Edward Said: a considerable figure who intervened in my work at this time, maybe somewhat later. My first encounter with Said was, in fact, not *Orientalism*, but a long interview he gave to the theoretical journal, *Diacritics*. I thought this was a really fascinating display of that kind of intellectual who lived not only in two worlds, but between many worlds. I remember a moment in this interview, it was a primal moment for me, when he was talking about how his own reading of Orientalist images was more concerned with significant form, than with the content in subject. And how he had found various French intellectuals useful to him, like Roland Barthe and his work on social and cultural mythology, the semiotics of the image, or Michel Foucault on forms of inclusion and exclusion. He then turned, dramatically and suddenly, in the interview, from the Left Bank to the West Bank, and talked about his Christian/Islamic roots, about the cultural iconographies and landscapes of that experience, his political commitments to the Palestinian cause, and the Palestinian diaspora.

I think that was a very important perspective for me, of the possibilities of being, somehow, *in between*, of occupying an interstitial space that was not fully governed by the recognizable traditions from which you came. For the interaction or overdetermination often produces another third space. It does not necessarily produce some higher, more inclusive, or representative reality. Instead, it opens up a space that is sceptical of cultural totalization, of notions of identity which depend for their authority on being 'originary', or concepts of culture which depend for their value on being pure, or of tradition, which depends for its effectivity, on being continuous. A space where, to put it very simply, I saw great political and poetic and conceptual value in forms of cultural identification, which subverted authority, not by claiming their total difference from it, but were able to actually use authorized images, and turn them against themselves to reveal a different history. And I saw this little figure of subversion intervening in the interstices, as being very different from the big critical battalions that always wanted to have a dominating authority, opposed by an equally powerful subordinated agency: victim and oppressor, sparsely and starkly blocked out. However much one was politically and ethnically convinced of the imbalance and inequalities of power, I felt that there was always, in the very structure of authority, certain strategic ambivalences and ambiguities, and I felt that those who were oppressed, were actually empowered, by pointing to these, by being able to use these ambivalences and ambiguities, instead of representing power as a kind of homogenous, hegemonic block. So you can understand how the work I did, initially, was considered to be quite heretical, because people felt that the cause of materialist theory, or the cause of political liberation, was best served by setting up and I was very sceptical of that.

My interest in psychoanalysis, and the way in which it also talked about partial and ambivalent identifications, was also very central to my rethinking of the structures of power and authority. I realized that there was something inadequate in the literary concept of character, which was used to talk about the problem of identity in colonial literature, as indeed, in other literature. I felt that the concepts of character and identity being used were really rather banal.

It didn't measure up to the particular complexity of identity and identification, in the psychoanalytic sense, that seemed to me to constitute the crisis of a colonial psyche. There was a very fixed realist epistemology to the notion of literary character, and there was an unquestioned Western individualism implicit in the notion of identity. Some of these inherent values, I felt, were inappropriate. For instance, there is an impossibility or implausibility of identity in *A House for Mr Biswas* that displays the tragic destiny of a colonial/post-colonial individualism: Biswas's belief in a teleological history, the hope that he would finally build the perfect house, or that a perfect mode of dwelling would be achieved. And what was tragic about it, to me, was not just the fact that Biswas, as colonial character, couldn't achieve it in the colonized world. I think much of the literature of Empire, including *The Jewel in the Crown*, is about the limitations of liberalism, about its internal limits. And psychoanalysis, with its great emphasis on the ambivalence of concepts, and the importance of social fantasy, seemed to me to be an essential interdisciplinary move to make in colonial or post-colonial discourse.

Studies in that area had largely been dominated by political theorists, demographers, geographers, historians, sociologists, and anthropologists. The place of the literary critic in that world was often reliant, either on a tradition of literary theory largely based on the European novel and its sense of time and space and value, or on the work of area studies specialists, development sociologists, or economists. So you were always relating a problem of identity and culture, through the literary axiomatics of character, back to the historical or the sociological colonial 'facts'. For me, this was never a satisfactory *modus operandi*. I was interested in seeing how the very form of the colonial psyche had registered a number of these historical/cultural texts and influences, and also how it had its own history. And to allow colonial psyche and social fantasy a real space in the work required, I felt, that interdisciplinary move towards psychoanalysis.

And here comes one of the greatest influences in my own thinking: the Martiniquan/Algerian psychoanalyst and political activist, Franz Fanon. He held a passionate belief in a reconfigured, post-extentialist humanism; in the empowerment of the oppressed, in the autonomy of peoples. But Fanon was aware, too, that the psychic world of oppression was a very complex world, and that its problems could not be adequately, or indeed, appropriately resolved through national liberation. There has been a very proper criticism of some of his great shortcomings on gender and sexuality, his theory of violence. But Fanon is a deeply complex and contradictory writer, who wrote for many audiences, who wrote his case-studies in the midst of the Algerian revolution, who was fascinated by the polymorphous and perverse effects of a political struggle. And he died tragically young at 35, leaving us with only fragments of the larger work that he could have produced.

Psychoanalysis clearly has a context which belongs to a particular bourgeois European family form. It has a primitive ethnography derived very much from the early anthropological thinkers. But within psychoanalysis there is always this tension between the cultural institutions that inform it, and its desire to construct the symbolic, fantasmatic account of a realm of psychic reality that cannot be equivalent to material reality.

You can say that Freud was mostly working with rather patriarchal, nuclear Jewish families. Whereas the family form in *Biswas*, for example, is more matriarchal, complicated, quasi-feudal, semi-rural, borderline culturally diverse and hybrid, a Hindu post-slavery family in the diaspora. So you can set up those two different sociological realities, and then you can say, from a psychoanalytic perspective, nevertheless, that the Oedipal drama, which is about the accession to a certain kind of social and psychic authority, works with a phallic mother, as you have in Biswas. But that, to me, is an allegorical use of psychoanalysis for cultural analysis, which is not that intriguing, or interesting. It proposes a universalist reading, which I don't find that appealing.

The other way of conceiving of a use of psychoanalysis is much more strategic. To go back to Biswas, I felt it was important as a way of thinking about colonial identity, because psychoanalysis, in the most general sense, takes identity as never being complete, identity as being a scenario, or a circulation of meanings and values and positions, identity as being an illusion of totality, and yet that illusion, that ambivalence within identity, can be strategically, historically, socially, deployed. So it seemed to be, using it as I was, for a particular kind of literary critical cultural endeavour, a much better way of talking about identity than by saying, as was popular in certain traditions of literary theory, and indeed in certain kinds of psychological thinking, that what you had in the colonial space was a kind of inauthentic or imitative subjecthood. That's not to say that those things don't exist. But it just seemed to me much more interesting to see the 'misrecognition' of identity, not as a problem of negation or confusion, but as the working out, or working through, of an ambivalence between the 'real' and the phantasmatic, between the social and the psyche that structures the subject. The role of fantasy in the construction of identity could have very significant implications for a social regime that depends, for its authority, on the projection of 'inferiority' on other races, cultures, and histories. You work *with* identification in psychoanalysis, you *negotiate* identity in psychoanalysis: it's not about 'having' or 'losing' it. Psychoanalysis is concerned with more fundamental questions: what does it mean to 'represent' a relation to another? And how do we regulate relations of difference?

In recent years you've been moving between continents quite a lot. Could you reflect on the different ways in which identity is being constructed in Europe and the United States?

One of the clearest lessons that I have learned, is to make a distinction between the problem of identity as it relates to the issue of racism, in England and in the United States. And the difference is this. Until I spent some time in the US, I was, somehow, persuaded that forms of modern racism in the West had a kind of global equivalence—the ways in which they expressed themselves, the way in which the city became a space of racism, the way in which the state reacted. And clearly, in modern Western democracies there is a lot in common. But there is a big difference. We have to think very differently about a culture where the matrix of racism has been slavery, where the 'ex-slaves' are now the racialized subjects, in their own country. We have to make a distinction between the will to identity, the will to violence, the experience of terror, that prevails in the United States, from that of a very different diasporic history, which is the history of contemporary racism in Britain or France. In the British case, the oppression happened elsewhere, migration is largely post-Second World War, and, in many cases, the societies of origin, in the Caribbean, Africa, or India, were societies experiencing the chaos, the economic difficulties, and social disjunctions of an early post-independence period. People migrated to England, partly because their colonial education had prepared them to expect the land of milk and honey, but also they were coming with an economic motive, and they were coming, certainly in the 1950s and

1960s, to a potential job market. They were able to establish themselves with homes, education for their children, a Health Service, ways in which they could never have established themselves in their own countries. But all these forms of social amelioration must be seen in the context of institutional and individual racism that kept migrants in subordinate positions. I think we might even require a different definition of racial victimage for these different situations.

Black British film-makers and video artists are often critical of what they see as a kind of Afro-centred, cultural nationalism, cultural essentialism amongst some US practitioners. It seems to me that talk about identity construction in England is sometimes more experimental and conceptually daring. However, one has to think from the other side, that the cultural deprivation and devastation of black American populations, and the ghostly repetition of slavery in their everyday economic lives fuels the need to form communities built around some more solid identification, with an essential figure, even a totemic ancestor. It also needs to be said that Americans of colour can articulate a national interest and identification because a migrant or minority polity constitutes the ethos of belonging. Whereas in England, however successful or prosperous the migrant may be, he or she will always be accommodated on the margins of the myth of Englishness.

The prevalence of a post-Second World War ethos of social welfare in Britain, although in many ways discriminatory and racist, provided a certain kind of support, and prevented the bone coming through the skin of the knuckles. It prevented the rawest realities of racism. I have no doubt, now, that racism will become—is becoming worse, with the effects not only of Thatcherism, and the contemporary Conservative ethos, but also of a fortress Europe, which will harden its borders, and may even, as you see in Germany and parts of Italy, whip up a tremendous paranoia in relation to those who are outside the fortress, the 'predatory' others, the job-seeking, or job-snatching Third World peoples, the refugees who want to slip in through the borders. We're in a very problematic position, with a whole new discourse of paranoia emerging on the rim of Europe, just at the time when people are trying to persuade us that within Europe, it's going to be porous frontiers, a new amity, and a new comradeship.

Do you see any important differences in the forms of resistance to racism in the United States, Britain, and Europe?

Well, first of all, the factor that must be considered when we talk about racism and racial violence, is the armed nature of the American population. The implications of the gun laws for the racial tension are both obvious and very striking. But I think there is another difference.

I feel, in Britain, that the promise of a consensual culture, which is the heritage of welfarist/Labourist traditions—although those traditions are being eroded—produces pluralistic dreams of resisting racism through multiculturalism—a belief that we can educate people out of racism by exposure to or the knowledge of cultural diversity—Indian food, African dresses, and so on. I am less convinced that these ideas of cultural relativism and political pluralism, that are part of this sense of a consensus, are now very effective ideas. I think the tension has gone beyond that. The other influence which shapes resistance to racism differently in Britain, is the long tradition of class politics, where the question of class has dominated all other forms of subordinate identities. So race or gender issues were always seen as second-order oppressions.

Americans have resisted discrimination and oppression by constructing forms of community, often around single issues. In America you can construct a community of subversion, and that produces an energy in public discourse which I find invigorating. It creates a form of resistance which can at times be more utopic or visionary. The contribution of radical black theology, taking its inspiration also from Latin America, is quite stunning. I was most moved and stimulated by black preachers of a radical gospel, who were able to give you a sense of the sacred as a form of survival, of a theology which wanted to deal with the intangible effects of racism, with despair, melancholy, desire. In some ways the discourse around race is more advanced in the United States. You do have some instances of narrow-minded 'political correctness'. But at least the issues are out on the table. In the schools, too, school students from an earlier age are made more conscious of the complex polity in which they exist.

In the late modern world, however, a concept of culture based on the wonders of pluralism and relativism is inadequate as a guide for dealing with issues of racial conflict. We may enjoy a range of cultures, we may enjoy opera, or cricket, but culture becomes a biting issue, or a striking issue, when there is a conflict of choice or of resources.

The Rushdie event is an example of this. This may sound very counter-intuitive because, on the one hand, you have the sacred propriety of the Koran, and on the other hand, the liberal tradition of the novel, and its desire to question and interrogate, and write against the grain, and produce readers who read against the grain. So, you have the great conflict between the magus and the mullahs, and that's the way it's often represented. But I think something else is going on which is more subtle.

The reaction of European liberals was the assertion of universal rights of free expression. But what we also saw was the inadequacy of those ideas to deal with an ethnic population, with a history of racial discrimination in the North of England. Those liberal ideas were not dealing with the other forms of social outrage and disturbance, that were being experienced by the migrant populations of Bradford. On the other hand, whereas the Bradford Muslims were quoting their unshakeable belief in the authority of the Koran, you could also see, in that extreme position, their anxiety that the questioning of religious authority, initiated by *The Satanic Verses*, was seeping into their own community. The assertion of fundamentalism is a disavowal of many of the things that Rushdie is talking about, the questioning of patriarchal authority, of religious precept and tradition, that is already rife amongst the younger generations of those communities. So there's a kind of liberal fundamentalism and an Islamic fundamentalism, and I think both don't want to see what is actually on the ground, which is, that we have a new complex, culturally problematic kind of cosmopolitanism developing. And that cosmopolitanism does not have its origins purely in Enlightenment concepts of social virtue and civility. It also is a cosmopolitanism of migration, which has very specific post-colonial and Third World history.

I wanted to ask you about multiple identity. In a sense, we've been talking about that, haven't we?

Yes. Multiple identity is a concept that is really circulating quite rapidly, and the origins of that concept, I think, are quite interesting. In Britain, social identity used to be discussed largely in terms of class, and then race and gender came afterwards. But now you have a situation where 'communities of interest' are increasingly constituting the elements of political organization. The concept of multi-identity is actually a misnomer. It introduces, once more, a kind of illusory pluralism as if there are many identities to choose from. But who is free to choose? As Lacan pointed out, in the matter of identity nothing comes for free: he typified the construction of identity in the demand,

'Your money or your life'. That is to say that the 'choice' of identity and its psychic and ideological representation is an agonistic, agonizing struggle. Identities are formed through differential, non-equivalent structures of identification and it is through these borderlines of being that our social relations are articulated and established. Contemporary society challenges us to recognize a culture and a politics built around communities of interest. They're not necessarily communities of origin, they're not communities which have a kind of holistic or totalized view of the entire political structure. They are strategic: no less effective for that, no less principled for that. And the problem of identity that emerges from that is how do you constitute a set of identities, or a range of identity, which does not locate you principally in one or the other? The positive side is that there is a greater democratization of difference. But when you combine these elements, do you still trace these forms of social difference? How do you recognize the element of, say, sexual determinism, in a struggle against racism? There isn't a part of the body that is racialized, and a part of the body that is sexualized. It's this complex turning of these categories, of one into the other, that is, I think, really the point at issue.

Very often, the model for talking about multiple identities has been a spatial model, or a voluntaristic model: that it is possible to occupy a number of different nodal points, and you're one, or two, or you move from one to another. That seems to me to be based on a notion of the subject as existing in a voluntaristic space. I don't think that's the real issue. The real issue here, I think, is better represented through psychoanalysis, which always sees the subject as a kind of ambivalent, negotiated phenomenon, in relation to a number of models, priorities, and norms, but, at any one point in which the subject is negotiating its identifications, it is not multiply poised, but it is ambivalently structured in relation to itself—the notion of splitting, or the notion of repression, or the notion of surmounting, or the notion of sublimation. I have some problems with some of these concepts. But what I want to stress here is that it is not the multiplicity of subjects, but the actual agonistic struggle in constructing 'one' subject which, in some sense, is 'less than one'. It is the doubleness of the subject, rather than its multiplicity, that is at issue.

Do you see the distinction I've made? The doubleness, and ambivalence, and contradictoriness of the subject, rather than its multiplicity—that I think has to be theorized for work in social and cultural analysis. I think it's a kind of post-Althusserian structuralist notion that you have a number of ideological institutional apparatuses, and that parts of your identity are constructed and claimed by each. My suggestion is that may well be a convenient mode of description, but at the point at which you are trying to understand how, in between and across various identities, people constitute something specific, it is not very helpful. When I speak about the doubleness of identity, I don't mean two: I mean to suggest the negotiated iterability of identity, its constant repetition, revision, relocation, so that no repetition is the same as the preceding one. I think this model of repetition with a difference is a much better way of looking at constituted identity than the model of multiplicity.

You have described much of your own inspiration as coming from novels. Do you see a potential for autobiography and life stories in these areas, or not?

Yes. Very much so. Talking as we did about the doubling of identity, about hyphenated identities, about borderline or borderland identifications, I think that the emphasis on these areas of cultural experience are, in some ways, a quite recent development in cultural and historical studies. We're talking about migrations within living memory. And I think one cannot stress enough, two things. One is the specificity of particular experiences. The other is the need to theorize questions of narrative and identity, to try to make that theoretical work deal with the very specific configuration and conjunction of different cultural and social elements. So apart from the inspirational interest of a lot of autobiography as forms of testimony, and the uniqueness of that inspiration, autobiography is also important, because life stories display that very peculiar weave of elements of lives lived iteratively, lives lived interstitially, and challenge those, like myself, who are interested in a theoretical understanding about these processes; they challenge us to think beyond what our concepts enable us to do.

Are there any particular examples you might point to?

One autobiography which very much impressed me was by the South African activist Hilda Bernstein, *The World That was Ours* (1967). It gave me a new sense of the meaning of time, or timeliness, both in the conflict of personal and political demands, and also even in the moment of her fleeing. I think also of Steve Biko's *I Write What I Like*

(1978). And all Indians would say, and it's actually quite true, that Mahatma Gandhi's *Experiments with Truth* (1948) is quite a striking attempt to address the public as the private, and the private as the public. I think that's a very significant autobiography. And he was a migrant too: South Africa, Britain, India were the scenes of his life. I have also been very interested by the refugee statements that Jackie brings home. Sometimes they are dictated, sometimes they are just written by themselves, and there are different genres or elements of formality. They're very often life stories, to plead for a refugee status.

Which leads to the other vital point. Many of those who constitute these new communities of interest, such as refugees, underclasses, diasporic—by their very nature many of these people often don't have access to their own representation. And I think their experiences, and their voices must be heard in their own words in order to make us rethink what we understand by nation, national belonging, or national culture: to question nation, to question citizenship, to question community. It's never adequate to say their voices must be heard as voices, because none of their voices are just innocent voices, their voices are mediated through the dialogue they have with the questioner, through their own sense of what it means to represent themselves, through their own ideologies, so they are also framed voices, if you like, and produced voices. But in just that sense they are testimonies of the construction of a changing identity, of a changing polity, of a changing transnational community.